Archbishop Donald Arden

Reflections on serving in Malawi, Southern and Central Africa, England 1943-2014

TSL Publications

First published in Great Britain in 2025
By TSL Publications, Rickmansworth

Copyright © 2025 Donald Arden & Jane Arden (editor)

ISBN: 978-1-917426-12-1

The right of Donald Arden and Jane Arden to be identified as the author and editor of this work respectively has been asserted by the author in accordance with the UK Copyright, Designs and Patents Act 1988.

All rights reserved. No part of this publication may be reproduced, stored in a retrieval system or transmitted, in any form or by any means without the prior written permission of the publisher, nor be otherwise circulated in any form of binding or cover other than that in which it is published and without a similar condition being imposed on the subsequent buyer.

Cover photos: see pages
206 & 218

Photographs courtesy and copyright of
Jane Arden and family

Foreword

This book gives an account of the remarkable life of a remarkable man, Donald Arden. From his early globetrotting with his parents, through his ordination training and curacies in Southwark and St Albans' dioceses during the bombing of the Second World War, he had a resilient formation which was to serve him well in his almost twenty years' service as a priest in Pretoria and Swaziland, his twenty years as a bishop in Malawi, and then his over thirty years ministry in the Diocese of London.

And the pattern throughout his long and varied ministry was for Donald to add value to what was going on in church by paying attention to what was going on outside as well. So, for example, in Swaziland he became the chairman of the Swaziland Pineapple Growers Association which developed the fruit which is now a major crop in the country's economy. I think that there's a parable there for Donald's ministry which has brought many projects to fruition.

The early sixties were busy years for Donald. He became Bishop of Malawi in 1961, shortly before the country became independent, steering his new diocese with skill through turbulent and divisive times. He met and married Jane and before long they were the parents of Bazil and Christopher. At this stage, his ministry was still less than half-way through, but I would claim that Donald's ministry has been a game of two halves in a rather different way.

My wife, Barbara, and I first encountered Donald's ministry when we went as USPG missionaries to Zambia in the late sixties for, with the sad accidental death of Archbishop Oliver Green-Wilkinson, Donald was shortly in 1971 to be our archbishop. As Bishop of Malawi he was well placed to play a pivotal role as Archbishop of Central Africa in a turbulent province which consisted of Botswana, Southern Rhodesia, Zambia and Malawi, three countries that had recently become independent and one, Southern Rhodesia, later Zimbabwe, where the Smith regime had declared UDI and Robert Mugabe, amongst others was waging a fierce war of liberation. The borders had been closed between Zambia and Rhodesia, but the one country where all the dioceses of the province could meet was Malawi, and Donald's sensitive handling of that potentially destructive scenario was part of the glue which held the churches together and enabled them to make a significant contribution to nation building in each of the four countries.

He was also very busily at work in his own diocese, adding value to the Church's mission through enhancing the training of both clergy and lay people, upping the contribution of the churches' health care until it was providing some 45 percent of all the health care in the country. He played a leading role in the "Malawi Against Polio" campaign which eventually saw the eradication of polio from Malawi. When he arrived in the country in 1961 Donald had written to friends saying that the next bishop must be a Malawian, when he left in 1981 there were three.

I've said that for me Donald's ministry was a game of two halves. Let me explain why, for we haven't yet quite reached half time. Up until then those, like myself who had benefitted from Donald's ministry as priest, bishop and archbishop, judged him to be rather austere and formal, a formidable presence to a young priest like myself.

Imagine my astonishment, then, when some seven years later when Barbara and I were living in Canterbury, where I was university chaplain, I dutifully popped my head into an international church leaders' conference which was taking place on the campus. For church leaders they were making a lot of noise, and as I entered the hall where they were meeting, I was met with sounds of ecstatic singing and indeed dancing, and the first person I saw was Donald, not only waving his arms in praise but linking them with a neighbouring African priest. I was astonished. Whatever had happened? Well, of course, renewal in the spirit had happened. A wave of charismatic worship and praise had swept through Southern Africa and Donald and Jane had been caught up into it. From then on we were in the second half of Donald's ministry which had a looser, more joyful and relaxed style than what we had known in the first half.

Three years later the Diocese of London benefitted from it. I was by that time an archdeacon in the diocese and hearing that Donald was retiring from Central Africa it was agreed that he should come to Uxbridge as priest in charge of St Margaret parish church. He was soon sharing the joys of the gospel with his new flock and the parish entered a new and confident phase seeing considerable church growth.

Of course, we not only now had a dynamic priest in Uxbridge, we also had a dynamic assistant bishop in area and diocese and Donald, then and until well into his eighties, was always willing to play his part in confirmations and ordinations, particularly the ordination of women as priests at several services in 1994 – a model of how a retired bishop can provide a safety net for harassed episcopal colleagues.

The diocese benefitted yet more from the Ardens' arrival. I had become the Chair of the newly created Diocesan Board for Schools and we were appointing new staff. I remembered that Jane looked after the Diocesan Building Department in Malawi, designing and building a variety of buildings. Might she have the gifts to advise the new Board of Schools on building matters? She might and she did with an energy mirroring Donald's own.

On retirement at seventy, Donald began twenty-five happy years as an Honorary Curate in St Alban's Church, North Harrow. During this time he co-led several group visits to Malawi. Often he stayed on to visit neighbouring Mozambique where the struggle for independence was still being fought.

At the invitation of the Bishop of London, Richard Chartres, Donald marked the fiftieth anniversary of his consecration as a bishop in Malawi in 1961 by celebrating the Eucharist in St Paul's Cathedral on 30th November 2011. Bishop Chartres served as deacon and preached. People came from parishes where he served in England before sailing to Africa in 1943, friends from his thirty-eight years in Africa, together with many from the UK.

This book is a rich and readable account of a kaleidoscope of the experiences of a remarkable person, I much enjoyed reading it.

Tom Butler
Former Bishop of Southwark

Contents

Australia	8
England and Bombs	18
South Africa	25
Swaziland 1951-1961	31
Nyasaland 1961	43
Travelling and making links 1963	69
Family interlude	86
Developing a Malawian Church	99
Political turmoil and Independence	125
Companion Dioceses	133
Province of Central Africa (CAPA)	137
Travelling by Josiah Mtekateka	154
Unity amongst Christians	158
Health in Nyaslaand 1899-1996	179
Malawi Against Polio 1977	192
Building Department	201
Ardens leave Malawi	204
St Margaret's Uxbridge	208
St Alban's North Harrow	210
St Alban's interludes	213
Romsey and Postscript	219
Appendices:	221
Staff List March 1962	222
Four Outstanding Clergy	224
The building of Likoma Cathedral	231
Peter Kilekwa - Slaveboy to Priest	239
The SS *Chauncy Maples* and my Uncle Ernest	241
Archdeacon Christopher Lacey 1905-1968	244
Index of Names & Organisations	246

Australia

I was born, to my dismay, at Boscombe, on the edge of Bournemouth. I say Boscombe, not Bournemouth because it sounds less dull. My brothers were born in more colourful places, Felix in Penang, Mike in Tebin Tinggi, Deli, Sumatra in the Dutch East Indies. Mike had a birth certificate in Dutch of which I was very jealous.

The reason for being born in Boscombe was that Dad caught a tropical bug, which was not identified until some fifty years later. It may well have been Hong Kong encephalitis B, a slow-acting tropical corona virus resulting in a horrendously high temperature.

Family History

The Cheshire Ardens from which I was descended were traced by Felix in a burst of genealogical interest in the 1990s. They belonged originally to the Ardens of Warwickshire, Staffordshire and the Forest of Arden, one of only four families in England whose roots can be traced back with certainty to Saxon times.

Arden was the name of the great forest of Warwickshire and is of Celtic origin, meaning "well wooded." The main branch of the Ardens have always been based in Warwickshire, but somewhere before 1229, John de Arden, son of Eustace de Arden, was "named as his knight by Ranulph III, Earl of Chester" and had a grant of Aldford Fee, in Cheshire. There the family split into two halves, the western half being associated with Alvanley and Aldford, near Chester, the eastern half with Stockport, spreading over to the edge of Derbyshire.

Felix traced Dad's ancestry back to a William Arden of Norbury, born at Disley, six miles south-east of Stockport and close to the Derbyshire border, on 30 March 1728. From then on the family lived at a small yeoman farmhouse there, known rather grandly as Stanley Hall. This has been beautifully preserved and is now lived in by the green keeper at Disley golf course. Jane and I sought it out and photographed it in the 1980s. The base of the main branch of the Ardens however remained in Staffordshire and Warwickshire. It was a Mary Arden from Stratford-upon-Avon who gave birth to William Shakespeare.

My Parents

My dad Stanley Arden was born in Heaton Norris 24 September 1874 and given the name of Stanley. His father, who was also called Stanley, was a law clerk of Cheadle Heath and a member of the Hallé Choir. Heaton Norris has long since been absorbed by Stockport but the lovely half-timbered Underbank Hall, the town house of the Cheshire Ardens, still stands in all its glory and, in 2024, is owned by the Natwest Bank. The Arden country house, Harden Hall, is a ruin on the edge of Stockport. Dad was a choirboy at Cheadle Hulme and had a great love of music. Perhaps the hardest part of his disability was that it prevented him from playing the piano. He tried to teach me without lasting success, despite my having composed "The March of the Tin Soldiers" when I was ten.

In June 1898, he headed for London and joined Kew Gardens, where he served in the Tropical Department. The last year of his time was spent as a foreman in the Ferneries. At the end of 1900 he was sent from Kew to Malaya to work on methods of growing and tapping *Hevea brasiliensis* – the rubber tree. This is a native of the Amazon region. The Spaniards, then the colonial masters of Brazil, had tried by every means to prevent its being planted elsewhere. However, seeds had been smuggled to Kew a number of years earlier and multiplied there. H.N. Ridley had already taken seeds to Malaya a few years earlier and the trees showed every sign of being at home in its rain-forest climate. Coffee was the main crop in Malaya but horticulturalists knew that it could fail at any time through a disease sweeping the tropical world. The message from Ridley and Dad was to plant rubber as shade trees among the coffee. Should the coffee fail, then the rubber would take over. This was exactly what happened.

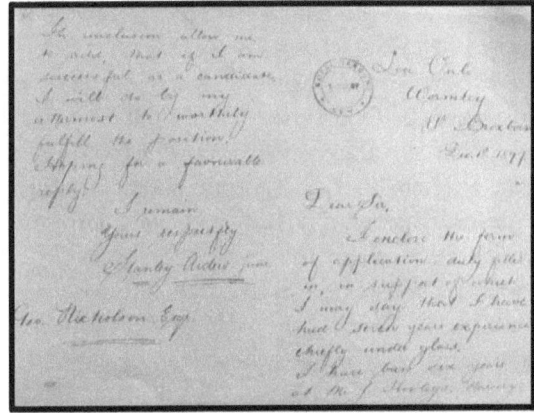

Stanley's application to work at Kew – 1897

Mum began life in 1880 as Winifred Morland, the descendant of Thomas Morland, born 1729, farmer and inn holder of Ravenstonedale in the Lune Valley of Cumbria. Thomas migrated to Rotherhithe to work with his brother who had gone there as a shipwright when things were hard in Cumbria and himself became a ship's carpenter and a Quaker.

I am glad that we have northern blood in our veins. When I returned to England from Australia in 1934, I found life in Surrey stifling. The aunt designated to be my guardian was interested only in playing bridge and our relationship came to an end when, playing as her partner at her bridge club, I trumped her ace out of sheer boredom. Even when you escaped to the North Downs, every attractive path seemed to have a notice on it: Trespassers will be prosecuted. But a week or two later when I found that you could escape from the grime and bustle of Leeds to the Yorkshire moors, I felt able to breathe again. Many of my friends at college were fellow-students who had lived in Burma, Africa or Canada or were Yorkshire born.

Mum had found life in an all-female Victorian household in Surrey stifling and escaped at an early age to train at Charing Cross and Ipswich as a nurse and midwife. She loved telling us of her work as a district nurse in the Land of Green Ginger in Hull, where the policemen would go only out in pairs. At 26, she took off for a nursing post in Singapore Hospital and it was there that Dad and Mum met and were married in Singapore Cathedral. In 2000, Jane and I found some of the likely sites where they would have done their courting and we had a stengah cocktail in the Raffles Hotel in their honour.

South East Asia

Dad's work with the Colonial Service took them to North Borneo and then to manage a rubber estate in Sumatra, in the Dutch East Indies. Mike was born there on Mum's birthday in 1909. Felix, always Fee to us, came along a couple of years later when they were managing an estate five hours by launch up the Johore River, just north of Singapore.

All this suddenly changed just after they opened their own rubber plantation – Bintang Estate at Sitiawan in Lower Perak, about 30 miles southwest of Ipoh. *Bintang* means "Star with a Tail" and the estate was named after Halley's comet, which made one of its rare appearances in 1911. Our son Christopher visited what remains of the estate when back-packing around the world in 1985. Mum was in England showing off her first baby to his grandparents when she received a cable saying, "Come urgently.

Stanley dying." Apparently he was in hospital with a temperature of 106°F, having caught an undiagnosed tropical bug. She had to board a ship at Marseilles and travel for another two weeks not knowing whether she would find him alive or dead. Dad was just 37.

Over the following two years, the slow-acting virus caused him to lose his balance. He remained like that for the rest of his life. He was never paralysed, his speech was unaffected and his mind was perfect until the day he died, but he could walk only if he had something or somebody to hold on to. He used what today we would call a zimmer frame but known to us then as a walking-machine, a heavy wooden thing on castors. For out-of-doors he had a wheelchair operated by two handles with gears. In top gear he did about 6mph and from age five I chased behind during school holidays. Small wonder that in Swaziland my nickname was Impangeli or Guinea-Fowl. There is a Swazi proverb which says, "*Impangeli ikhala igijima* – The guinea-fowl cries as it runs."

Back in England

Boscombe with its hills was no place for a wheelchair, so when I was three, we all moved to Worthing and stayed there until 1925. They were happy years, though I was always jealous of Mike and Fee who lived an exciting life as boarders at St Edward's School in Oxford. During the holidays they were able to go on long bike rides around Sussex with Mr Pocock, who seemed to come from nowhere but was a keen naturalist and took them to Bramber Castle and across the Weald and up the Arun Valley. I learned about these romantic places second-hand from helping Mike develop and print his photos of windswept trees and Saxon churches but I really only got to know Sussex by proxy later when I found Hilaire Belloc's poems and books in the school library in Australia.

Worthing 1921

Donald, Mike, Felix and Granny Morland – Worthing 1925

Australia Beckons

Mum often begged Dad to take her somewhere where the sun shone. I agreed heartily. Whenever we planned a picnic on the prehistoric Cissbury Ring or at the windmill at High Salvington (both within my reach), I seemed to end up with my nose flattened against the window watching the raindrops run down like tears for another cancelled expedition. Mike wanted to go farming but there were no prospects for this in Britain without capital. Then came the Wembley International Exhibition in 1924. The Burma pavilion in carved teak was unforgettable and so was the Indian building, inspired by the Taj Mahal. But our thoughts were all on Australia. The Exhibition made us decide on Adelaide as the next base for our peripatetic family. It had flat roads for Dad, sunshine for Mum, agricultural college for Mike, a medical school for Felix and St Peter's College for me. Though personally, aged nine, I was more interested in the vast vat of free orange juice at Wembley, perpetually being squished out of a limitless supply of oranges, and hoped there would be lots of such vats in Adelaide.

We sailed from Tilbury in December 1925 on SS *Bendigo*, an emigrant ship packed with twice its normal number of passengers because of the shipping strike, which had just ended. We spent Christmas at Las Palmas in the Canaries, calm after an especially stormy Bay of Biscay. My first view of Africa was through the porthole over Dad's bunk before sunrise. Here magically was Table Mountain, painted in the palest of pinks and silvery greys. In the five days we spent unloading, Dad must have walked miles, arm in arm with Mike on one side and Fee on the other, as we explored the Cape peninsula by train and on foot. Mum must have been nearly dead from exhaustion, looking after three children and a disabled husband on an appallingly over-crowded ship.

Adelaide

In February 1926 we disembarked at Adelaide from SS *Bendigo*. It had been a six-week voyage from Tilbury.

At Adelaide's outer harbour we had a rude shock. The immigration officer took one look at Dad, supported by Mike and Felix and said, "Who gave **you** permission to come to Australia?" I have no idea how that was answered, other than that my mother assured him, as a nurse, that Dad's condition was not infectious.

The Medical School for Felix said he could attend lectures when we arrived in February but would not be allowed to register till his birthday –

he would not be 16 until April 1926. He used to say he was probably the only medical student in the world who began his training not knowing how babies were made.

Jane and I, together with our son Christopher, his wife Nadine and daughter Olivia, and many friends and relations, celebrated Felix's 90th birthday in Brisbane in 2000, where he had earned a CBE for his work as a paediatrician.

In Adelaide, Dad had trouble brushing flies off his face, either missing the fly entirely or giving himself a mighty whack on the cheek, but in other ways it was ideal. We bought a newly built house with what in England would have been thought of as a large garden. Dad revelled in planting every possible variety of grape over all its boundary fences and a dozen different fruit trees. Some of the peaches were so huge and delicate that you could hardly pick them without bruising them. The apricots cropped so abundantly that Mum had to take over the clothes-washing copper to make them into jam. There were nectarines and quinces, fruits I had never heard of. When the grapes were ripe, I spent half my time filling my cycle-basket and taking them round to every friend we could think of.

I enjoyed Adelaide, not realising what a wonderful place it was to grow up in until after we left. Ten miles to the west was St Vincent's Gulf, bordered by mangrove swamps north of the Outer Harbour, where the mail ships came in every Thursday and where the Sea Scout boats had their moorings. Six miles to the east were the Mount Lofty ranges, partly gum-tree scrub (Aussie for eucalyptus forest), partly fruit farms, with German-speaking villages dotted about where Australia's wine industry began in the nineteenth century.

Sailing the sea scout boat White Star *in Adelaide Harbour*

Sea Scout

St Peter's College – Adelaide

There were six years between my older brothers and me. I was a replacement for Dennis who died on his first birthday, so I was rather like an only child when I was young, with Mike and Fee away at boarding school or college. I went to school at St Peter's College. As I was only ten I began in the Prep School. Father Julian Bickersteth the Headmaster was an important part of my life from 1926–33. My first memory was of Fr Julian coming down the drive from the Upper School to the prep school where he took VIa for Scripture. There was a craze at the time for flashing the sun into people's eyes with bits of mirror. KJFB (our name for Bickersteth) must have been fifty yards away and I had only a small broken bit but I happened to get him fair and square.

He came into class furious. I was late into stowing my bit into my pocket and was told to get the cane. There was a slender, whippy one in the cupboard but also an old blunt one buried under papers. I managed to get the blunt one out. Just as I was getting two of the best, a boy came round with the mark-book, astonished to see someone being beaten by the Head. I can see him now standing open-mouthed. It was unknown for a boy in the prep to be beaten by the Head and he spread the news to each class as he went round. I became a person instead of being just a pommie. Shortened to Pom, that became my nickname all my time at Saints.

My parents felt there was a risk of my becoming "bookish" and fortunately pushed me into joining the school's Scout Troop. I transferred to the Sea Scouts after about eighteen months and this became the joy of my life. They had a boat, *The Pioneer*, which had been the captain's pinnace on the first warship ever to visit South Australia in the 1840s, so was then about 85 years old. Her bottom was filled with concrete and she was an open boat with no buoyancy tanks. If swamped, she would have gone to the bottom like a lead weight.

At the age of 16, I held a Charge Certificate entitling me to take the boat out into St Vincent's Gulf, which can get very rough, crewed by Sea Scouts without any adult on board or any of them wearing life-jackets! Our Sea Scout Master, Mikka Forbes, had served as an apprentice on square-rigged ships in the 1900s, in the days when sea shanties were still used as working songs. I used to produce them, in bowdlerised form, to lull our grand-daughters to sleep when they were small.

I never enjoyed ball-games and found cricket especially unappealing when the thermometer could go up to 113°F in the shade so I took to rowing. The

Torrens River was only a mile from the school, a pleasant bike-ride through the Botanic Park except for the time when a magpie stole the blue cap off my head. I began as a cox and took our house crew to victory.

On another occasion, I was coxing a school four which was a good length behind our opponents in the last 50 yards of the race. To my horror I saw too late a stake in the water just ahead of number two's oar. There was no time for evasive action and a moment later his oar hit the stake with a noise like a rifle crack. To my astonishment our opponents gave up rowing and cheered themselves. I suddenly realised that they thought the noise was the single revolver shot, which meant that the north side – their side – had won. And we were both 20 yards from the finishing line. I bellowed through the voice-trumpet "Row like bloody hell!!" They did and we won. I met Major Hill, our coach, in the changing room a little later. He had not seen the race and said to me, "Congratulations! I hear their fool of a cox hit a stake or something." I said, "A bit like that sir." Later I achieved the sole sporting success of my life, rowing bow oar in the Farrell House boat that won the house races of 1932.

The Senior Literary Society was a joy. There I first met the poetry of T.S. Eliot, introduced to me by Herb Piper, the only open atheist in the school, who went on to become Professor of English at Canberra. I also spent much time rehearsing with the Theatrical Society. Their greatest achievement was the *Iphigenia in Aulis of Euripides*, performed in the new Memorial Hall, which had almost insuperable acoustic problems. My part was that of Queen Clytemnestra, a role that Sybil Thorndike had played. She was then perhaps the best-known British actress of her time and was on tour in Adelaide. She attended our dress rehearsal and at one point leapt up on the stage with a copy of the book and started playing my part. I still have the copy with her signature in it.

Our Headmaster Julian Bickersteth had been an army chaplain, decorated for bravery in World War I, which also turned him into a pacifist. He formed the Bolshie Club – a group of boys thinking vaguely about ordination. We met for the office of Sext in a tiny chapel in his attic at lunchtime every Friday. On one occasion we visited the Community of the Ascension, a men's religious order at Goulburn in New South Wales where we put on for them the *Iphigenia* we had just produced at school.

I had applied to the College of the Resurrection at Mirfield to train as a priest but since I could not attend an interview in England, it was arranged that Fr Barnes, who was visiting Adelaide and belonged to the Community, would see me then. The Head organised a picnic for the Bolshie Club and I had a few words with Fr Barnes but nothing that resembled an interview. When I reached Mirfield a year later, Fr Barnes greeted me like a long lost friend. After the Head, the most formative influence at school was Cammy, a one-time form-master of Scots origin, decorated in World War I, with an infinite capacity for resisting boredom. Friends and I used to drop in on him perhaps at nine o'clock at night and just talk, sometimes until midnight. He was never shocked, dropped in the occasional wry comment and almost never looked at his watch. It was only years later that we realised what we owed him.

Our last four summer holidays were spent on Mike's small mixed dairy farm, called The Snuggery. It was at the southern tip of mainland Australia, near the Victorian border and had been settled by Irish immigrants around 1870. The land was originally a tea-tree swamp, so dense, the old people said, that a dog couldn't walk through it. All the farms in the area had been started by old man McCourt who had eleven sons and one daughter, Julia. She lived, as her parents had lived in Connemara, in a tiny cabin with the pig in the end room.

Old man McCourt used to sit with a telescope on the chimney stack while his eleven sons were sent out, each to clear his own patch of tea-tree, while he kept watch to see that they were all working. By the time Mike arrived in 1929, all except two had drunk themselves off their farms. The two were the local butcher and Jim on the next farm. Jim had only one leg that worked, and travelled in a light dray with a hole in it for the leg was too arthritic to be bent. He had not got round to building a milking-shed in the 50 years he had been farming and used to milk his cows with the daily rain pouring down his neck. At The Snuggery, it took Mike a full day to clear the mountain of whisky bottles in his yard.

Possum, Mike's black pony at The Snuggery, was the love of my life. He only had one vice. He could not resist thistles and at full gallop would suddenly stop to nip off a tasty one in full flower. He had never been broken in and had never heard of trotting and cantering. He had only two paces, a walk and a gallop. Mike had inherited him from Jack McCourt who used to ride him six miles at full gallop to the "Tantanoola Tiger." There he would get drunk and relied on Possum to bring him home. Often Possum arrived back alone.

Back: Mike, Stanley, Felix, Winifred
Front: Zetta, Donald

In 1934, soon after I left school, Mike's lovely wife Zetta died in giving birth to Rosemary and I rushed down to be with him. He was learning the hard lessons of being a dairy-farmer. If your wife dies in the morning, the cows still have to be milked in the evening. We had a wonderful couple of months together. One of my jobs was to get the cows in. At half-past four in the morning you first had to catch Possum who was loose in the paddock. That was a game he loved. I could trot around for a quarter of an hour before he condescended to accept the bridle.

It was he who rounded up the cows – I was still half asleep. If they were a bit sluggish, he would just bare his lips and nip their bottoms. The more spirited cows would land him one under the jaw with their back hoof. He would stop in his tracks and I had to avoid shooting over his head. I never actually came off him and I usually rode bare-back to get an extra five minutes sleep. I loved Possum dearly. He was a shiny jet black in the summer and in winter a dark woolly brown. At eight in the evening we started cooking – after separating the cream and feeding the calves – usually an all-purpose soup stew that changed slightly from day to day, followed by riz-au-chocolat.

Following Zetta's tragic death my parents offered to look after baby Rosemary for which Mike was very grateful. After I arrived in England they decided to return to England and Worthing, together with Rosemary.

England and bombs

In September 1934 I headed for Leeds to begin training for the priesthood. I travelled by SS *Bendigo*, calling at Colombo, where I had an introduction to a businessman and my first glimpse of colonial life when I dropped in for a coffee. He was in an enormous room in a flat and called "Boy!!" and in stalked a tall man in a turban who handed him his pipe from four feet away and stalked out again. My cabin companion from Colombo to Southampton was perhaps the most brilliant youngster I have ever known. I remember him being able to give me the names of every member of the Australian cricket XI who had visited his school two years earlier. We filled up the washbasin in our cabin with limes, a fruit I had never met before except in the sea-shanty, "Lime juice and vinegar boys, according to the Act", learned from Mikka Forbes.

On arriving at Mirfield, Fr Barnes greeted me with, "What on earth have you done with your hair? It was red and curly when I interviewed you in Adelaide." I realised that he had interviewed Bob (Rufus) Ray, thinking he was me, but I was too far from home to be sent back. Bob later became my brother-in-law when Felix married his sister Dot.

In Leeds I was at the Hostel of the Resurrection attached to Leeds University. The Mirfield course, run by the Community of the Resurrection, lasted five years, three at Leeds and two at the College at Mirfield itself. I had never seen the north of England before. I had never seen such poverty, only read the descriptions of slums in Dickens and thought it was a thing apart. I thought I had seen poverty during the 1929 depression when the price of wool collapsed and young men were applying to Mike to work "for their tucker" which meant for no pay at all. Poverty seemed more supportable in an Australian climate.

I remember approaching Leeds by train and all I could see was grey slate roofs through the drizzle, with everything dripping. I could not imagine how anyone could live in such conditions. A Yorkshireman in the compartment asked, "Where's tha goin' lad?"

"Leeds."

"What t'hell for?"

I began to wonder. In those days you never saw the sun because of the thick smoke, except perhaps on a Sunday when a dull red disc might float in the grey sky. If a library shelf had not been dusted in the morning it would turn your fingernails black.

The only other colonial was Hugh Harker from Natal. We found each other on the first evening and wondered aloud, leaning over a canal bridge, whether we could take it. We did, and although Hugh has died, his wife and I were still in touch, 60 years later. That is also true of Dick Herrick, a little older than the rest of our year and (believe it or not) the only one who had worked for his living. We two often broke the rule of Great Silence, from 10 p.m. to 8 a.m., sharing thoughts and uncertainties about everything in earth and heaven. You could get no slovenly talk past him. "Donald, why do you talk about things you haven't thought about?"

Leslie Cumberland took me up and down most of the major Lakeland peaks during my first Easter in England and in our second year we shared the "married quarters", the only double room in the Hostel, at the top of the tower. Dick Tatlock took me and Alan to his home in St Helen's on the coast in Lancashire to show me what "the real England" looked like. I only remember a rowdy evening in his house with a couple of Lancashire girls and being reproved by his mother, "I think the devil must have got into you two tonight!" Alan was always having trouble with celibacy and surprisingly ended up being admitted as a member of the celibate Community of the Resurrection, though that lasted for only a few weeks, after which he switched career to the prison service.

At the end of each year, we spent a fortnight at Mirfield itself, rehearsing for Commemoration Day, when we presented a play to 5,000 people in the quarry theatre, out of which the stone for the College had been taken. It was long before sound equipment became available and we had to compete with trains puffing up and down the busy railway linking Huddersfield with Wakefield in the valley just below. After returning to England in 1981, I went up several times to attend Commemoration Day to reminisce with old friends, including Dick Herrick, Tom Butler and others.

In our final two years at Mirfield, my closest friends were Ernest Southcott and George Tidey. Ernie had come from Canada and was a free spirit. He and I were active in the Anglican Young People Association (AYPA) founded by a Canadian priest and recently started in England. He later became Provost of Southwark Cathedral. In December 1962, Jane and I stayed with him and his wife Margaret in the lovely Provost's house on the edge of the Thames. Ernie died in 1976.

Before Mirfield, George had taught in Burma. After Mirfield, George returned to Burma with his wife Rosmaund, sent by the Society for the Propagation of the Gospel (SPG), arriving in the Karen Hills before the Japanese invasion in 1941. His SPG booklet *Trek from Burma* vividly describes how he, Rosamund and thousands of others survived the gruelling seven-week trek out of Burma to India. They served in Burma for many years after the war. It was wonderful to meet them in London in 1981 not long after returning from Malawi. George died soon afterwards.

As a student, I took part in several work camps of the body then called IVSP – International Voluntary Service for Peace. This was inspired by a Swiss Quaker, Pierre Cérésole, who had been gaoled for refusing military service. I worked with IVSP on two projects in Switzerland where Quakers had organized an exit route for anti-Hitler activists when the Gestapo were breathing down their necks. With them, I helped dig out a coal-drift in Brynmawr, Wales, alongside miners from the four pits that had been the life-blood of the town, but were now all closed. A co-operative set up by Jim Forrester, a Friend who in alternate weeks was Lord Forrester of Verulam, sold fire-damaged goods, faulty but edible tins of food and other necessities of life – but, until then, not coal. The mine-owners refused access to unemployed volunteers. But Jim had persuaded one of them to open up a disused drift in the mountainside and volunteers and unemployed miners worked together to get the coal out.

One day, Jim took us on tour to show us what life meant for an unemployed miner's family. In one street a smouldering slag-heap reached up to the bedroom windows, its sulphurous fumes seeping into the room where the children slept. It was there that I first made the connection between Jesus's sayings about the rich and the poor and the realities of a life I had never imagined.

I have also always been attracted by the Friends (Quakers) who seem to me to put into action the life of Jesus and The Twelve better than most of us.

Felix came over to work for his Member of the Royal College of Physicians. We climbed Yorkshire's Three Peaks together after which he nearly collapsed with exhaustion. During holidays, Dad would hire a small car which I would drive. We had memorable times together visiting his favourite places around the country. It was lovely to hear in 1940 that my brother Mike had become engaged to Elizabeth, who came from Austria. Dad died in Worthing in 1942. Mum and Rosemary returned to Australia in 1945 when Rosemary was 11.

Winifred Arden 1945

Donald – London 1940

Kennington and the Blitz

I was ordained deacon in St Mary's church, Kennington, in the Southwark Diocese on 24 September, 1939, a couple of weeks after war was declared. Wearing a dog-collar for the first time while sitting in a tube on the way to the church is a lasting memory. The sirens went off at the beginning of the service but no one took any notice. The "all clear" went off just as it finished.

I served in St Catherine's Church Hatcham, near New Cross in South London where Fr Bill Fenton was the much loved vicar.

London, 1940

A year later, on the first day of the London blitz, the planes arrived at six o'clock in the evening whilst it was still light. I was visiting a sick woman, she was in bed and her husband was also in the room. Suddenly there was an almighty row from aeroplanes and falling bombs. The man dived under the bed and I found myself holding the hands of both of them, the woman in the bed and the man under the bed. When the noise stopped, I went outside into the street expecting to see devastation. Boys were playing football and one shouted out, "Hey, Mister, your church is on fire!"

The planes had dived through the canopy of barrage balloons and dropped a canister of incendiary bombs on top of the church. This was quite deliberate. It had a spire and being on a hill, was a prominent building about four miles from Rotherhithe. The plan was that when the bombers were over the fire the crew would press the release buttons and then the high explosives would fall on the dock area. The Old Kent Road gas works was also set on fire. Every fire brigade in the district was sent there and the church was left to burn. The congregation managed to pick up all the incendiaries with shovels, except for one that lodged in the peak of the wooden roof of the high Victorian gothic building. There it smouldered happily for two hours with no way of getting near it. Finally it burst into flames and the whole of it caught fire. The fire brigade arrived a quarter of an hour later, just as the roof crashed in.

At eight o'clock the proper air raid began. Fortunately an Air-raid Warden's post had just been completed in the church grounds, built to withstand light bombs with deep concrete foundations. Some hours later, when the raid ended, I went out to have a pee and nearly fell into a big hole bored at an angle underneath the shelter. We discovered later that the hole went 15' deep into the back-filled earth where it failed to explode. It was still there at the end of the war.

Early the next morning we prepared for the eight o'clock Communion service in Haberdasher Askes School across the road. I recall being reprimanded by Fr Bill Fenton for being improperly dressed. Somehow my green Leeds BA hood had disappeared in the turmoil of the night. I have never worn one since. About three weeks later, our temporary church at the school was bombed and blown to pieces so we moved back to the vestry, the one part of the church that had not been burned out.

Many people in the parish lost their lives. I remember one night when the Christmas Club was having its pay-out and the men were all in the pub. The basements of the terraced houses opposite had been shored and joined together to form a common shelter. The women and children were there. A bomb fell on the pub killing about sixteen of the men. In the shelter opposite, where I was, none of them knew till the next morning who was dead, who was alive, who was in hospital.

One of the images I will never forget was when a lone bomber dropped a bomb on a house early in the morning. Rescuers knew there was a woman in it. The house was just a pile of rubble. They dug down. The woman had been in bed on one side of the room and a baby in a cot on the other side. In the instant between the bomb hitting the house and exploding she had thrown herself right across the room and spread-eagled herself across the cot in order to try and protect the baby, sadly to no avail.

On another occasion I was conducting a funeral. We were processing from the chapel to the grave when the sirens went and German planes came overhead. I kept on walking but had the feeling that nobody was following me. I turned round and found I was alone with the coffin, the pallbearers had all jumped into another open grave. I could just see their heads sticking out.

Amazingly people adapted to the situation. They were quite put-out on nights when there were no raids. They would be sitting in the shelter and would say, "What's going on, it's eleven o'clock? I'm going to bed!"

With the church burned down and the children and many of the adults evacuated, it was decided the new curate was bad luck and I was told I was free to look for another job.

Potten End and Charing Cross Hospital

I joined the vicar of Holy Trinity Church at Potten End in Hertfordshire. Nearby was Ashridge House, the main Sector-4 evacuation address of Charing Cross and University College hospitals and a few smaller hospitals. Potten End itself was full of children from Stepney. Green Line coaches would arrive in the morning with the people from the inner London hospitals. There were a few military wards, full of men picked up from the Dunkirk beaches.

I recall Desmond, aged 14, with cancer of the spine. He was undersized and could have passed for 9 or 10. He had spent most of his life in bed and in very considerable pain but there was nothing they could do for him. He was one of the brightest lads I have ever known.

Desmond wanted to be confirmed so I prepared him for confirmation and the service was arranged to be on his birthday. A week before his birthday I went to see him and asked how things were going and he replied, "Not so good, I couldn't get to sleep last night." He said he had come to a big decision. If he came through his illness he would become an MP. My reply was, "For crying out loud, who wants to spend his time polishing his bottom on a hard wooden bench?" "No, I had a good idea about midnight while I was watching the night nurse. She was so tired that she could hardly keep her eyes open. She told me she had been on duty for twelve hours. I want to get a law passed that no nurse in this country should work more than eight hours at a time."

They moved him into the "other ranks" ward from the civilian ward because they thought he would do their morale good. Some of them were sorry for themselves because they had lost a limb. Here he was, a chap who was going to lose his life. They loved him so the confirmation was held there. The Bishop of St Alban's, a great character from South Africa, standing about six foot four inches strode into the ward with his gold cope and mitre and we had a wonderful confirmation. Then they joined in the birthday party. He died four days later.

I was active in the Student Christian Movement and was able to attend a memorable conference at Swanick in Derbyshire. There I sat at the feet of William Temple, then Archbishop of York; spoke with George Macleod, from the slums of Glasgow, who was founding the Iona Community and beginning on the building of its Abbey; listened to C.F. Andrews, missionary and friend of Gandhi. I was given enough to think about for years to come. In 1988, Jane and I had a wonderful day visiting Iona and Macleod's glorious Abbey.

At about the same time, I heard that my vicar was intending to join the navy and discovered I would be left to run Potten End and Ashridge forever, so I went to SPG (The Society for the Propagation of the Gospel, now USPG) and asked what the possibilities were of work overseas. While at college, I had signed a form to say I would give equal consideration to work overseas or in the UK. I intended to go back to the Far East some time. All my family traditions and our private family language were connected with Malaya and the place fascinated me. SPG had a scheme where they were going to train people to reignite the church as soon as the war died down a bit, either in China or S.E. Asia after training people in mission work in Basutoland (now Lesotho) in a kind of bush brotherhood. I spoke on the telephone with the Appointments Secretary and said I would like to join the scheme. He asked me a few questions and said there were six or eight members on it, most were leaving the next week, but I could join them on the next convoy. This was the nearest to an interview I had.

I sailed in a convoy from Liverpool in October 1943. We were dodging the German "U boat" submarines most of the way to Cape Town.

South Africa

We arrived in Cape Town on Christmas Eve. The priest who was my cabin companion was entranced after a day's visit with the coloured community on the Cape Flats and worked there for the rest of his life.

When the organiser of the party arrived in Cape Town a week later, he took a look at me and said, "I have the perfect job for you Donald – the Railway Mission in Bechuanaland (Botswana)." It was the one job I knew something about as I had had a friend who had worked there and from her stories taking to drink was an occupational hazard! It was a complete non-job. It had been started some fifty years earlier when the expatriate railway workers were all British. They had since been replaced by Afrikaners, members of the Dutch Reformed Church. The caboose one lived in was hooked on to the end of a goods train and one was shunted up and down the railway in Bechuanaland at odd hours of the morning. One got out and tried to find the one in twenty who might be English speakers.

I refused the offer to join the Railway Mission and was given option number two – something called "The Pretoria Native Mission". It really was enormous fun, with a wide variety of congregations. Some services were held in European churches in the suburbs. The centre was a wooden building that had been there since the year dot, just out of Church Square in Pretoria, right in the heart of government. Others were out in "native locations", as they were called, on the edge of Pretoria, some on Dutch farms and others on "native reserves", up to sixty miles from Pretoria. This was the terminology of the day. It was a complete cross-section of society. My boss during my time in Pretoria was Father Pip Woodfield, who had previously been the head of a teacher training college. I respected and liked him.

Apartheid had not been named at this time but it was there. It was practically impossible for people in Pretoria to know what was happening. Some of the "native locations", were guarded and whites were allowed in. In any case, who would ever want to drive ten miles to a "native location"? There were horror stories about what might happen to you.

In Pretoria there were two quite different townships. Atteridgeville and Lady Selbourne were the only two places in the Transvaal where Africans had been able to buy land freehold. The conditions in Lady Selbourne were terrible. There was no police station. The nearest was in Pretoria itself. There was a women's mission called Tumelong (the place of faith). On one occasion when there were four women missionaries working there, somebody broke into their house, they all jumped on him and pinned him to the ground. Three managed to hold him down whilst the fourth went to telephone the police. The reply was, "Where are you speaking from?" "From Tumalong Mission, Lady Selbourne." "We can't go there at night, it's not safe!" "We live here and we are sitting on this man. What do we do with him?" The final reply, "Continue sitting on him. We'll come and collect him in the morning!"

Atteridgeville was a model township and a great deal of imagination had gone into it. It was named after Mrs Atteridge who was an imaginative mayor of Pretoria and somehow had got it through her hardline Council. It was very well done, as things were at the time. The roads were not all in squares. The houses were of many different designs and had gardens! Each road was planted out with a different species of tree. It really looked extremely human and one of the most inspiring places I had ever seen. It is still going. It was just too good to knock down when apartheid was introduced in 1948.

Ishmael, one of the clergy team, was an absolute saint and lived in Atteridgeville. Among his many congregations was one at the big ISCOR steel works. He used to hold a Eucharist at 4.30 in the morning for the day shift before they went on duty. I remember Ishmael telling me once that he had got up at 3.45 a.m. and tried to start his motor-cycle. He tried kick-starting it for half an hour and it just would not fire. He had to give up and came to me later in the morning and said, "Father, I've failed." He was one of the hardest working people I have ever met.

South West Township was built at the same time in Johannesburg, Orlando, now renamed Soweto. They ordered a thousand houses and began by building the loos, so there were a thousand loos laid out in straight lines across the African veldt as far as you could see. Then came the houses, absolutely identical, in straight rows. They did not even name the roads. They had one set of numbers running throughout it, so your house might be "893 Orlando". I had never seen anything quite so impersonal and awful. Fortunately I did not work there.

School feeding programme

There was concern about malnutrition in the schools connected to the mission and their ability to feed the school children. One of my jobs was running a feeding scheme for several schools. We had 2d (1p) per child a day with which to feed 5,000 children, including overheads. We were able to achieve it and kept the children reasonably fit.

We could not afford to spend much on transport and some of the schools were fifty miles away. We decided to supply food that could be sent once a term: maize-meal, which was cheap as the staple food, as much high-protein food as they could afford and vegetables. The cheapest protein was cheddar cheese. A cheese weighed about a hundred pounds, like a barrel of tar, and could keep a school going for a term. It was about 10d (5p) a pound.

The schools could not grow any fruit. Those in the country were on Afrikaans farms and in the townships there was no land. Cheap oranges were available. They were graded into five different sizes, the smallest were almost given away. A thirty-eight pound "pocket" cost 20d (10p) and held up to one hundred oranges, so it was possible to give each pupil an orange a day for about 0.1p per head.

They varied the diet as much as they could. Some of the schools were on the route of an Islamic baker, a member of the Aga Khan's Ismaeli sect, who lived in Pretoria. He said to me that if I ever wanted money for my school I should just ask his accountant. As a Muslim he was bound to give ten percent of his income to the poor. The ten percent automatically went into a special account. It was there for the asking. He thought I would make good use of it.

Periodically there were bread shortages and the van was empty when it reached a couple of schools thirty miles out of Pretoria. I went to see the baker who immediately told his driver to go to the furthest schools and give them all they wanted. He would then ration the European outlets on his way home. It reminded me of the generosity of the Islamic Faith.

I was in Pretoria for eight and a half years. I had two "Cape Coloured" congregations. They were a small community, 5,000 out of a total population of 150,000. They had little place in society and found it hard to find work. Employers already provided loos for "Whites" and "Natives" and could not be bothered to build a third set for "Coloureds". The Coloureds had just one mediocre school and a smaller but much loved church school called "The Good Shepherd". I am still in touch with two SPG missionaries who taught there in the 1940s.

At the School of the Good Shepherd I suggested starting a Scout Troop but there were problems. There were white Scouts and native Pathfinders and never the twain could meet. No time for Baden Powell and all that stuff about being a brother to every other scout – unless he was the same colour as you.

The Pathfinders had only recently been accepted into the worldwide Scout Movement. Until then, everything had to be a little bit different. The patrol-leaders' stripes had to be horizontal, whereas in then white Scouts they were vertical. Now that the Pathfinders were recognised as part of the Scout movement, the stripes could be vertical – but the rule that they must never attend gatherings of white Scouts remained absolute. Our boys decided to throw in their lot with their Black brothers and so became the 4th Pretoria Pathfinders.

They had no equipment or money. Everything had to be begged for their first camp. The Black troop at St Peter's Rosettenville on the Witwatersrand lent us two tents – fine, except that they were full of holes. One tent came from a white Scout troop on condition that only Europeans slept in it. That ruled out the Assistant Scoutmaster, as he was Coloured. Beggars could not be choosers. The cooking-pots were borrowed from the Jewish community – no colour restrictions but no pork products were to be cooked in them.

At 3.00 a.m. on the first night of the camp we had the biggest downpour I had ever experienced. The heavens burst open and just poured water – not rain – on to us, accompanied by a high wind. There were shouts and laughter and two tents collapsed. The contents of both arrived in my tent, the only one still standing. No question of who was which colour, just 25 bodies in one tent. It was hilarious and none of the 4th Pretoria will ever forget their first camp.

In 1950, a camp was held at Umgababa on the Natal coast. None of the scouts had ever seen the sea. Pretoria is about 400 miles from the Indian Ocean so it was quite an expedition to get there, especially as I was not allowed to travel third class on the train. I had to travel at one end of the train and the boys at the other. I held all the tickets to add to the complications. On the way back there was a kindly ticket inspector who said that the law only applied in the Transvaal so I could join my boys until midnight, when I would enter the Transvaal, and then I would have to leave them. At the other end of the carriage was a tall bearded Zulu. He never took his eyes off me. After a little while he got up and stalked the whole length of the carriage to where I was sitting. He pulled a half-crown out of his pocket, gave it to me and said, "That's for being without apartheid." Half-a-crown was a lot of money – as much as a farm labourer earned in a day. Each of the four provinces had its own traditions regarding this. The

Cape was the most liberal, the Coloured had a vote, which the other three never had. Natal was mildly liberal.

Umgababa was a "Native Reserve" south of Durban, just outside the "White" part of the Natal coast. We descended on it in 1950. None of the boys possessed a swimming costume so they bathed in the Indian Ocean. Then the owner of the local hotel came and said he had had a complaint from one of his guests. Through her binoculars she could see the boys were bathing in the nude and was offended. The hotel was half-a-mile away. I said I was sorry but the boys could not afford bathing suits. It was hard to expect them not to swim on the only time they had ever seen the sea. I suggested that his guest should turn her binoculars in the other direction.

One morning a telegram came from one of the parents in Pretoria, 400 miles away: "Please deny or confirm drowning tragedy." There were 30 boys in the camp and they had gone off in four different directions (on patrol hikes?). It was impossible to know who was there and who was not. I phoned my boss in Pretoria, Fr Pip Woodfield and found he was being besieged by parents. I told him I couldn't guarantee that they were all safe because they had gone off at the crack of dawn, but nobody had told me anybody had drowned! I would count them when they returned. The Coloured community was so tight that once a rumour started, everyone heard it within minutes. All the boys returned to camp in one piece.

4th Pretoria Scout Troop
Willie is on the left in the front row
2005

The Coloured people in Pretoria spoke among themselves a dialect of Afrikaans laced with a few Malay words. They kept English for important things such as school and church. To me they would only speak English. I had to learn enough Afrikaans to know if they were swearing.

The troop kept going for another 40 years after I left it in 1951. It was entirely run by successors of the boys who joined in the 1940s. Willie Hoods visited me in Uxbridge in 1985. He joined in 1946 as the smallest Cub in the Pack and became a very good Scout before I left five years later. I had lost touch with him for a long time and was astonished to learn that after Independence he ended up as Deputy Administrator of the Transvaal. Long before then Willie and his wife Gloria had started a school for handicapped Coloured children and had been raising funds for it ever since.

I had visits from others. One was working in Canada; the wife of another who went to Australia wrote in Christmas 2010 to say that he had died. The 4th Pretoria has been an important part of all our lives.

In 2005 Jane and I stayed with Willie and Gloria Hood. Willie Hood gathered together 11 members of the troop from all over South Africa for a wonderful reunion in his home in Pretoria when I handed over the Log of the 4th Pretoria that I had made and kept. What a party!

Swaziland[1] 1951-1961

Having said "Yes" to Bishop Tom Savage I drove the two hundred and fifty miles from Pretoria to Swaziland in the new Bedford half-ton pick-up to begin my work as Director of the Usuthu Mission in September 1951. Apart from Wilmot Jali, the parish priest, his wife Rosina and the few labourers employed on the mission, I found the congregation at the Mission on strike. They had vowed never to enter the church again.

The Diocese of Zululand, based at Eshowe, three hundred miles away in Natal, was congratulating itself on its decision to keep only 120 acres for the mission and to sell the other 5,000 acres to the Swazi nation at half the normal price. The nation was far from being grateful. The diocese was unaware that the land had been given free of charge to Jekeseni (Jackson, missionary at Usuthu in the 1890s) by Mbandzeni, the Paramount Chief and the father of Sobhuza II, who succeeded him in 1900 and remained Paramount Chief until the 1980s. They were saying, "Your neighbour's wife has a new baby but she has no milk. You lend him a cow. Two years later, the baby is weaned. Does he then sell it back to you?" Everything depended on good relations between the Church and the Swazi nation.

Paramount Chief Sobhuza II and one of his wives

I sent a telegram to the bishop saying, "Please cancel sale or I will return to Pretoria." He did so and I stayed. The strike was over.

The Usuthu Mission had responsibility for the work of the Anglican Church in half the country. Its centre was a small church in the Malkerns

---
[1] Renamed Eswatini in 2018

Valley built before World War I, a primary school and two new rondavels (round huts). One was to be our living quarters. The other, the bedroom. Later we built a small house. The Usuthu had been closed as a mission station in 1913 because of malaria and was an outstation of Bremersdorp, a town twelve miles and now called Manzini, the place of waters.

The Usuthu was to become the home of the Mirfield Old Students' Mission to Swaziland for the next ten years. The first Old Student to serve was Anthony Molesworth who had been a curate at St Mary's, Blyth, in Newcastle diocese. He was a great linguist and storyteller but not all his stories were printable. Others who joined later were Peter Burtwell and Anthony Salmon.

Left to right: Geoff Harrison, Wilmot Jali, Jack Dobson, Donald, Anthony Molesworth

Sobhuza was a wise ruler in an age when autocracy was already out of date. He moved with ease in and out of traditional Swazi culture and language into the modern world. Fortunately he agreed to attend my unveiling and came with his indunas (advisers) in colourful Swazi dress and an appropriate wife out of the hundred he had acquired. He spoke perfect Swazi and English. Before the feast of two whole beasts was devoured, Sobhuza graciously welcomed me but said pointedly that the Anglican Church had so far done very little with the land his father had given us. His followers seemed to agree. I chose a Swazi proverb with which to open my reply. "The mouth can cross even a river in flood." If your people and we can work together, there may be something to see in a few years' time. Six years later I referred to this meeting when speaking at the official opening of St Christopher's school.

Paramount Chief Sobhuza II and Donald

Members of the local community joined us for worship on Sundays. As a young girl Jean Ions (who later married Jack Dobson) recalls: "We used to go to Church on Sunday at the Mission. It was the little old church in its original state. It was kept clean and neat by the local ladies. The one thing they had to do before each Sunday was 'polish' the floor which meant getting some fresh cow-dung to smear on it and polish it. Some of the 'ladies' didn't fancy it! I just remember thinking what a pleasant smell it gave off and how meticulously they polished it."

The Malkerns Valley was dramatically beautiful. To the west, the slopes of the Drakensberg mountains, which Usuthu Forests (a wing of the Commonwealth Development Corporation) was just beginning to cover with pines. Eastwards you looked across the lowveld to the Lebombo mountains, 50-60 miles away marking the border of Mozambique, then known as PEA (Portuguese East Africa). Alongside us flowed the Great Usuthu River, which provided constantly replenished building sand. Work was just beginning on the Malkerns irrigation scheme, which was to turn the whole valley into rice fields and citrus orchards. Over the next 20 years it would provide all the electricity the country needed and irrigate vast acres of rice paddies in the lowveld.

A Zulu priest, Wilmot Jali, was in charge of the parish when I arrived and was a huge help to me. His wife Rosamund was the very competent head of the primary school. Bit by bit we managed to get the church going again. The parish covered the southern half of Swaziland but little was happening except at the Usuthu, Mankaiana and Hlakikulu. There was an old and decrepit mission station at Endlozana, just across the Transvaal border in South Africa. I had a motor scooter – a Vespa, and then a Lambretta – and went off on a hundred and twenty mile trip once a month.

Fortunately I had learned to sing mass in Zulu from the Mandebele congregation at Broederstroom, Pretoria. They had migrated 550 miles from Zululand in the mid-1600s and had clung tenaciously to their language, though surrounded by Sotho-speakers, whose language was as different as German is from English.

Most Swazi followed African Traditional Religion and were polygamous. Large numbers of men went as migrant labourers to the Johannesburg gold mines, which then employed 350,000 men, creaming off the most go-ahead from Swaziland, Lesotho, Zululand, Mozambique and Malawi.

Men and boys did the ploughing with oxen, other agricultural work was done by women. As the boys were herding cattle for the five months when the maize was growing, few of them got very far at school. The top classes were mainly girls: western culture came into Swaziland through women. It was the other way round in Malawi, where gardens are tilled by hoe and that is women's work, so the boys went to school.

Stephen Makandanje

One of our "bush-brotherhood" team was a Malawian, Stephen Makandanje. He had walked 1,000 miles to Swaziland in search of work in 1915 and had worked all his adult life as a hospital orderly. He built a church in Hlatikulu with his own hands, having asked to be on night duty at the hospital so that he could work on the church during the day. It took a year to mould and bake the bricks, another year to build the church building and a third year to build up a thriving congregation.

I thought Stephen would make an excellent priest and asked him if he would like to be ordained. He said, "No, that would spoil it all." I asked him. "Why?" He said, "The work of God has to be done from your heart. To be paid for it would spoil it." I replied, "If I asked the bishop to ordain you as a priest and promised to pay you nothing, would you accept?" "Father, that is what I have always longed for."

Stephen inspired me with the idea of voluntary ministry. Years later when in Malawi, diocesan synod welcomed the idea and when we finally left in 1981, many of the clergy were voluntary priests.

Usuthu pineapples 1956

I was due to go on leave in 1956 to Australia – I had not seen my family for seven years. We had just planted a quarter of a million pineapples. I was Chairman of the Swaziland Pineapple Growers Association.

Nobody had grown pineapples in Swaziland before; the pundits said they would only grow within ten miles of the coast. The entire pineapple industry was near Port Elizabeth in the Eastern Cape, five hundred miles south. We had started irrigation farming, using water from the Great Usuthu River and planted some pineapples to see how they would do.

We had a lot of other things happening at the time, including starting a secondary school, and I was doing most of the farming. Anthony Molesworth knew nothing about it so it was essential that somebody be found to look after the farm for six months while I was away. We were employing a dozen or so Swazis but they needed direction. We had a long meeting and couldn't think of anyone, when Anthony said he knew a chap who used to be in his scout troop in Tyneside. He had been doing his military service in Kenya and was probably at a loose end as he had just lost his job. He was working underground for the British Coal Board.

I said it sounded just the job for fruit farming and building in Swaziland, write and see what he says! We did not hear anything and then we had a cable from the Canary Islands saying, "On the way. Arriving in Cape Town next week." And so arrived Jack Dobson, who was later ordained priest and then became Archdeacon of Swaziland.

The pineapples have done extremely well and it is still a major industry of the country. The people who said they would not grow with us did not know what they were talking out. Never believe experts! The farm next-door was owned and run, but not directly managed, by the Director of Horticulture for South Africa who lived in Pretoria. He was responsible for all the pineapple growing in South Africa and was one of the initial growers of pineapples. He went bankrupt! We did not make a lot of money but we did not go bankrupt.

For various reasons, partly to do with the factory and partly due to the cost of exporting and finding markets, the pineapples were not a financial success but profits were good enough to keep the industry going. The Director of Horticulture, at one stage, was employing one hundred people on his farm trying to pull out the weeds by hand, which was not much fun with all the spines along the edges of the fruit.

My leave in Australia taught me much. I found that their methods were totally different from those in South Africa. The pineapple has a very vulnerable root system. They are small and fleshy so are easily broken off and then the fruit ceases to grow, although they may live. It is impossible to hoe so they were planted feet apart and weeds were left to melt around the plant. In Australia they plant them half the distance apart, only twelve inches, with the idea to get them to grow together as quickly as possible so they form a total shade over the ground to prevent weeds growing. They also applied a weed-killer spray, which kept the weeds at bay for six weeks. If the fruit was growing well in six weeks a canopy grew over the ground preventing weeds growing. We planted our pineapples using this method and they did very well. A Pineapple Growers Association was formed and I was made its Chairman.

There was no problem getting the produce to a port as the railway was being developed primarily to take the products of the forest that had been planted along the Drakensberg Mountains. Maputo, the new name for Lorenzo Marques, was one of the best natural ports in Africa. A river with sixty feet of water right along the wharfs, completely protected by islands.

I saw Swaziland from the air in 1980 and, as we circled the airport, all we could see was blue-grey – pineapples. A much, much bigger industry than when I left it twenty years earlier, now stretching miles along the Malkerns Valley.

St Christopher's secondary school

When I was in Australia in 1956 people generously gave enough money to get the school started. Jack Dobson, the coal-board man and a surveyor, was in charge of the building as well as the farming. The school was built on a fairly steep hillside. The amount of soil we had to excavate was considerable and we had no proper excavating materials at all, but we did have a tractor at this stage.

Jack built St Christopher's for 120 boys for something under £10,000. I think it was originally for 60 boarders and expanded to 120 students, just 100 yards from where our houses were. A glorious view looking right down the Mzutu valley, with the mountains in the distance.

Jack was the best man at my wedding in Malawi in 1962.

St Christopher's campus, Usuthu

St Christopher's chapel

The Paramount Chief came to the opening of the school in 1959. We were very glad that he had marked the occasion by sending one of his sons as a student.

Community life was what interested me most. The Usuthu semi-brotherhood was good but something was lacking. Perhaps we could learn from the ashrams (mini-communities) of India, and from the West Queensland Bush Brotherhood, where I hoped to spend a fortnight.

On leave to Australia

My leave in Australia in 1956 was part of my second "furlough". SPG (The Society for the Propagation of the Gospel) allowed missionaries their second "furlough" after seven years. The next would be after ten, then no more. You belonged now to the local Church. I left Anthony Molesworth in charge with Jack Dobson looking after the farm.

I was keen to see something of Asia, where our family history began. I sailed for Australia on a White Star cargo ship via the east coast of Africa, to Bombay (now Mumbai). Two miles off Zanzibar the wind already carried the scent of cloves.

At Mombasa, Arab dhows were in the harbour. I watched one being repaired. The Arab boat-builder was using a drill operated by a bow, rather like that for a violin. The bit spun backwards and forwards as the skilled craftsman moved his hand left to right, with the cord wrapped round the drill bit. I later saw exactly the same technique being used in Penang harbour. Arabs had been trading on both sides of the Indian Ocean from the time of Christ. The bow-drill, like Islam in Indonesia, Malaysia and East Africa, was one of their legacies, as was the Swahili language, made up from Arabic words and Bantu grammar. At Karachi an enormous squatters' camp provided a kind of temporary home for perhaps a hundred thousand Muslims, some of the millions who had left India for the new state of Pakistan established in 1947.

At Tiruppattur station – mid-way between Bangalore and Madras – I was glad to find an ashram bullock-cart waiting for me. The ashram church was in the style of a South India Hindu temple. It had a white tower covered with carvings, not of Hindu deities but of trees and wildlife. I found nine members of the ashram, but some were out in villages. They lived in a community of eighty or more, the rest being students, mostly Hindu, who had come to spend their vacation working with members of the ashram.

The two founders, one Scots and the other Tamil, were both eye-surgeons and had met during World War I. From time to time the ashram divided into small groups who would each stay in one of twenty or so villages, looking for new patients with eye problems and helping with other community needs, such as clean water.

At sunrise each morning, all of us – Hindu volunteers, ashram members and myself as a guest from Africa – spent an hour in silent meditation, cross-legged on an inner verandah that surrounded a patch of grass and a palm-tree. I think I felt nearer to Jesus and his Twelve than at any time of my life.

Gandhi once visited Tiruppattur. When he left, he said to the Hindu members of the group, "This is the kind of Christianity you should be afraid of!" The rest – symbolised by the very English parish churches I saw, even in villages – would have no future.

I left by bullock-cart after three days, caught another train and in Madras met a South Indian Bishop. I disgraced myself by calling him "My Lord" and trying to kiss his ring. I thought this was what one did to bishops. I received a gentle rebuke, "This is the Church of South India. We don't have Lords."

By train again down the Coromandel Coast (what a lovely name!) and then the long Adam's Bridge that spans the twenty miles of the Gulf of Mannar between India and Sri Lanka. Sri Lanka had just won its independence and my hostess took me to the top of a mountain overlooking the beautiful city of Kandy. The results of the election of Sri Lanka's first President were about to be announced. There, 500 feet below us, the whole of Kandy was in a party mood – fireworks, music and dancing. Then the news broke – Sri Lanka's first Prime Minister would be Solomon Bandaranaike, leader of the Sri Lanka Freedom Party. He was succeeded by his wife.

I continued on my passage by ship to Fremantle, the first bit of Australia we saw as a family when we arrived as immigrants thirty years earlier.

Impopotha and outreach work

It was good to be back at the Usuthu Mission after a worthwhile leave. Fifty years ago one of the early missionaries found a little Coloured boy, the son of an English colonial officer and a Swazi woman. He put him on his horse, clothed him, taught him and when was grown up sent him off to find his way in the world, just saying: "When you get a chance, do something for the Church in return."

This man, now grey-headed, said that he had bought a little farm and wanted to give a piece of it to the Church.

So we built the little church of St Anthony on the small hill overlooking half of Swaziland. At one end is the round apse in the chancel. It was closed off by two big doors so that it could also be used as a school. Outside the building was whitewashed so it could be seen from miles away with its great cross of sky-blue tiles.

St Anthony's Impophota

On one visit Ruth, the mission Land Rover, was towing a big trailer picked up on a scrap heap and we nearly got stuck in the mud several times but Ruth carried on for 30 miles. It was nearly dark when I arrived at Mpopotha, a hot meal was waiting at William's house.

Mission work and Siswati language

We did quite a lot of active mission work during which the number of church congregations grew from two to twenty-five. Our priority was to build up a Swazi priesthood. I think there were only one, possibly two, Swazi priests in the entire world at that time. There were a few Zulu priests, one of whom was Fr Jali, a member of the team at Usuthu. The Zulu language is quite different from the Swazi language and this had to be an indigenous church so one of our first jobs was to find candidates for the priesthood.

We found a couple in the secondary school we had in Endhlozane, which was 100 yards outside Swaziland in the Transvaal, and they were trained. I forget whether they were both ordained but one definitely was and there were others later on. One of our fights was to have the Swazi church recognised as independent of the Zulu church.

They had nothing much in common, except we were speaking the Zulu language in church because the Zulus had a greater profile in British consciousness and both of these places, you might say, had been under British administration. Zululand was attached to Natal, and Swaziland one of the three High Commission Territories – Swaziland, Basutoland (Lesotho) and Bechuanaland (Botswana).

The British had prescribed that Zulu should be the language taught in schools and when education first arrived in Swaziland, Zulu was the language imposed. It seemed to us quite ridiculous that people should be speaking a foreign language on top of another language that they had to learn as the main business language – English. I felt there was a place for people to have two languages, but not three. People would always need English as being the language of higher education, also being the common language of the black population of Southern Africa. Swaziland is necessarily a part because it is, physically and geographically, almost with South Africa. The same applied to Basutoland (Lesotho) and Bechuanaland (Botswana).

The other language is the one you spoke as a child, the one you say your prayers in, make love in, the intimate language of the heart, and that has to be the real language. Swazi is not the correct name as the letter Z does not exist in Swazi. The language is called Siswati and people do not refer to their country as Swazi, it is Kangwane, the name of the founder of the nation, who originally migrated from Mozambique somewhere about the end of the eighteenth century.

There was no good reason for Zululand and Swaziland to be in the same diocese. The Swazis suffered from having a bishop three hundred miles away in Eshowe in Zululand and saw him twice a year. I was a member of the Standing Committee and had to make a six hundred mile round-trip for every meeting.

So we did two things. One, to try and establish the Swazi language of Siswati. There was a small local newspaper mainly in English but with a page or two in Zulu. They agreed to print anything we could produce in Siswati. We invited contributions in Siswati – folk tales, autobiographical pieces, anything. There was an enthusiastic response, even though few had ever seen written Siswati before. The only printed material in existence was a catechism of the 1860s, long out of print, and a grammar book from the Department of Linguistics at Pretoria University in Afrikaans (Cape Dutch) and Siswati.

Superficially Siswati is a bit like Zulu but there are important differences, for example, the letter "z" is replaced by a "t" and all nouns begin with a consonant, not with a vowel as in Zulu. The vocabulary is perhaps fifteen percent different.

Simon Nxumalo

One set of contributions to the local paper was outstanding. Whoever wrote them was an artist with words. One was about a thunderstorm. "Great black clouds filled the sky; the rain came down and then the hail and the herd-boys shivered and pulled their skin cloaks over themselves." It was brilliant writing. I said to Jack, "Let's go and dig this man out." He had written from a little school on the top of the mountains in Usuthu Forests, perhaps twenty miles away. We went off on a Sunday afternoon to find him.

Simon Nxumalo was a teacher in his mid-thirties and excited by our visit. He pulled out a tin trunk from under his bed full of Siswati manuscripts. He hadn't been able to find anyone interested in reading them. We picked out the best and printed them week by week. There was a centre in Johannesburg promoting Southern African languages. They offered to take Simon Nxumalo and train him to lead a Siswati team and to write the necessary materials. In due course he came back, published the first literary books in Siswati and launched a literacy campaign on a national scale.

Siswati later became the official language of the country. The prayer-book and the New Testament have both been published in Siswati.

Off his own bat he also set up the Sebenta Society – self-help movement. "Sebenta" means "work" in Siswati. I left Swaziland at this point and am hazy on detail but I know he went into politics and ran a party in opposition to the Paramount Chief – a brave thing to do. He finally did a deal with the King's party and ended up as Deputy Prime Minister. Right out of the blue, some eight or ten years ago, he telephoned me from Swaziland and we had a long talk about AIDS. He was then the Chief Scout of Swaziland, and as I had been a former Commissioner for Training, I recall suggesting that he use the Scout and Guide movements as a way into the need for behaviour change in the anti-AIDS campaign.

As part of our campaign for recognising Swaziland as an independent country in a Zululand Synod that was being held in Swaziland, we called for the name of the diocese to be changed to "Zululand and Swaziland". Bishop Tom Savage was not best pleased. Now he had to sign every document with the cumbersome signature "+Thomas Zululand and Swaziland". It was another eight years before Swaziland became a separate diocese with its own language, history and culture, no longer the poor relation of South Africa's Bantustan, KwaZulu.

Bernard Wrankmore

We welcomed a variety of people and groups to work with us at the Usuthu. One of the most colourful was Bernard Wrankmore. A letter came from the Archbishop of Cape Town saying, "We have an excellent but unusual man in mind for ordination. Could he come to you for some of his training?" So Bernard joined the team. He had worked in several countries, amongst other things he had been a camel-driver, organiser of prize-fights and country-dancing.

I travelled with him to Cape Town and found myself sitting in a small dinghy while Bernard searched the seabed for abalone – large edible snails. I was given a hand-pump to supply him with air. He had no mask and told me there was a limit of thirty seconds without air, after that he would be drowning. It was a terrifying experience. It was wonderful to see him again at my wedding, where he fixed our departing Land Rover, three times!

I learned much from the people of Swaziland and the team with whom I worked for ten years and was sorry to leave for Nyasaland in November 1961.

Nyasaland – 1961

Quite out of the blue I received a letter from the Archbishop of Canterbury in January 1961 asking me if I would allow my name to go forward for election as Bishop of Nyasaland.

I did not know the first thing about Nyasaland except a sixty-year old bit of family history – Ernest Crouch, my uncle, had been a UMCA missionary who, amongst other things, built the *Chauncy Maples* steamer there in 1901. (There is more about them both in the Appendix.)

I needed to ask someone whose opinion I could trust. I phoned Anthony and Mags Barker, doctors at the Charles Johnson Memorial mission hospital at Nqutu in Zululand, to tell them I needed their advice about something. After hearing my news, they said they would pray about it and tell me in the morning. In their bedroom, Anthony turned to Mags and said, "Thank God for that. I thought he might be calling to tell us he had developed VD (venereal disease)!" In the morning they told me I should go.

Consecration

Before leaving Swaziland, I became aware that there had been controversy about my appointment as Bishop of Nyasaland. The struggle for independence and state of emergency were in full swing. There had been agreement that a white bishop was needed. Apart from a handful of white UMCA (Universities Mission to Central Africa) missionaries, hardly any African clergy in the diocese had more than primary education, followed perhaps by vernacular training as a teacher and certainly none had experience of finance. But there had been a strong feeling that if a priest from South Africa was made bishop, he should have at least a whiff of Trevor Huddleston's anger at apartheid. Luckily, it helped that I could describe myself as Australian, having been to school there and all my close family still living in the country.

Chief Gatsha Buthelezi, with whom I had paired up on the Zululand Diocesan Standing Committee as a two-man opposition, had promised he would write to Orton Chirwa, the most outstanding figure in Dr Banda's newly formed cabinet, to certify my lack of respectability. I was therefore relieved to find Orton representing Dr Banda at my consecration, at the Church of the Ascension, Likwenu. This beautiful thatched church, aptly named as it was high up on the slopes of the mountain, was sadly destroyed by a bush fire in 1965. Orton, the brilliant and brave Attorney General, subsequently joined the opposition to Dr Banda and while in Zambia was seized by a Malawian police task force and later died in prison in Malawi.

It was 1961. Past violence, present poverty and future uncertainty, were all in the air. During the State of Emergency, declared during the struggle for independence from the hated Federation of Rhodesia and Nyasaland, a number of people had been killed and many imprisoned, including Dr Banda in Gwelo prison in what was then Southern Rhodesia. There were high hopes for the future of this beautiful country, the size of England, then with a population of three million, but still much to be agreed before it became independent. (At its independence in 1964, the United Nations listed the new country of Malawi as the poorest in the world).

St Andrew's Day 30th November 1961 at Mkuli – Malosa

At my consecration on St Andrew's Day 1961, 30 November, the Archbishop of Central Africa presided, assisted by Bishop Cecil Alderson of Mashonaland, Bishop Obadiah Kariuki of Kenya and Bishop Tom Savage of Zululand. Tom Savage preached and passed on the few words that Jesus spoke in his own Aramaic language:

Abba – Father. You, Donald, can only be a father-in-God if your whole life is one of loving dependence on God the Father.

Ephrata – Be opened. Your task is to open the ears of the deaf – those who do not know Christ and the faithful that they may hear more clearly.

Talitha cumi – Little girl, arise. Expect new life to come to the church through your ministry.

Eloi, eloi. My God, my God, why have you forsaken me? Your hands are to be signed with the cross. Accept the agony of bringing people to God, and in that sign go out to conquer.

Also present at the consecration was Canon Petro Kilekwa. Petro had been captured as a slave in Eastern Zambia as a young boy in the 1870s. He was marched nearly a thousand miles to Zanzibar, sold in the market there and taken in an Arab dhow to the Persian Gulf.

I felt about three inches high as I gave God's blessing to the huge crowd outside the church, wielding the great diocesan ivory and silver crozier which contains part of the wooden staff wielded by Bishop Charles Mackenzie, who died of malaria and enteritis on the banks of the Shire River nine months after entering Nyasaland in 1861. The ivory had been presented as a peace-offering by a Yao chief after the murder of one of the early lay missionaries on the eastern lake shore.

After the service, Dr David Stevenson, the diocesan doctor, famous for playing his bagpipes before dawn each morning on the Malindi lake shore, called me aside. He said he looked forward to continuing to serve in the diocese but wanted to warn me that if war were to break out between Scotland and England, he would have to leave without notice to fight for Scotland.

Challenges in the Diocese

The first year in the diocese was heavy and I was not sure that I would survive. The twenty-three African clergy earned the equivalent of five pounds a month, hardly any of them had a bicycle that worked and their housing was dreadful. Their average age was around sixty. We were allowed two places every two years at the provincial theological college in Northern Rhodesia (Zambia) where students came from the four countries in the Anglican Province of Central Africa – Bechuanaland (Botswana), Southern Rhodesia (Zimbabwe) and Nyasaland. This would just allow us to replace the clergy who were retiring. Growth was out of the question.

When the *Chauncy Maples* was sold in 1957 and Likoma Island became virtually unreachable, the headquarters of the diocese was moved to Mponda's (Chief Mponda's place) on the edge of the Shire River at the southern end of the lake. This was ninety miles from the nearest sizeable town. In the wet season the road was flooded for days at a time, the post was erratic, there was no telephone and few visitors. If the church was to play any significant part in the new Malawi, it had to be closer to the centre of things.

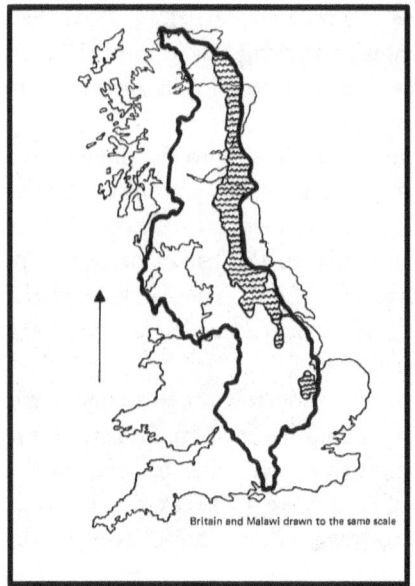

Britain and Malawi drawn to the same scale

The new Bishop, 1961

Showing the relative sizes of Britain and Malawi

Financial problems

In the post soon after my arrival was a letter from our bank manager. "Would I kindly refrain from signing any further cheques?" Our overdraft limit was £12,000 and we were now £20,000 in the red. That would represent perhaps £100,000 at today's values. I asked the missionary treasurer for a balance sheet. He produced a statement showing we had a deficit of £3,000 for the past year and said that my predecessor had never asked for a balance-sheet. I drew a veil over further conversations.

In April, I wrote to my brother Felix, a paediatrician in Brisbane:

> In the diocese we are boiling up for a frightful financial row. We borrowed an auditor from Northern Rhodesia diocese who says there is around £10,000 missing and unaccounted for in the books. He doesn't think it could be the treasurer's fault "because he is such a nice man" but he did say that every fact had to be prized out as with a corkscrew. Anyway, there seems to be enough evidence to give him the push which will be a great relief.

For seven days a non-stop meeting went on at Mponda's – teachers, medical assistants, business people, black and white, trying to find some way of making the financial wheels of the diocese go round. Amongst other things it recommended we move the headquarters of the diocese to Malosa/Likwenu where we already had nearly a square mile of land.

Likwenu had been an old tobacco farm of about three-quarters of a square mile. High on the list was to move the headquarters from Mponda's to Likwenu/Malosa. It was in a largely Muslim area within seventeen miles of Zomba, then the seat of government, and on the main road to the central and northern provinces (as they were then called). It already had the embryonic Malosa Secondary School (named after the 6,000 foot mountain ridge behind it), a small primary school, a leprosarium with about one hundred patients, a church at the top of the hill, appropriately named the Church of the Ascension, and a small clinic, built above the school in the hope that mosquitoes would not find it. Mosquitoes were not deterred but patients were.

Mponda's

Mponda's was my home during 1962. It is a very large traditional village and the headquarters of the most powerful Yao chief in the country. The apostrophe is an important reminder that the area belongs to Chief Mponda. At Mponda's you are in no doubt that you are in the heart of Africa. On any night you would hear the barking of innumerable dogs, drumming for Muslim dances, hyenas as the treble, human voices and hippos as the deep bass.

In 1960, Chief Mponda had boycotted the visit of Michael Ramsey, Archbishop of Canterbury, seeing him as a puppet of the hated Federal Government of Nyasaland, Northern and Southern Rhodesia.

A colourful place but hardly a suitable centre for a diocese roughly the size of England. It had no telephone. The nearest was in Fort Johnston, later renamed Mangochi, four miles away. When the road was under water, we could get no post. Zomba, the government capital, was 75 miles to the south and Blantyre, the main commercial centre, another 42 miles further on. Bishop Frank Thorne had left me a car which only kept going through the creative ingenuity of its wonderful driver, Robert Malidadi. The missionary nurses and priests visited their health centres and parishes by hitch-hiking on one of the few vehicles that used the road.

I wrote to my mother in Australia a few days after arriving at Mponda's:

> The flamboyant trees are all covered in red flowers. The mission is in the middle of the largest Muslim village in the country. Fortunately Chief Mponda consented to see me. As a keen member of the

Malawi Congress Party, in its fight for independence, he refused to meet the Archbishop of Canterbury, Michael Ramsey, three years ago because in his sermon he had commended the British Government's policy of linking Nyasaland, Northern and Southern Rhodesia in a Central Africa Federation.

The mission consists of a very lovely church in the middle, with the *mezane* (a Swahili word meaning mess and common room) and for each missionary a small thatched two-roomed house. Mine is the same but newer and in better condition. There is a big and flourishing primary school with Justus Kishindo as its excellent headmaster and a small maternity hospital that sees up to 400 outpatients a day. Joan Knowles is in charge of the hospital and is sister to Jonathan Knowles, who was with me at Mirfield and was killed at Dunkirk.

On the other side of the lake is Malindi mission, 15 miles away. To get there you go through Mponda's village to Fort Johnston and there you wait for up to two hours, eventually crossing the 200 yard wide Shire River on an antique hand-pulled ferry, powered by a team of Yao men who sing hauntingly. Archdeacon Habil Chipembere is in charge there, father to Henry Chipembere, who invited Dr Banda to come back to Nyasaland to break the Federation and eventually to head its new independent government. Henry was imprisoned with many others by the Federal Government – I hope to visit him soon in Zomba prison.

At Malindi there is St Michael's Teacher Training College, a large primary school, a church designed as a small version of the cathedral on Likoma Island, a very busy hospital and the all important workshop on the lake shore that used to service the *Chauncy Maples* and other boats. Now, through the gifted, pipe-smoking Francis Bell, the workshop provides an invaluable service to the various institutions and local villagers by mending and making anything mechanical. Francis has trained many mechanics who have become highly regarded throughout the country. Most buildings date from the 1920s and most of them leak!

At Mponda's, the ever loyal and encouraging Ron Tovey, at 35 the only young missionary priest in the diocese, knocked at my door one morning. Rain was steadily dripping through the thatched roof onto my desk, which I had covered with old newspapers, leaving only the typewriter exposed. "Let me show you something to cheer you up," he said, leading me to

Christine Moss's house. She was away on a hitch-hiking visit to health centres. Ron pushed open the door of her house and opened the cupboard where her few dresses hung. Everyone was soaked and the rainwater dripped through them onto the mud floor. It was a good way of stopping my self-pity.

This was the first time I had worked with UMCA missionaries and I developed considerable admiration for them. Committed to being celibate, those who became engaged were asked to leave. Sixty of the first one hundred and fifty died from blackwater fever. They lived a frugal life, although even that was far more comfortable than those amongst whom they lived. There was a common purse to cover every day living and £30 a year with which to buy clothes and go on holiday.

Meeting Jane and getting engaged

Jane and I became engaged on the slopes of Mulanje Mountain in Easter Week 1962. I had gone there to take Easter services. I had been working quite hard and felt I needed a day off so I wrote to the church warden of the little expatriate congregation at Mulanje called Mel Crofton. His wife Brigid was Jane's twin sister. I wrote to Mel and Brigid to confirm that I was coming and asked if it would be too much of a bore if I stayed on for a day and climbed their mountain. It is a magnificent mountain 10,000 foot high, with 3,000 foot vertical rock faces. Its plateau covers one hundred square miles with birds and trees not found anywhere else in the world. At its base are rolling green tea estates.

Brigid opened my letter and is reported to have said to her sister Jane who happened to be staying there, "The bishop wants to spend an extra night here – you'll have to entertain him!" After I left, Jane said to Brigid, "I hope the entertainment was adequate!"

On 27 April 1962 I wrote to my mother:

> Thanks for wishing me a happy Easter. Before I tell you just how happy, please get three of your anti-dilatant drugs and suck them for five minutes ... right? We're getting married on Michaelmas Day. I'm too happy to write about this coherently but am more certain of the rightness of it than anything I have ever done. Her name is Jane Riddle, at present teaching in the St Andrew's Prep School in Blantyre, born and brought up in East Ogwell in Devon, educated at a school run by the CJGS sisters (Companions of Jesus the Good Shepherd), taught in Stepney, came to Nyasaland three years ago,

where her twin sister Brigid is married to a young Assistant District Commissioner, Mel Crofton. They are at present stationed at Mulanje, whereby hangs the tale. We first met when she arrived at Mponda's with a car full of paint and Coloured Sea Rangers and started to paint out the whole mezane – a frightful job which involved spending a week up in the rafters – which were actually the slipway of the *Chauncy Maples* laid down by uncle Ernest – cleaning out the accumulated bat-dirt, cobwebs and lamp-oil grime of half a century. When I was in Blantyre on Maundy Thursday, she poked her head round the door, where the Rector and I were having a serious discussion about finance, to ask if I would like to help her photograph a beaked snake, a rare variety that a professional snake-catcher had found. When I saw her also taking a portrait of a boomslang (a very venomous type of tree-snake) from about 6" with a close-up lens (even the snake-catcher was getting worried!) I noted that she had that touch of recklessness that anybody taking me on as a proposition would need. It was quite by chance that my hostess at Mulanje was Brigid. I had picked that church out of a number where I could have gone for Easter. As it happens to be in the shadow of the finest mountain in Nyasaland, I thought I might stay on an extra day or so to climb it. On the Monday, we all had a wonderful picnic in Mozambique and on the Tuesday, Jane took me to climb Mulanje, the toughest day's climb I have done for a long time – in alternate sun, rain, mist, more sun and finally dark. The next day we toured tea-estates, ending up with a film-show by a planter from Darjeeling. By the time we parted, I think we must have been engaged. It seems that we are likely to meet about three times before the wedding at Michaelmas, as I am hardly going to be at home at all and Jane is tied to the school. Our marriage will probably rock some of the UMCA staff a little, though not seriously, as she is well known by many of them. She is one of the very few Europeans who is completely at home with Africans, who call her by her Christian name without embarrassment – something you rarely meet. She has many accomplishments – officially a secondary school music teacher with PT and religious knowledge, enjoys small boat sailing and photography, does typing and shorthand, drives a car fast and well, is a running repairs mechanic, plays the organ, says her prayers, has a tremendous sense of vocation and an equally robust sense of humour, very calm and sure on the surface but rates about 99 on whatever scale it is that starts with frigidity at 0. One of Jane's children, home from school, rushed into her mother full of excitement: Miss Riddle's getting married. Who to? The Pope. Don't be silly, the Pope doesn't get married. Well, the Bishop, it's the same thing. Is this enough for one letter?

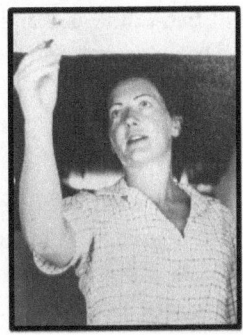

Jane Painting the roof   *Jane with Guides*

Breaking the news of our engagement to the UMCA missionaries at Mponda's was a problem. One of them remained totally silent. Part of the mythology was that my predecessor, Frank Thorne, had been so overcome by the engagement while on leave of two serving missionaries, that he had left the room and was physically ill. But generally they were accepting and those I most respected, such as Archdeacon Christopher Lacey and Fr Ron Tovey, were clearly delighted.

A few days later I had a letter from Bishop Frank, then in Tanganyika, asking, "Are you a Jane (Austen) fan, like me? Would you please put my copy of *Pride and Prejudice* into the post." He also asked about Jane Riddle, "She's far too nice to be a spinster." I felt the Lord had delivered him into my hands and posted the book the same day, with a note saying, "I am a Jane fan, but not in the way I think you meant. We have just announced our engagement and hope to be married in Michaelmas." Frank responded at once with a delightful letter saying, "If I can come to terms with this and even be enthusiastic, I am sure that younger members of UMCA will do so even more quickly."

Ecclesia

The diocese had other problems; how to communicate with clergy and laity in a country the size of England but with only one railway line in the far north where there was no Anglican work. A country with almost no all-weather roads, a skeleton bus system and a trunk telephone line which on the Nkhotakota lake shore at least consisted of one single strand of fencing wire. Our answer was to launch *Ecclesia*. *Ecclesia* was a monthly eight-page magazine consisting of two sheets of foolscap size paper folded. It sold for one penny (0.5p in today's money) and the annual subscription was 15p, to cover paper, envelope and stamp. It came out in two editions, English and Nyanja/Chewa. With rare exceptions it appeared every month for seventeen years.

The first editorial made the point that the missionaries of today are all of us:

> The diocese is one. Whether our birth-places were in Portuguese East Africa (Mozambique) or Britain, in Tanganyika (Tanzania) or Australia or Nyasaland, we are all involved in mission. Those of us who come from other countries – as do most of our clergy, African and European – we come as your servants for Christ's sake.

Chaplaincy and Diocese

The five "white" congregations – Blantyre, Limbe, Zomba, Mulanje and Thyolo – were not diocesan parishes but part of something known as the "European Chaplaincy". This had its own structures and finances and never met the African church except at a brief annual synod. So *Ecclesia* announced a joint meeting of the Diocesan Standing Committee and Chaplaincy Fund representatives to be held on 4 May 1962 to decide on "many urgent matters".

It was not an easy meeting. The "Winds of Change" announced by the British Prime Minister, Harold Macmillan, acknowledging the number of countries in Africa becoming independent, were only a gentle breeze in Nyasaland. It had always been a protectorate where few expatriates were allowed to buy land. It was not a colony like Kenya and the two Rhodesias, where expatriates were allowed to own land.

This had ceased to mean much in the Central African Federation, with Roy Welensky as Prime Minister of the Federation calling the shots. Even in the tiny capital of Zomba, where most of the inhabitants were European and African civil servants, the Club was "Whites only." Consequently, the Governor, Sir Glyn Jones, refused to enter it. Feelings about independence were even stronger in the tea estates of Mulanje and Thyolo.

There was, however, one highly respected tea-planter, Arthur Westrop. He had a background in Sri Lanka and in Scouting and had built All Saints Church in Thyolo. With the passion of an Old Testament prophet, he supported the merging of the Chaplaincy and the Diocese. When he sat down, the two became one without a single dissentient. It was agreed unanimously that henceforth the Chaplaincy churches were fully part of the Diocese.

We were in desperate need of younger clergy. Of the twenty-three African clergy serving this five hundred mile long country, most were over fifty. A much welcome letter from Bishop Tom Savage, from whose diocese I had come, provided support in this area. He told us that all the Lent offerings of Zululand-and-Swaziland would be sent to us as a gift. On the strength of this, we were able to send five young men for priest training instead of the two for whom we had budgeted.

Early days

Exploring the diocese and learning its rich history, was the next task. The first missionaries to arrive in Nyasaland came in response to David Livingstone's plea for Christians to come and stop the ravages of the slave trade. Bishop Mackenzie and his companions arrived in 1860. Many died of malaria and the survivors withdrew. Twenty-two years later, in 1880, two UMCA priests arrived. William Percival Johnson and Charles Janson walked eight-hundred miles from Zanzibar and six weeks later were the first Anglicans to see the lake. Charles Janson died a few days later, Fr Johnson soon lost the sight of one eye and eighty percent vision from the other. With twenty percent vision in just one eye, he continued to work around the lake for the next forty-six years. During this time he translated the Bible into Chinyanja by the dim light of a hurricane lamp. His name is in the Calendar of Saints in Central and Southern Africa.

Likoma Island being a dry, rocky island (five miles by one and a half miles), lies two miles from the Portuguese East Africa (Mozambique) coast to the east. It was chosen as the headquarters of the Diocese because of its safe harbour, its insulation from raids by slave traders and its comparative freedom from malaria. It was the headquarters of the Diocese until the *Chauncy Maples* steamer was sold in 1957.

As befits the headquarters of a diocese, between 1902 and 1905, there arose on the island a magnificent cathedral only slightly smaller than Winchester Cathedral, complete with cloisters, library and Chapter House.

Chauncy Maples, or the CM as she was universally known, used to do a monthly round of lake shore mission stations in Portuguese East Africa

(Mozambique), Nyasaland (Malawi) and German East Africa (Tanzania). It was not until 1906 that a party led by Canon Petro Kilekwa opened the first church at Kayoyo in the Ntchisi hills, midway between the Nkhotakota lake shore and Lilongwe.

The first months in the diocese were times of almost continuous travelling and my mind was a blur of new scenes and new faces, with many standing out vividly: the Muslim village headman in blue robes kneeling for confirmation, after facing the opposition of his family and the surrender of his chieftainship. Blessing Christians kneeling in the sand from the bow of *Boatie Paul* as one arrived at lake shore villages. Being taken with pride by a village congregation to see the huge kiln of bricks they had burnt for their new church. The double baptism of an African and a white baby, where the godmothers on each side happened to be wearing identical dresses.

Evensong on the lawn of a government headquarters after being driven out of the building by swarming nkhungu flies – tiny flies that erupt in their millions from the bottom of the lake. Little things perhaps, but they all make up the joy and life of the Church in Africa, which went into the new era full of vigour, however inadequately equipped.

South West Tanganyika

Five days after our engagement, I left Mponda's on a six and a half week *ulendo* (journey) to attend the consecration and enthronement of John Poole-Hughes as Bishop of South West Tanganyika – part of the Diocese of Nyasaland until 1953 – and to explore the Northern Region of Malawi. For this, I took *Boatie Paul* from Likoma Island. She was an iron flat-bottomed barge designed for work on the placid canals of Holland and would ride the often large waves of Lake Malawi by thudding down into the valley of the waves with a shuddering smack. There was a lively discussion among the crew about the weather prospects, of which I understood almost nothing. I was acutely conscious that only sixteen years earlier the newly built *Vipya*, a large passenger steamer, had turned turtle a few miles out of Nkhata Bay and three hundred and thirty-nine of her passengers and crew drowned. I was grateful that the consensus of the crew of *Paul* was that we would make it to Mbamba Bay in Tanganyika.

Karonga

From Tanganyika, I headed back to Likoma Island and from there to Karonga in the far north on M.V. *Ilala*, the only passenger ship on the lake, and efficiently run by the Nyasaland Railways. I wrote to my brother Mike from Karonga:

> I got up at four this morning as *Ilala* sailed up to the top of the lake – a lovely pearl-grey morning with the Nyika plateaus to the west looming out from the mists and the first light of dawn coming over the Tanganyika escarpment to the east. As the sun rose, it picked out great pillars of nkhungu flies – a curious phenomenon on the lake. The eggs hatch underwater on the lake bed and you can see the spiralling great columns, going several hundred feet into the air – they stand out while like steam coming off the water.
>
> At six, *Ilala* cut off her engines opposite Karonga, and one of the lifeboats was lowered to take me to the beach, where I was left feeling very small and lonely until Tony Mott, the District Commissioner, arrived a few minutes later. From then on, I was passed on from one centre to another, and in each there was a group, most of government servants and their families, some British, some African, clearly delighted at the chance of sharing evensong or a Eucharist – this is a region where I had been told the Anglican church hardly existed. It was something that at that time you could only dream about in Pretoria or even Swaziland.
>
> The north is the Scotland of Malawi – beautiful, mountainous, thinly populated, mainly by Tumbuka speakers. In 1962, it was mainly Presbyterian, the fruits of the work of Dr Robert Lawes and others from the Church of Scotland. Lawes held doctorates in medicine, theology and philosophy and worked from Livingstonia for thirty-three years.
>
> In contrast, there was no Anglican priest on the northern mainland in 1962. There were small and lively inter-racial congregations, usually of civil servants, meeting in government buildings or private houses. These were visited occasionally by priests from Likoma Island. Here I met for the first time Alec Rubadiri, the first African Assistant District Commissioner (ADC), an outstanding man.

Mzuzu and Likoma Island

There was panic when I reached Mzuzu, now the capital of the Northern Region. A telegram had been received from one of the lay missionaries on Likoma Island: "For God's sake send police reinforcements." A government launch was laid on to take Canon Jameson Mwenda and myself, together with twenty armed police, to the Island where Chikanga, a witch-finder had set up business. It turned out to be mostly panic. Some women had been hauled off to be tested for witchcraft by Chikanga and many Christians had broken church law by bowing to public opinion and seeking an all-clear from Chikanga, without that all-clear their neighbours would have regarded them as witches.

I then returned to Nkhata Bay on *Paul* and after more visits took *Ilala* back to Monkey Bay, where we arrived forty minutes ahead of time. And there to meet me was Jane on the wharf! We swam and talked and swam and talked. What we didn't realise when swimming out to the anchored *Chauncy Maples* at Monkey Bay, was that people watching from the shore were taking bets on whether we would return. The day before they had been watching a large crocodile sunning itself on the rocks near the CM! Back at Mponda's there were some two hundred and fifty letters of good wishes on our engagement to be acknowledged. I took the easy way and sent a circular letter, churned out on the ancient hand-turned duplicator.

The letter ended:

> In this lovely country – I had heard about her lake, but why did nobody tell me about her mountains? It is easy to be bemused by the beauty and the pulsing life, and to forget her real problems. How to provide food for the most densely populated territory in Africa; how to tackle malaria and TB; how to find work for the tens of thousands of young men that stand idle round every village market-place; how to provide schools for the half million children still without education – these, in this desperately poor land, are problems to crack the head of any economist.

Canon John Kingsnorth and Jane to Likoma

The far-sighted John Kingsnorth was coming to explore the Nyasaland church. He had worked for many years in rural Zambia and had just taken over as General Secretary of UMCA in London. He also had the prophetic touch and was awake to the new reformation happening in Rome and with the World Council of Churches in Geneva. He needed to see the diocese at first hand and so did Jane – she would be spending four months talking about it in the States. So they went off together to Nkhotakota, Likoma Island, Nkhata Bay and Mzuzu.

Jane would have had a good reception on Likoma. The UMCA practised strict housing segregation. Male missionaries had their houses on the west side of the square, women on the east. A church elder had said to me after our engagement was announced, "We're glad you're being open about it. We always thought they did but it's good to be honest!"

Jane and I met up again at a Student Christian Movement conference at Chongoni.

Birth of Chilema Lay Training Centre

I attended an SCO (Student Christian Organisation) conference at Chongoni, near Nkhoma, the headquarters of the Central Region Synod of the CCAP (Church of Central Africa Presbyterian). The Presbyterians, together with the Roman Catholics, were by far the largest churches in the country.

The CCAP problem was the same as ours: how to staff a rapidly growing church from a non-elastic seminary. Their solution was training the laity and they were planning a small centre: one staff member and twenty students. I said that was odd – we were considering an identical plan. Where was their centre to be? The answer – Domasi, just eight miles from our new proposed headquarters at Malosa. It was crazy!

What God was calling us to do became clear. We quickly consulted our own church committees on the proposal to join together and establish an ecumenical centre on land at Malosa on independent land cut off from the diocesan headquarters and placed under the control of ecumenical trustees. Both churches agreed at once. The centre would be called Chilema Ecumenical Training and Conference Centre, named after the small stream that flows through the land. We were later joined by the Catholic Church, until some years later they developed their own catechetical centre. A fourth partner was the Churches of Christ, a body dedicated to ecumenism.

At this time, Jane and I were just about to leave on a four-month fundraising tour in England and the United States – we were asked to re-route ourselves via Geneva and to secure the backing of the World Council of Churches for the proposed new centre. Today, Chilema Ecumenical Training and Conference Centre is known throughout the country. The Churches of Christ and Roman Catholics later became members of the Board.

Matope

In June, I visited the parish of Matope for the first time (a parish in Malawi can comprise anything up to twenty or more widely scattered congregations). The name means "mud" and is at the point where the Shire River, after flowing broadly and gently out of the lake for seventy miles, hits its first cataract. This mass of water then tumbles down from the lake level of 1,500ft to the Zambezi, a fraction above sea level.

It was here, in 1884, that Archdeacon William Percival Johnson was stranded by the dry seasonal fall of the river level. By this time he was blind in one eye and had twenty percent vision in the other. Being stuck in the mud at Matope for a few months was for him an opportunity. In three months, he baptised the first Christians and built the first Anglican church away from the lake shore.

After two confirmations in the parish on the Saturday, I ended up at a village called Malawi. This was before the whole country adopted the name. Malawi is thought to refer to the glinting of the rising sun on the waves of the lake. The children had been waiting for me from around noon and by this time it was quite dark. Thinking the church was a hundred yards away, I took a couple by the hand and the whole pack followed. The church turned out to be about a mile away. Anyway, it warmed me up on a chilly night!

The rest-hut was freshly smeared and looked damp and uninviting so I set up a camp-bed outside. I found it rather chilly so I got a couple of cassocks to put on top. The next day, I woke up in broad daylight in the middle of the village street in a bed decorated with a purple cassock and all the children standing around expectantly!

Another confirmation there and on to the old Matope mission station. The boat that served as a ferry was locked up and it took an hour to find the man with the key. We launched the boat to cross the wide river back to Matope but it turned out it had only one oar. That was not enough to stem the flow of the river and the rapids were unpleasantly close. So we manhandled ourselves up the reeds for half a mile then paddled furiously with the one oar to cross the river.

There was a wistful look about Matope at that time. It had a fine set of buildings, church, school, hospital, and clergy house but the old bridge that had been nearby had been washed away and the new one built four miles lower down on the new main road. Most of the people had gone there also, the passing trade of hungry bus passengers being their main source of income.

The 1962 Synod

The Diocesan Synod had not met for three years and I called for one in August. This would be make or break time. Would we be able to catch up with the "winds of change" blowing through Africa and the world – or would we die a slow death? I isolated myself for a week with Cecil and Maude Winnginton Ingram in Zomba to devise a new constitution for the diocese. Cecil's father had been Bishop of London and Maude was an excellent typist and we all worked on it together.

The Diocese met for its fourth Synod in August at Malosa. The Bishop's charge began with a tribute to the saintly, witty and tough Bishop Frank Thorne, whose twenty-five years of leadership had ended unhappily. The police, then controlled by the Federal government of Southern and Northern Rhodesia and Nyasaland, had shown him a list of people who, they said, were on the list to be murdered. Frank had quoted this in the *Diocesan Chronicle*, one of the world's least known publications. The *Chronicle* was printed by the Likoma Press and had a circulation of perhaps two hundred past and present UMCA missionaries. By some extraordinary chance, Frank's comments came into the hands of a *Daily Mail* reporter.

Frank had said he was himself a supporter of African independence and never dreamed that Dr Banda's Malawi Congress Party would even think about political murder had he not been shown compelling evidence that very day. Next morning saw headlines in the London *Daily Mail*, "Bishop confirms murder plot". Frank never forgave himself. Years later, when I saw him in London, not long before his death, he was saying over and over again, "How could I have been so stupid?"

The points I tried to make in my charge were:

> *The new age.* The great feature of the new age in Africa is that power has passed from Christians to other Christians, not to atheists, as in France, or to Marxists, as in Russia.
>
> *An age of the laity.* We need lay men and women who, like Stephen, are "full of faith and the Holy Spirit." People are not to be judged by the colour of their skin, nor by the colour of their politics as in Germany or the Soviet bloc; nor by the size of their car as in the West. They are valued because women and men are the children of God.
>
> *Readiness for the new age.* We could hardly be less ready. There were only twenty-three African clergy. The poverty of Nyasaland hinders our development. (It was listed by the United Nations as the poorest country in the world when it became independent in 1964). Government grants for schools and hospitals are a fraction of those in neighbouring countries with revenues from copper or from industry.

Our needs:
A nerve centre. Most of our work in the past was in Portuguese East Africa (Mozambique) and Tanganyika (Tanzania). Ten years ago, the diocese was divided into three and the *Chauncy Maples* sold. Mponda's is not a suitable centre for a diocese. The Bishop is out of touch, both with the government and his own diocese.

We have hesitated between Lilongwe and Malosa for the new centre but it is too early to move to Lilongwe. Perhaps that is where a suffragan bishop should be? Here at Malosa we already have a secondary school, a primary school, a hospital, a leprosarium and plenty of land for future development.
Adequate clergy. In twelve years from now there will be ten clergy who have not retired and the population will be a million larger. We have relied on our three hundred teachers until now to take charge of out-station churches. We can no longer do this as they will be deployed by the government. Let us learn from the South West Tanganyika diocese. When they were divided from us ten years ago they had fourteen priests; next year they will have forty.

We need to train clergy at three levels:
1. At least a handful of graduates who will have to be trained in other countries.
2. The majority of at least Junior Certificate standard, trained at St John's seminary in Lusaka.
3. A single group of ten or more older men for a shorter course, to tide us over the next fifteen years.

Self-help. How can standards be raised and the number of clergy increased? There is only one answer: every parish must learn rapidly to support its own priest. At present, the total cost for all the clergy is £5,000 a year. Their parishes provide £250 of this.
A Diocesan Training Centre is needed to train older ordinands, full- time catechists and a new voluntary army of Readers. (As the letters "r" and "l" are often interchangeable in Chichewa, they have appropriately been known since as "Leaders"). Other openings for lay volunteers are as Youth Leaders, Sunday School teachers, Church councillors and Stewardship Campaigners. We all need to see our daily work as work for God.
Self-government. We need more than a Synod every two or three years. There must be organs empowered to take decisions between meetings. This is so urgent that I am presenting a new set of Draft Acts for experimental use until next Synod. These will give us a Diocesan Standing Committee (DSC) invested with the full powers of Synod, except for a very few vital

areas. The DSC will have full authority in all matters of finance. The new Acts provide for elected councils in every parish. They give us our own trustees so that church property will be no longer held by trustees in London. They give us a Diocesan Secretary to share the burdens that threaten to overwhelm your Bishop and auditors to see that our finance is properly accounted for. These new Acts will help us to cut the apron-strings and grow into an adult church.

Money. Our financial position is disastrous. No audited accounts have been published for seven years. During this time, we have spent between £25,000 and £30,000 more than our income. To help meet this gap we have been given an emergency grant of £15,000 by UMCA. A special grant of £10,000 made to each of the four UMCA dioceses to put buildings into working order has also been given to the bank manager to pay off part of the overdraft. But this does not help the future. We have got used to living at £6,000 a year above our income. You are all too familiar with the forced economies: selling the *Chauncy Maples*; closing St Andrew's Theological College, the printing works on Likoma Island; the ordinands not sent for training; the closure of churches at Namwera; the leaking roofs...

There are four steps that we can and must take:

1. Control our finances through the DSC.
2. Decentralise: parishes and institutions must take their own steps to survive.
3. Make new friends overseas. My wife and I propose to spend five months fundraising in the UK and USA. We ask for your prayers.
4. We must learn to give. Our troubles would end tomorrow if every one of us, rich or poor, gave each month one day's earnings – in cash, crops or fish.

One thing I know. This Diocese **can** find the resources to grow, human and financial. This is already happening in a diocese that until ten years ago was part of our own, equally rural, equally poor – South West Tanganyika. We have invited Mr John Nkoma, a lay member of their Finance Board, to this Synod to tell us how to do it. We look forward keenly to hearing what he has to say.

One Church. I quote from Bishop Stephen Bayne, the first Executive Officer of the worldwide Anglican Communion, "It is not enough that missions should grow into self-governing churches. They must grow into one self-governing Church."

Our diocese was born in two separate places: on the eastern lake shore where Archdeacon William Percival Johnson arrived, coming overland on foot from Zanzibar; and in the south, where the little overseas community had organised the Chaplaincy. We need one legal framework for both and we need the experience of both.

Equally urgent is the need to be at one with Christians of other traditions. We must be strong to bear witness against all the forces of the devil that divide us. I commend most earnestly the Week of Prayer for Christian Unity from January 25th, if possible with Christians of other traditions. I ask you to take any other steps which will lead us to our goal of unity in Christ. Let us pray to the Spirit:

>Come Holy Spirit;
>Come in gentleness as a dove making us to be at one;
>Blow within us as the wind, filling us with new life;
>Burn within us as fire,
>setting us aflame with the love of God.

Wedding

Jane and I were married in St Andrew's church, Mulanje on Michaelmas Day, 30th September 1962 from the home of her twin sister Brigid and her husband, Mel Crofton, who was Assistant District Commissioner. (We learned much later that St Andrew's was not licensed for weddings under Nyasaland law and a special Act of the Malawi Parliament was passed to legitimise Bazil and Christopher. But legitimacy was the least of our worries.)

The dramatic backdrop to the wedding, out of the back garden of Brigid and Mel's house, on the slopes of Mulanje Mountain, was a sheer wall of granite rising 5,000 feet to the Mulanje plateau, on which another more jagged range runs up to Sapitwa (The Place You Don't Go To) at 10,000 feet.

The previous day, the Usuthu team from Swaziland – Jack Dobson, Peter Burtwell and Bernard Wrankmore – arrived in Bernard's battered jeep. Bernard had driven from Cape Town, picking up the others on the way. They drove one thousand three hundred miles non-stop, taking it in turns to sleep and drive.

Guided by Brigid, everyone was involved with stuffing olives and preparing the wedding feast until after midnight. Habil Chipembere and Christopher Lacey – the two archdeacons in the Southern Province – took the service and a mixed choir from Malosa Secondary School and St

Andrew's Prep School led the singing, including a hymn that took us both back to our school days:

> Breathe on us, Breath of God, Till we are wholly thine,
> Until this earthly part of us Glows with thy fire divine.

Preparing food for the reception. From left to right, Bernard Wrankmore, Brigid Crofton, Peter Burtwell, Bette Riddle, Jack Cormack, Dorothy Riddle, Jane, Jack Dobson (facing camera).

Jane was a photographer's dream in a glorious white dress made by Brigid. In the bright September sunshine, a brisk wind blew her veil around like a ship's pennant, in front of the rolling green of tea bushes that surround the granite walls of Mulanje Mountain.

Archdeacon Christopher Lacey, Archdeacon Habil Chipembere

Nephew Julian Crofton and nieces Moyra and Janice Riddle

When we came to make our getaway, the ancient Standard car which I had inherited from Frank Thorne was true to type and broke down after the first half-mile. We coaxed it back up the hill to Mel's house where, while we thanked the prisoners from the local gaol for tidying up after the party, Bernard swapped his suit for overalls, adjusted something underneath, and so we made a second farewell. A mile down the road, a repeat performance – after which Mel offered us his Land Rover and, at the third attempt, we made the one hundred and eighty miles to Namaso Bay and the cottage of a friend.

David Eccles, of the Fisheries Department, kindly lent us a small sailing dinghy and our fortnight was a glorious mosaic of the rare Pel's fishing owl, listening to the haunting call of the magnificent fish-eagles, grey louries, three types of kingfishers, two types of hornbills and a friendly one-legged wagtail, a couple of crocodiles on the rocks, and, out in the lake, a huge turtle, the only one we ever saw – and each other. It was the first time since our engagement we had both been in the same place for more than two days. Back at Mponda's we changed an ancient thatched house with some beautiful 1901 brickwork into a family house by putting two single iron beds together. Unfortunately the matt-resses were a size larger and Jane fell out of her side in the middle of the night.

Diocesan Standing Committee

The first Diocesan Standing Committee – the new power-sharing organ set up by synod – was held in late October with nineteen clergy and lay members. It had eighty-seven items on its agenda and the minutes filled thirteen pages. It decided that:

Our home in Mponda's

1. The move to Likwenu should happen, despite the cancelled grant. The new bishop's house would be taken off the list (it was 1965 before it was built) but the office and houses for the Secretary and Treasurer would go ahead.
2. The new office would have its own telephone.
3. A layman, Frank Chithila – the Medical Assistant on Likoma Island – would represent the Diocese at the 1963 Toronto Anglican Congress – the last that has ever been held. In the event, Frank was unable to go and Clement Marama took his place.
4. Professional auditors were appointed for the first time.

5. A bilingual Eucharist – Nyanja and English on facing pages – would be published immediately
6. A new ecumenical training centre would be established at Chilema. This would not only train catechists, it would also enable laymen who had proved their worth as catechists or as voluntary helpers to be ordained as priests.
7. Michael Blackwood, a solicitor in Blantyre, was appointed Chancellor and did sterling work for the next fifteen years.
8. Justus Kishindo, the excellent headmaster at Mponda's and Supervisor of Education on the lake shore, was appointed Diocesan Secretary.

I doubt if the diocese would have survived had Justus not made the decision to sacrifice his government pension as a teacher and come to work with the diocese. He was later joined by his friend, also a teacher, Maxwell Zingani, who made the same sacrifice and who became our Stewardship Adviser and Literature Secretary.

Quite apart from their own areas of responsibility, they would now and then make an appointment to see me in the evening and say – ever so gently – "Bishop, we are not sure you made the right decision when you said ..." Invariably they were right and I changed course.

Preparations for America

A four month visit to the USA had been planned for some months. It was the only hope of finding the resources to pay off our many debts and to bring into reality even a fraction of the many hopes for the diocese.

At Malosa, the site for the new headquarters for the Diocese, there was a lot of land suitable for farming and building and steeper land where trees could be planted. Government had already taken back a small part and was threatening to take much more if it was not put to use to benefit the community. UMCA had offered £20,000 to enable the diocesan headquarters to be moved to Malosa, but on terms the diocese could not meet financially.

The only hope of a new beginning was to find help from America. I had no contact with the Episcopal Church of the USA, known as ECUSA, other than with a priest in Chicago called Dick Young, so I had gone ahead before our engagement and arranged with him a four month visit early in 1963. For a time it seemed as if Jane would be an abandoned wife within a few months of our promising to have and to hold each other, till death parted us. Then her family generously stepped in to make it possible for us to keep those vows and accompany me on the trip.

I had met Stephen Bayne at Provincial Synod in Lusaka, Zambia. He was an American bishop who had just been made the first Executive Secretary of the Anglican Communion. He was impressed by the needs and possibilities of Nyasaland and encouraged me to go ahead with plans for a visit, mentioning the possibility of companionship with the Diocese of Texas. This meant going a month earlier than planned. Texas was holding its diocesan convention in February; our plans had been to arrive in March.

Stephen's enthusiasm communicated itself to the Diocesan Standing Committee which generously gave me leave to be away for six months.

Much had to be squeezed into the next two months. Dick Young wanted lots of photos – we had none larger than 6"x4" and could not afford commercial enlargements. So the Swaziland enlarger, operated by a car battery, was called back into service. Each night, after supper with the mission staff in the mezane (eating place), we would set up the enlarger in our new bedroom. The danger point came at around 8.30 p.m. when the missionaries would leave the mezane and head for their rooms, swinging paraffin Tilley pressure lamps. Every dish had to be hastily covered to protect them from light until people and lamps were safely in their rooms. Mosquitoes in the developer didn't help either. Often the production of photographs would be accompanied by noises from hippos grunting on the banks of the nearby Shire River. Eventually we reached the target of fifty 8"x10" photographs. Many other dreams were reduced to a fifty-year plan and I began to feel more confident about the forthcoming trip to the States.

The unexpected, good and bad, continued during the last few weeks before we left for our American odyssey. The £20,000 grant from the UMCA for the headquarters at Malosa was suddenly withdrawn – no reason given.

This was counter-balanced by a letter from Dunstan Choo, a fine Nyasaland priest whom I had known in Pretoria in the 1940s, when he was a priest in the northern Transvaal copper mines. His letter asked if he could return and work in Nyasaland. There he was provided with a car and, by South African standards, a modest salary. I thanked him and said I could offer only a push-bike and a salary one-tenth of what he was receiving. I received an immediate reply: this was a call from God and his intention was fixed, no matter what the salary, the transport or the housing. He came in due course and was the first priest ever to be based in the mainland area of northern Malawi. Later he became the first archdeacon of Northern Malawi, which, in 1990 grew into the Diocese of Northern Malawi.

As we left Blantyre in mid-December after a week with little sleep, a small team from Blantyre Synod of the Church of Central Africa Presbyterian (CCAP), led by the Reverend Jonathan Sangaya, came to the airport to see us off. I had earlier been asked to re-route ourselves via Geneva and to ask the World Council of Churches to support the building of what would be the first ecumenical institution Malawi had ever known. There could not have been a more encouraging send off as we left for Europe and the United States.

Athens

We took advantage of the free stop-overs on our flight to London and Athens was our first stop. I had been learning Greek for nine years in Australia, Leeds and Mirfield but had never had a chance of seeing Greece. We enjoyed plodding from ruin to ruin and seeping in the wonders of the highest culture the world has known. The oracle of Delphi had always fascinated me. It was the age when sharp-witted Athenian statesmen, historians and philosophers, generals and heads of state would still consult the oracle before making great decisions. How do spirit and mind interact? How do science and the humanities cross-fertilise children's education? I asked the Oracle of Delphi, "How do you become a rounded human being in a world of specialists?" As usual the reply was oracular.

We visited Cape Sounion which was fittingly being battered by a winter storm as the sun set in a red glow. Jane and I were almost alone, imagining the women from Athens and Peiraios peering through the salt spray for a glimpse of Triremes returning from battle with the Spartans. Were they wives or widows? They would know today or tomorrow. On the bus returning to Athens there were only two young women beside ourselves. By one of those freak chances, both were from Queensland and one a doctor whom my brother Felix had taught.

Rome

It was our first time in Rome, again a bitter winter's day. St Peter's had its seating arranged for the Second Vatican Council which had begun its work in October (it ended in December 1965). We had little idea of what it would mean in the years that followed. Already, by calling together the Second Vatican Council, the eighty year old "caretaker" Pope, John XXIII, had sparked off an internal reformation as significant, but more peaceful, than that launched by Martin Luther four hundred years earlier. Names previously unknown to me, such as the Swiss theologian, Hans Kung, were opening doors that could never again be shut. Little did I think that we were to follow him in Chicago.

We changed our route to London to include the stop-over to see the World Council of Churches in Geneva and a helpful airport official in Rome said, "Let me book your luggage through to Heathrow rather than Geneva and you won't see it again." How right they were! That was the last we saw of the case with all our plans and all our photos until it turned up, three weeks later, just before we left England for Chicago. An agonising wait.

World Council of Churches (WCC)

The only day we could be in Geneva was a Saturday which fortunately then was still a working day. I discussed the proposals for the ecumenical lay training centre at Chilema with people in the Department of Laity, who gave it a very warm welcome. The meeting with the WCC went well as they very much wanted such centres to be ecumenical. Substantial funding followed this meeting. In due course, grants came which enabled Chilema to open its doors in 1964.

England welcomed us with a frozen Christmas beauty we've seldom seen before or since. The country was sparkling white in the sun when we landed at Heathrow and the snow was still virgin when we left for Chicago a month later. It was the first time I had seen England for twenty years – what a welcome! The airline had lost our luggage and we had no warm clothes. Mercifully Norman and Barbara Gilmore – now returned from Zululand and living in north London, took us in and clothed us until our suitcases eventually arrived. To have lost our clothes would have been inconvenient but to have lost all our photographs and slides, would have been disastrous. Mel and Brigid Crofton, Jane's sister and brother-in-law, together with their children Julian and Nicola, were on leave in England and we had the joy of sharing a white Christmas with them in their home county of Devon in the lovely village of Holne, on the edge of Dartmoor.

Travelling and making links 1963

During our cold January month in Britain I was first timetabled to meet staff of the Universities Mission to Central Africa (UMCA). This was the missionary society formed in 1857 in response to the challenge of David Livingstone to the universities of Oxford, Cambridge and Durham to help supplant the slave trade in Central Africa with Christianity and legitimate trade.

The Society supported work in what was then Northern Rhodesia, Nyasaland, Portuguese East Africa, Zanzibar and part of Tanganyika. One year after our visit, UMCA merged with another missionary society, the 260-year-old Society for the Propagation of the Gospel and USPG – the United Society for the Propagation of the Gospel – was formed.

In London our hosts were Ernie and Margaret Southcott, old friends from the 1930s at Mirfield and in the AYPA (Anglican Young Peoples' Association), from whom I had learned more about communicating the gospel to the young than Mirfield itself was able to give. Ernie was then Provost of Southwark Cathedral and we stayed in the ancient Provost's house on the edge of the Thames, our bedroom having a magnificent view across the river to St Paul's Cathedral. One day we had the thrill of seeing a red-sailed Thames barge sailing by. Ernie and Margaret generously arranged a glorious gathering of old friends and we shared and partied in true Southcott style.

The most alarming experience was a press conference in Fleet Street. I was expecting a handful of journalists from the church papers but walked into a room full of journalists representing all the national daily papers and the international press agencies, the lot! Unbeknown to me, Bishop Frank Thorne's "murder letter" had made headlines in the *Daily Mail* (mentioned in chapter 5).

The first question was a googly from the *Daily Mail*. "You will know that 'Messiah' is being used of Nkwame Nkrumah, the President of Ghana. We now hear of similar language being used of Dr Banda. What are your views?" I felt the earth opening up under my feet. Anything I said would undoubtedly appear in tomorrow's CAT, the *Central Africa Times*, then hostile to the independence of Nyasaland. It would also be on Dr Banda's desk. I murmured something about African politicians using biblical expressions because many had been through church secondary schools. This went on for ten minutes and suddenly the room was empty. I remember being comforted by the Vicar of St Bride's, who had arranged the press conference.

While in London we met Bishop Stephen Bayne, an American who had just become the first Executive Officer of the Anglican Communion. I was relieved to know that he approved of Dick Young, the priest organising our visit to the United States. Also in London we met Stuart and Sue Brand, former colleagues of Jane when she was teaching in Stepney. Stuart was vicar of a parish in Notting Hill but he and Sue came with their family at the end of 1963 to serve in Blantyre.

We travelled north from London through thick snow to visit the Community of the Resurrection at Mirfield, whose old students had been the mainstay of the work in Swaziland. At York, we met John and Alison Leake who were to serve so well as UMCA missionaries at Chilema in its most creative and formative years.

In York, we also met Ann Fox, who, by a strange chance, was already well known to both Jane and me. Ann knew my family in Malaya and in Worthing before we emigrated to Australia and maintained contact with my mother. She was also Jane's godmother, having been a friend of her mother for many years and often staying at their home in Devon.

Making friends in the USA

Two days later we were in a plane headed for Chicago. When the air hostess passed round the papers we noticed that Moscow's temperature was −14°F, the coldest in Europe. But in Chicago it was −22°F. Below us the gold of the setting sun on the Welsh mountains was so beautiful that we forgot the figures, totally entranced as we travelled west in a sunset that seemed to go on for hours.

A very able but eccentric priest who ran a student centre in Chicago, Canon Dick Young, looked after our visit to the USA. Dick was a member of the Order of the Good Shepherd and knew George Braund, a priest who was at one time on the staff of UMCA. He knew many people across the States and was genuinely interested in the new Africa. In four and a half hectic months, Jane and I visited twenty-five States and averaged two and a half talks a day between us. We had two goals: to raise awareness amongst Episcopalians (Anglicans) in the United States that there was an Anglican church in Africa other than in Liberia, and to raise funds needed for the church in Nyasaland to develop.

We arrived at Bishop Anderson House in Cook County, Chicago, at 9.00 p.m. local time – 3.00 a.m. English time. An interesting link was that Dr Banda had trained as a doctor in Cook County Hospital before taking further qualifications in Scotland. It was a five-storey building, open to university students until the small hours of the morning. Food and drink were free. Counselling with Dick Young on the fifth floor was also free, all paid for, it seemed, by generous benefactors. Dick never wasted time, so, after our first introduction to a home-delivered pizza, he drove us around Chicago for over an hour. We eventually collapsed into bed at midnight – 6:00 a.m. English time.

Dick was efficient down to the last detail. He was horrified that I had no episcopal robes, so the next day bought some on approval from clerical tailors in New York and then asked his secretary, who was a competent seamstress, if she and her friend could copy them. The originals were returned to New York the following day and I still wear Dorothy's handiwork, forty-three years later. Dick seemed to be on first name terms with every bishop in ECUSA (Episcopal Church in the United States of America) and for the next four and a half months arranged our travel programme, often conducting two conversations at the same time with a telephone in each hand.

Our first agenda was a visit to Nashotah House, a seminary on the Canadian border, where the temperature was –34°F and the icicles hanging from gutters 18" long. Three of the students were interested in working in Nyasaland – two, Jeff Schiffmayer and Louis Luchs, actually came and did good work.

An early and most productive conference at which I was a speaker was that of the Overseas Mission Society (OMS), the brainchild of Sam van Culin, a Hawaiian priest, who later became Secretary General of the Anglican Communion. Episcopalians were proud of the "Episcopal Jurisdiction" in the Anglican world. Sam had the courage to say that it did not really exist. We were told it was part of our job to help widen understanding of the Anglican communion.

At that time, the "Jurisdiction" only consisted of the Philippines, where members were outnumbered about ten to one by the Philippine Independent Church and a handful of dioceses in Central America, almost all having fewer confirmations each year than many "outstation" churches in Nyasaland, in Africa, there was only Liberia, with one hundred and twenty confirmations a year, most of them in the hinterland where the Cowley Fathers were at work.

Sam wanted to break down the walls so that every diocese in the world in real need could benefit from the resources of the whole Anglican Communion. Sam van Culin and Stephen Bayne were both on fire with the theme of John Newton's hymn, Let Every Nation Rise and Bring Peculiar Honours to Our King.

Asia, Africa, Latin America and the West all had something to offer the world. This was crystallised in a conference in August 1963 at London, Ontario, into the clumsy but prophetic phrase "Mutual Responsibility and Interdependence", known by its code name of MRI. More on this later.

On to Houston, nine hundred miles south and centre of the Diocese of Texas, Stephen Bayne's choice as a possible partner for Nyasaland. We stayed with the bishop, John Hine, who had taken an uncompromising position on racial equality. This was six months before Martin Luther King's speech, "I have a dream."

We arrived just as their Convention (diocesan synod) began. John's stance had provoked stormy opposition. I was on the floor with convention members and found myself in the centre of a small group of very angry laymen advancing on John Hine and chanting, "You communist! You communist!" After that, I wondered how people would react to John's proposal that the dioceses of Texas and Nyasaland should enter into a companion relationship. John won out however and *Ecclesia*, our diocesan monthly newsletter, recorded:

Jane and Donald

> The Texas Diocesan Convention, equivalent to our Synod, decided unanimously that we should be a companion diocese for the next three years.

I believe this was the first time that any American diocese had formed a companionship outside the "Jurisdiction". Such links were for three years and could be renewed once only. It brought an immediate grant, backed and doubled by Episcopal Church headquarters in New York, which enabled us to wipe off past debts and to move the Diocesan Office from Mponda's to Malosa.

John Hine was elected Presiding Bishop of ECUSA a year or two later and gave a powerful lead in committing ECUSA to the human rights campaign. The three years grew to twelve and, in an unofficial way, the friendship still

Dr Art Johnson and wife Nan who came to work in Malawi

exists 40 years later. The real credit for the companion-ship getting off to a good start goes to a priest, George Carlisle, secretary to the link, and to Milton Richardson, the Suffragan Bishop who made Malawi his special cause, and who later became Diocesan Bishop. They both visited Malawi.

The renewing of the companion diocese link coincided with the creation of the new Diocese of Lake Malawi in 1971 comprising the Central and Northern Regions, and the ECUSA allowed a new link to be formed with them. Somehow, this continued until the early 1980s. The Diocese of Texas underwrote the building of a new diocesan centre in Lilongwe, which had become the capital of Malawi in 1972. They rightly felt that the diocesan bishop should not have his headquarters one hundred and twenty miles from the capital.

The general pattern of our four and a half months in the States was to spend around a week in each of the twenty-five States and dioceses we were visiting. The people and bishops who drove us around on the days we spent in their diocese were always aware of the agenda. The OMS message was seeping through. The dioceses stretched from New Mexico in the south-east to the San Juan Islands on the borders of Canada in the north-west. They included Utah and Salt Lake City, where Episcopalians felt themselves a minority in a Mormon State; several mid-Western dioceses; New Mexico, and the Pacific coast from the San Juan Islands down to San Diego on the Mexican border.

The San Juan Islands were all one parish and the rector took us out to some of them in his boat. We chugged our way to three of them where the welcome was warm and sincere. One of the small groups we met remained faithful supporters of Malawi for the next twenty years. An abiding memory is of the humming-birds hovering outside the rector's kitchen window, feeding from the syrup he put out for them.

Typically we would have a TV or radio interview and lunch-time and evening meetings, together with visits to other centres in the diocese. Often Jane would go off to speak in one direction and I in another. Wherever we went, we were enveloped in American hospitality. The beds were enormous by Mponda's standards and very soft, something Jane's back did not appreciate, so often we slept on the floor, much to the consternation of our hostess. And the steaks: it was sometimes hard to show the proper enthusiasm when a twelve ounce steak at lunch was followed by a sixteen ounce one at dinner fifty miles away!

Interspersed between parishes and diocesan meetings were visits to a number of seminaries where both seminarians and staff usually showed particular interest. From Sewanee Seminary in Virginia, Jack Biggers came to work as a parish priest in Lilongwe. Several years after moving back to the States, he returned in 1995 to become the first bishop of the newly formed Diocese of Northern Malawi, retiring in 2000.

In a university library, we asked if they had any maps of Nyasaland. The librarian looked puzzled and then asked, "Now what State would than be in?" No one was to blame. A typical Mid-Western newspaper might allocate two of its seventy-two pages to foreign news. This was not so true of the west coast of California, but was so in the Mid-West. The reaction to our message was almost invariably one of deep gratitude. Some of the parishes we met remained generous supporters for years, fed only by monthly mailings of *Ecclesia*.

For the last month of our visit, our agenda was to try and find companions for the other three Central African dioceses – Mashonaland and Matabeleland in Southern Rhodesia (Zimbabwe) and Northern Rhodesia (Zambia). This idea appealed to Jim Pike, the fiery Bishop of San Francisco, and a great champion of the under-privileged. When the service in Grace Cathedral ended at which I had preached, he made an impassioned plea to his people to become involved. As we were leaving, one of the wardens said to me, "I've seen Jim on fire before, but never like this." Jim was as good as his word and companions were found and bishops did visit Mashonaland, Matabeleland and Zambia but no lasting links grew out of them.

New Zealand

Having reached the west coast of the States, and wanting to introduce Jane to my mother and family in Australia, we boarded *The Mariposa* in Los Angeles and sailed across the Pacific to Sydney. We called in at Tahiti, where we snorkeled inside the reef and marvelled at the fish and coral; Raratonga, where the singing was magical; Bora Bora, where the Catholic priest shared his grief over the death of Pope John XXIII by giving us a beautiful carved fish, and Auckland. Unforgettable experiences, enhanced by a generous fellow passenger stalking across the dining saloon on the first night to give us a bottle of wine and instructing a waiter to keep us supplied until we reached Auckland!

In New Zealand, we hired a little red mini car and in twenty-four hours covered much of the North Island on the most glorious May day imaginable. There had been six weeks of solid rain and this was the first day of sun. The sheep looked as though they had been freshly laundered and set out in emerald green pastures. We drove the thirty miles down the eastern side of Lake Taupo watching the most glorious sunset we should ever see. A volcano in Indonesia had erupted some weeks earlier and the stratosphere was filled with volcanic dust. It was a salutary reminder that we are one family on God's earth, though at the time we did not know this prosaic "explanation" of the glorious evening sky.

We spent the night near the southern end of Lake Taupo and decided to get as far up Mt. Ruapehu, a smouldering volcano, as we could. Just as we reached the turning point half way up, there were two punctures in quick succession. The first was easy to cope with the spare wheel. When the other tyre went, we had a problem. Auckland was 190 miles away and *The Mariposa* sailed at 2.00 p.m. By the time kind passers-by had come to our rescue and mended the second puncture, there were only four hours left to reach Auckland. Jane enjoys this kind of challenge. I am not so sure about the sheep or myself. But we made it – just!

Australia

We ended our two weeks on *The Mariposa* in Sydney and spent two days with my elder brother Mike, his wife Elizabeth and my nieces Patricia and Paula. Mike's first wife, Zetta, had died in 1934 following the birth of Rosemary. Mike, still a farmer at heart, lived on a small-holding and was supplementing his income by teaching. Then we were on the overnight train to Brisbane.

It was seven years since I had seen my eighty-three year old mother who was living in her own home in Brisbane. My other brother, Felix, a paediatrician, and his extended family were nearby. This was the first time they were able to rejoice in meeting Jane. It was good to be able to have some family time together.

The ever-generous Felix arranged for us to spend a few days at the incredible family-run O'Reilly's Guest House, high up in the rain-forest on the Macpherson Range, which separates Queensland from New South Wales. This huge area of rainforest has Antarctic beeches that are over two thousand years old and an amazing range of birds, flora and fauna.

We walked for miles under the high canopy of the forest, fascinated by what our guide was telling us about turkeys that hatched their eggs by controlling the temperature of a mound of leaves; bower-birds who surrounded their bower with anything blue, from clothes-pegs to bottle-tops; trap-door spiders who let down the door once a juicy insect was inside, and much else. Walking on our own, we had just finished our picnic lunch on a lonely cliff looking towards the Great Dividing Range, when a five-foot goanna – Aussie for iguana – emerged from inside a hollow tree alongside and ambled off.

Two weeks later, we sailed on the *Southern Cross* for Durban. She called in at Melbourne, giving us just enough time to visit Mike's daughter, Rosemary. Rosemary and Warren had a house full of five cheerful children, Roslyn, Sue, Mike, Marion and Peter, who gave us a lively welcome. And then on through some very stormy seas in the Australian Bight to Durban. Jane's trophy from the voyage was a silver spoon for winning the deck-tennis championship!

Durban

We arrived in Durban in mid August and I was startled to find a letter from Archbishop Oliver Green-Wilkinson asking me to fly to Toronto the next day to attend the Toronto Anglican Congress on behalf of the Province. This would be the first Anglican World Conference in which lay people would predominate.

My feelings were mixed. We had been away from the Diocese for eight months but there was no time to argue. So Jane travelled on her own to Zululand, hopefully to be met at midnight on Glencoe station by Dr Anthony Barker of Nqutu Hospital. We had both been due to be their guests for a few days.

I had hardly read a theological book since leaving England twenty years earlier. The war, the cultural isolation of Pretoria and the remoteness of Swaziland meant that I had little idea of who were the movers and shakers in post-war Christianity. Hans Küng, one of the sources of inspiration for the Second Vatican Council which had just begun, had been in Chicago two days before we arrived in January and had filled the main auditorium at the university twice over. It was the first time I had even heard his name. I knew about Bonhoeffer's martyrdom but had never even seen his *Letters From Prison*, said to be the most influential Christian book being read by students worldwide. The main benefit of conferences is that they provide opportunities for people to meet. The last major conference I had attended had been with the Student Christian Movement at Swanick in Derbyshire, twenty-five years earlier. This was a belated chance to catch-up.

Toronto Anglican Congress

The Congress was huge. Clement Marama, a leading layman, represented the Diocese of Nyasaland. Maurice Carver from Southern Rhodesia was also there, at his own expense. It was two days before we found each other. The pattern was two talks each morning, group discussions in the afternoon, and in the evening fun events such as going off in bus-loads to the Shakespeare theatre in Stratford, Ontario to see *Troilus and Cressida* – the first time I had seen Shakespeare in modern dress. On the Sunday, I preached passionately about Madagascar, which I had only just heard about from two Malagasy laymen in our group. In the afternoon, there was an outdoor Eucharist in which 16,000 people participated. Ideas were being floated by Australian delegates that I had never heard of, such as lay celebration of the Eucharist. It was still under discussion in Sydney diocese forty years later.

Two main themes emerged. The first was the vital importance of lay people. John Lawrence said that our strategy should be to ensure that trained lay people were seen and supported in places where minds are influenced and decisions made. Bishop Leslie Newbigin of South India sketched a caricature of the Church:

> It exists manifestly on Sundays, is in a kind of suspended animation from Monday to Saturday, and unlike most animals, hibernates in the summer.

My reflection in *Ecclesia*, our diocesan monthly newsletter, when applying the critique to our diocese, was:

> What a difference it would make if we thought of our job being done by 10,000 active communicants rather than by thirty-four clergy and four lay staff.

The second theme was interdependence. This was summed up in the conference message to the whole Anglican Communion:

> The Church that lives by itself will die to itself.

The most fruitful conversation I had at Toronto was with Janet Lacey. She had been, I think, an actress, and then was involved in resettling some of the millions of refugees in Europe after World War II. Recently she had helped found Christian Aid and was its Director. We discussed the growing chasm between health needs in Malawi and the poor state of most church hospitals and health centres. She said, "The longest way round is the shortest way home. Don't ask for financial help. Ask the World Council of Churches in Geneva to send someone to look at the Churches' health work." The Christian Council of Malawi did just this.

London, Ontario Conferences

From Toronto I went one hundred and twenty miles to two conferences in London, Ontario. The first was *The Advisory Council on Mission Strategy*. This meeting seemed to have two objectives. The first objective was to persuade the Anglican Communion to do more about Latin America. As I recall, we spent a long time watching presentations and listening to lengthy papers.

Here I met John Taylor, a young priest from the Church Missionary Society (CMS). I was not aware until then that he had already published perceptive studies of the Church in Uganda and on the Zambian Copperbelt. None of us knew then that after many years as General Secretary of the CMS he would become Bishop of Winchester and that he would write some of the finest theology that the Anglican church produced in the twentieth century, such as *The Christlike God*, and *The Go Between God*. His *Monthly Letters*, written for CMS missionaries in the field, were a constant source of inspiration to me over the next sixteen years.

The second objective was to sharpen up the concept of mutuality in mission which had emerged from Toronto. How could the world-wide resources of the Anglican Communion be released for all the churches struggling to meet the many new opportunities as the "winds of change" turned into a gale? Country after country in the former British, French, Dutch and Portuguese empires were winning their independence.

The concept had been given the name *Mutual Responsibility and Interdependence* (MRI) by Stephen Bayne. The group I was assigned to was not enthusiastic about the name but in the brief time available, nobody could think of a better one. MRI it remained. The most obvious result was the circulation of the MRI project list every year. Although often despised as "shopping-lists", they enabled numerous plans in the least-equipped churches in the world to emerge from the dream world to reality.

This second meeting held at London, Ontario was led by David Paton, a former missionary in China and now Secretary for Mission for the Church of England. He subsequently visited Malawi. David had recently republished a forgotten book by Roland Allen, *St Paul's Missionary Methods and Ours*. We became good friends and later, when he was prematurely attacked by Parkinson's, we used to visit him in Gloucester.

Roland Allen was a prickly mission priest in China in the early 1900s, who resigned after a few years and spent the rest of his life writing about how not to conduct mission. His thesis was that churches grow only if they trust new Christians and the Holy Spirit. The mission to China, he said, had largely failed because it had tried to transplant a western-style church into a Chinese culture.

St Paul, on the other hand, used to stay only a couple of months, or maybe a year, and then let the Holy Spirit take over. He might occasionally revisit them briefly or write them a letter or two. That was all.

As Mark Gibbs said in his book *God's Frozen People*, what did the church do when it had no buildings, no finance, no New Testament, no theological colleges, no paid clergy – none of the things we regard as essential? It converted the Roman Empire.

The church in developing countries, said David Paton, was taking the best educated men it could find – sometimes women, but not often – and sending them away to a theological college, often separating them from their families for two or three years. If they did well in their exams, they might also be sent to another country to do a degree in theology.

This diagnosis certainly applied to Nyasaland. When the Diocese became part of the Province of Central Africa in 1953, joining with dioceses in Southern and Northern Rhodesia (now Zimbabwe and Zambia), the vernacular college on Likoma Island was closed. The new students were sent to Lusaka, the bustling capital of Northern Rhodesia, seven hundred miles or more from home. All training was in English. There was no chance for local leaders to celebrate the eucharist in the church they might have helped build with their own hands. Very often, the growing point of a parish is the out-station with a charismatic local leader. This was clearly demonstrated by some of the men in Nyasaland who trained for the priesthood in the vernacular in the late 1960s.

I was reminded of Stephen Makandanje, the voluntary priest from Nyasaland who had built both the church and the congregation at Hlatikulu, in Swaziland. He had shamed me by saying, "I can't be paid for being a priest. It would spoil it all."

Africa bubbled with new energy, eloquently described in Trevor Huddleston's speech at the newly-formed All Africa Conference of Churches at Kampala in April 1963:

> A great new day is dawning, not only for Africa, nor for Africa's Church, but for the Church throughout the world, to share in an

outpouring of charity and sacrifice which will be, not the end of the missionary era, but its lovely new beginning. This is the real message – and the challenge – of Kampala.

Nairobi

On my way home I stayed with Paul Chadwick at Trinity College, Nairobi.

It was good that in Nairobi they were offering clergy a chance of updating and relating their theology in an African context. They learnt how the church could work effectively in the new towns of Africa.

It was also a chance for clergy from different parts of Africa and different traditions to meet and work together. Three of our clergy were later able to benefit by attending the college before it switched to using Swahili as the medium for teaching.

I was also impressed by a mobile book-van organised by the Church Army from their centre for training evangelists. They showed me a nursery school, an adult literacy centre, engineering and homecraft training-schools and a family life centre. Clearly we had a lot to learn.

Return to Nyasaland

It was almost the end of September before the diocese saw me again after a nine-month absence. The diocese was fortunate in having the superb Christopher Lacey as Vicar General. He had served in Nyasaland for twenty-six years, was forward-looking, equally at home with Malawians and expatriates and fun to be with. He was full of energy and constructive ideas. (see Appendix).

Jane had moved into one of the Malosa Secondary School houses adjoining the site for the new diocesan centre. This was an area of five hundred acres known both as Malosa, from the 5,000 foot mountain ridge on its western side, or Likwenu, from the river that ran through it. To the east, Lake Chirwa shimmered fifteen miles away, and on a clear day you could see beyond it five mountain ranges in Mozambique, the furthest one hundred and twenty miles away.

I wrote to my mother:

> It's a magical place. At 4.00 a.m. the dawn chorus begins all around us and during breakfast all sorts of interesting birds keep popping out of the bush, purple-headed louries and green-winged pytilia and cordon-bleu finches. A few days ago an anteater – the first we had ever seen – brown, just under a metre in length with a long snout –

emerged from the bush and snuffled around the ground while we were eating.

The first letter I read after my return was the resignation of Guy Carleton, Archdeacon of Nkhotakota and the Central Region, where over half our church members lived. He also asked me to go to Nkhotakota to help solve problems in the congregation.

So I set off on the hundred miles to Lilongwe on an earth road that was in need of a grader to smooth away the corrugations. There, Guy collected me in an ancient pick-up in which the cylinders fired intermittently.

At dusk, we gave a lift to a hitch-hiker. Around eight in the evening and by now totally dark, we started up a long hill. Half-way up there was a hammering on the window, "Faster bwana, faster!" We looked back and could just see the huge shape of an elephant trotting a couple of yards behind us. Guy leaned forward, accelerator hard down. His face was a study! The speedometer reached 10m.p.h. The hammering and the shouting reached a crescendo. Finally, we reached the top of the hill and the elephant wandered off into the bush.

Guy, like Christopher Lacey, was a missionary who had a clear vision of the church in independent Africa. Arthur Rawlings, a layman at Nkhotakota, was another and our building team grew out of his ideas. One of his students was Dunstan Mzokomera.

One of Guy's special enthusiasms was that the language in our liturgy should be in the form of Nyanja/Chewa used throughout the country, not in the lake shore dialect spoken only on Likoma Island and in Portuguese East Africa (Mozambique). He had, on his own initiative, translated and published the entire hymnbook in standard Chewa. This had been warmly welcomed by those using it throughout the Central Region.

Guy was aware of his shortcomings and said, "My trouble, father, is that I am paternalistic." So he went off to the West Indies, from where he wrote to me later, "I have learned my lesson and am heart and soul in Antigua's battle for independence." Unfortunately, he picked the losing side and was deported to another island, and finally had to return to the UK, where he died comparatively young.

Heading towards Malawian Independence

In the national political scene, the first cracks were beginning to appear in the Cabinet. The country was still in the run up to independence. Dr H. "Kamuzu" Banda, as he liked to be called, was Prime Minister and Sir Glyn Jones was Governor General.

No outsider could easily know what was going on. Even then, the radio was controlled by the government and at moments of crisis would go off the air. There were no newspapers except the CAT (the *Central Africa Times*) edited by a European. For us, the BBC World Service was, at that time, difficult to get as we were in the shadow of Malosa Mountain.

As a church we had little opportunities of input. I had been living in Malawi for almost two years, but at Mponda's, with no telephone and erratic post, communication with the world around us was difficult. The inter-church network was fragmentary and each church operated through its own links. Anglicans were at a severe disadvantage.

Almost all of the cabinet and Malawi Congress Party (MCP) leaders belonged to the Church of Central Africa Presbyterian (CCAP). The two exceptions in the cabinet were John Msonthi, the son of one of our priests but himself a Catholic, and Henry Chipembere, the son of Archdeacon Habil, at Mponda's. Henry was 33, a graduate of Fort Hare in South Africa, and had been Assistant District Commissioner of Kasupe, the area where we were now living. He was a powerful and sometimes intemperate speaker. He had been treasurer of the Nyasaland African Congress and was the most powerful and intelligent member of the cabinet. It was he who had invited Dr Banda to return to the Nyasaland he had never seen since he left it as a young man in the early 1920s. Henry and his wife Catherine were both from Likoma Island.

Henry and Dr Banda had been in prison together for thirteen months in Gwelo in Southern Rhodesia. They were moved to Zomba prison and released in 1960, but Henry was again imprisoned under British rule for two years until January 1963. Dr Banda never visited him during this second imprisonment but I did, and found him in a very cramped cell with no amenities. We were in England when he came out. He told Dr Banda, in a letter not released at the time, that he wanted to assure Europeans that he intended now to be "a man of peace".

Orton Chirwa, the Minister and lawyer who had attended my consecration, and who was generally held in high regard, chaired the MCP committee which elected Dr Banda Life-President. With hindsight, this set an unhappy future for Malawi and a disastrous precedent for other newly independent countries. But none of this did we know at the time. The stakes were high.

Travelling the Diocese

Much of the remaining three months of 1963 was spent in confirmation tours covering the whole country and the ordination of six deacons and one priest. Four new ordinands were sent for training to St John's, the provincial seminary in Lusaka.

Travelling was not easy. The roads were almost impassable to ordinary cars once the rains began in November and we had no Land Rovers. No tarred road existed anywhere north of Zomba, except in the town of Lilongwe in the Central Province and one mile in Mzuzu in the Northern Province, where the Queen Mother spent a night on an earlier visit.

Congregations on the lake shore north of Nkhotakota for the next 50 miles could be reached only on foot. The Bua river, ten miles to the north, had to be crossed by canoes. To reach Likoma and Chizumulu Islands, after the diocese's "*boatie*" *Paul* came to her sad end, we were entirely dependent on the sometimes erratic timetables of the *Ilala*, the passenger/cargo ship run by the Nyasaland Railways that steamed around the lake.

A Texan on the lake shore

During a visit to Nkhotakota we were joined by George Carlisle, the new Malawi secretary for the Diocese of Texas and chaplain to the NASA space station near Houston. I had met him in Texas and now he had been given the job he longed for. George was a heavy weight in every sense and I warned him that the parishes we would be visiting involved considerable walking but he was determined to come. We travelled to the Bua River in a pick-up and crossed over in canoes.

The next twenty miles – and back again – would be on foot. By mid-morning the group had split into small parties and someone came running up to say, "The bwana from America has collapsed!" We rushed back a quarter of a mile and there was George on the ground with three or four people fanning him hats and grass. I was beginning to think this was the end of the Texas link when one of our party arrived with a cup of tea. By an extraordinary chance, someone had started a tea-shop on this path. We were perhaps the first outsiders to use it. The tea restored George, but he looked relieved when I suggested he should go back at his own pace and cross over the Bua to Nkhotakota where we would meet up again in a few days. George dined out on the story back in Texas and became a dedicated promoter of the Malawi cause, doing much to help the new diocese of Lake Malawi.

Salima Confirmation

I began my confirmation tour in the Central Region at Salima, on the lake shore. There had never been an Anglican congregation within thirty miles or so. Now four had self-seeded themselves in the area and they were expecting me for a confirmation.

The beginning was unpromising. Nobody in Salima had even heard of an Anglican church. I tried, in mangled Chichewa, *"Chachi ya Englande? Chachi ya Provinsi?"* I even tried the curious name by which Anglicans were known in Pretoria, *Kereke ya Chachi* (literally, "Church of the Church", in Afrikaans and English – at that time up to 600,000 men from Nyasaland were working in the mines and farms of South Africa and Southern Rhodesia.

People really wanted to help and a group of four went into a private session. They came back looking triumphant. *"Chachi ya Likoma?"* "Yes!!" One of them came with me to show me the church, newly built and with a second-hand iron roof, on the outskirts of the town.

The name *Chachi ya Likoma* said something about the missionary zeal of the thousands of Likomans working on the mainland – but also of our limitations. The public perception of the Anglican Church was of a chaplaincy for migrant Likomans. I found exactly the same perception in Blantyre's township of Soche. It had a fine new church, recently dedicated by Bishop Frank Thorne, but the people saw it as for Likomans, not for "us".

At Salima I tried out some of the ideas I had heard at Toronto and mentioned the title of another of Roland Allen's books, *The Spontaneous Expansion of the Church*. The interpreter put the whole of Roland Allen into four words, *"Mpingo wokula mwadzidzi mwaokha"* ("the Church that went up whoosh!")

Laity and Worker Priests

Lay leadership was a key issue. The UMCA system had been to train teacher-catechists working in Anglican schools. They were responsible for teaching on weekdays and on Sundays for looking after out-station churches – preaching, teaching, burying and preparing people for confirmation.

This had come to a sudden end when teachers became employees of government and employed for school work only. A few teachers in an Anglican school would perhaps be Anglicans and might volunteer to look after a church on Sundays – but as teachers could now be posted to any school, it was very unlikely that the few Anglican teachers would end up in Anglican schools.

Rapid remedial action was needed: training local leaders in pastoral work, appointing an Education Secretary who could recruit Anglican teachers and build up relationships with government. There was no immediate solution. One day, Chilema Lay Training Centre would be able to help but it was still in gestation.

We had not lost sight of the Toronto emphasis on the laity. Clement Marama, in his report to the diocese, put this at the head of the things he had learned at Toronto. He wrote in *Ecclesia*:

> I am convinced that the most urgent need for the enrichment and invigoration of the Church is an honest look at the position of laity. The time has come for real action to listen to the voice of laity. This is urgent if we want a closer relationship with other Churches.

Maurice Carver, a layman who had made a huge contribution to education in Southern Rhodesia had asked if there was anything he could do in the diocese and we welcomed him with open arms. At his own expense, he had attended the Toronto Congress. Following Clement's report, Maurice contributed an article for *Ecclesia* on the tent-making ministry, the reference of course being St Paul, himself a tent-making layman. Maurice quoted an instance in South India where six men – a tanner, two drummers, a woodcutter, a foreman and a teacher – were ordained presbyters while continuing to earn their living in the village communities to which they belonged. The result was a quadrupling in the number of village congregations.

I was glad that 1963 ended with a joint meeting of lay people from the Blantyre Synod of the CCAP and the Anglican diocese and a three day Lay Retreat which I was asked to lead.

Family Interlude

On the 17th of April 1964 our son Basil eventually appeared. Jane was in labour for twenty-four hours and I was able to be with her for what seemed like an eternity. In the end, the doctor decided Basil needed some encouragement and put a suction pad on his tiny head so that he could help by pulling. The result was that Basil emerged looking like a pixie with a pointed head, but it soon returned to its normal shape. I don't know which of the three of us was most exhausted!

Here are a few highlights from letters to my mother, who died at 88 just after the 1968 Lambeth Conference began. She had suffered all her life from the after effects of rheumatic fever in her teens, but had raised three sons. She had cared for Dad since 1912 when Hong Kong encephalitis B destroyed his sense of balance. He was always mobile and by some miracle mentally unaffected. In the house, he relied on a primitive form of the Zimmer Frame called a "walking machine"; out on the road he used a tricycle chair propelled by two handles. From the time I was five, I used to accompany him for two or three hours every morning.

> 17 April. Basil took some 24 hours to come into the world at 9.45 p.m. in the old Zomba Hospital. He is a most scrumptious infant, has regained his birth weight in three days, with a greatness of very fair hair, a slightly sunburnt complexion (not all red and horrid but a pale tan) and now his head, about a foot long when he was born, has come back to his proper shape. He was assisted on the way out by a thing like a bicycle pump. Jane is fighting fit. Her only complaint is that Basil drops asleep halfway through his meals and drains port take-off point before beginning on the starboard one, so that she is becoming lopsided. The lawn is also lopsided as Jane got two-thirds of the way through mowing it when Percival, our cook, caught her and gave her a piece of his mind.

In July, Basil made his first visit to Likoma Island, travelling overland with us through Mozambique. I reported that he was in momentary danger of being pulled limb from limb by Likoman mothers who had never seen a pink baby before.

In September, I wrote: "Basil is trying to crawl and full of fun. His trouble is that he gets stuck upside down in the middle of the night."

By November, Basil was "mobile, with all the instincts of a juvenile delinquent but with an unfortunate charm and cheerfulness which makes it difficult to wield the heavy hand."

In April 1965, we introduced him to the lake. He took a bit of time to get used to the vastness of the water-supply, as there was a strong wind and waves that tended to break over his head, but by Wednesday, he was so enjoying himself that we resolved to build him a sandpit in the garden. Mark II is due to arrive at the beginning of December.

In September I was reporting:

> Basil is a bit like a beached whale. He gets stuck upside down in the middle of the night and can't get back again. But he's learning to crawl and is full of fun. The matins lessons are from Ecclesiastes, a horrible book mostly, but it has its moments like 4.9, added by the writer of Wisdom, "Two are better that one, for if the one falls, the one will lift up his fellow ... If two lie together, then they can have heat: but how can one be warm alone?" I am not sure I would dare the other one we ran into last month, but I'll leave you to read it: Proverbs 5.11.

I had hardly been at home and had seen little of Basil since he was born in April 1964. We had to cancel our holiday so in October Jane and I and six-month old Basil were spending a few nights on nearby Zomba Mountain. We took with us the few architects' plans that we could lay hands on. There was not an architect left in the country, apart from those in the Public Works Department and for the first time there was a little money for the clergy houses, health centres and schools that were so desperately needed. This space would enable us to sketch out plans for buildings that could be afforded. There is more in the chapter Building Department.

Basil baptised in April 1964 by Archdeacon Chimpembere at the Church of the Ascension in Likwenu

Nigel Crofton's baptism July 1964 Archdeacon Christopher Lacey, Donald, Jane, Basil, Mel, Gerald Riddle (Jane & Brigid's father), Julian, Brigid, Nigel & Nicola Crofton

A few months later Nigel was baptised.

It was during this time that we received the telephone call from Sir Glyn Jones, the Governor General to persuade Archdeacon of South Nyasa Habil at Mponda's to go to Likoma Island, and then to Malindi to convince Catherine, Henry Chipembere's wife, and her children to go with him.

Letters to my mother, then aged 87, were important to her and contained snapshots of our life. Here are a few:

> 12 October: An original excuse from a candidate for being late for a confirmation at Matope last week. Half the congregation lives across the Shire River, just before it starts on 100 miles of rapids. "A hippo put its foot in our boat and pulled the oarsman into the water." Fortunately, nobody was any the worse for wear. Francis Bell had one in his garden at Malindi which refused to go away, so he threw a bau-board at it – a massive wooden-board for a game a bit like the solitaire we used to play. It is played all over eastern Africa with beans or stones: a favourite game in the men's ward in Pretoria.
>
> We should have had our annual round of unity talks at Chilema last week, but it was rather an anti-climax. Livingstonia Synod didn't arrive – a car breakdown, we heard later. Blantyre Synod forgot to tell their team till the day before and it was too late for them to get off work. The Churches of Christ came in the afternoon, looking a bit bedraggled after fighting a bush-fire early in the morning that nearly wiped their centre out, saved by one of them throwing himself on a tin of burning aluminium paint in the oil-store that would otherwise have blown up all the diesoline drums and ignited the whole place which is all grass-roofed. However, we didn't waste our time. It was a chance to work on the first edition of the Liturgy which is being

printed in three editions: Nyanja, Nyanja-English and Yao-Nyanja on facing pages.

An innovation this year at the Clergy retreat: We got Patrick Kalilombe, a brilliant Malawian White Father, to conduct bible studies with group discussions. The clergy were a little shocked at the idea but thought it was a good one when it was over. The RCs have had a bad blow when their most outstanding Malawian, doctor of canon law in the Gregorian University in Rome, left to get married. Many of the priests here are Dutch and, with all the ferment going on in Holland about clerical celibacy, are shattered.

10.15: Adjourn to garage to confer on how to make a sun-printing frame for architectural prints (it worked well). Resume at desks. Complete final draft of new edition of Diocesan Liturgy: what is modern English for "Thou who takest" – you who take? You who takes? Fill in a very German form of several pages of small print to get the hydro-electric project working here at Malosa.

14.00: J off to hospital to see how the building of the A-frame Guardians' kitchen she designed is progressing (Guardians are relatives of patients who stay at the hospital and provide food for their sick ones). Arranges hospitality for twenty-two members of Standing Committee, due to meet in our house; back to check work at Hotblack House. The house named after Gerry Hotblack, soldier, schoolmaster, strawberry-farmer, who at 76 has turned missionary and is building himself a house across the dam from ours. His daughter Joan has come to look after him and our accounts at the same time. D is busy unloading on to her the accumulated accountancy problems.

Returning to the family, in November 1965, I wrote:

> The garden delights Basil. He delights in irrigation and the harvesting of Cape gooseberries, without too much damage to clothes or digestion. A less useful activity is playing darts with labels of cuttings on the back verandah. We are still on the nursery slopes of gardening – labels in one hand, text-book in the other – and the results could be alarming. If the oyster-nut vine, which grows 20 feet in six months, finds itself labelled as alyssum, we might need another house.
>
> 3 December 1965: We are now four! Christopher Donald weighed in last night at 8 lbs 13 ozs, gloves on, ready for the fray at 9.05 p.m.

Thanks to three midwives, one doctor and one husband – none of whom were really necessary. Personal data: fat as an Eskimo, dark brown hair, dark blue eyes far apart like Jane's. Kind of wide, in fact about square in contour. Kicks a great deal, both before and after birth. Favourite posture: like Rodin's "thinker", with chin in hand, following you round with eyes. Glad to have him as ten days overdue. A crisis was threatened if he came in the middle of Diocesan Standing Committee, the following weekend, for which members had travelled hundreds of miles.

A bit scary as the doctor at Zomba, a recent import from Scotland, is said to be an alcoholic and that anyone stitched after 7.00 p.m. is likely to be stitched together permanently as his hand shakes so much. Art Johnson, our Diocesan doctor, who'd been out at health centres in the country, arrived five minutes before the birth and did the necessary tailoring.

We think Basil will take the situation all right. He's been wandering into the spare bedroom for a week or two, looking at the cot and saying, "Baby!" He'll be glad to have another boy to play with. Jane has been persuaded she can't really come home and look after twenty-two guests for the Diocesan Standing Committee meeting and I have pockets full of notes on how to stuff peppers.

Basil welcoming Christopher

Early years

2 January 1966 (from Jane): Basil's bath now goes on indefinitely and I don't know who enjoys them most – Donald or Basil.

11 January 1966: Someone going on leave left Jane his light motorbike. She tears about Malosa on it, to Basil's delight. When he hears her coming home he pretends to grip the handlebars and shouts, "Mummy – tu-tu-tuu!" Susan and Paul Cole-King have been staying with us for a week with their three and a half children – good training for Basil having all his toys pinched.

Basil is quite sweet with Christopher and will hardly let him out of his sight. If he cries at the other end of the house, we all have to go and investigate to keep him quiet. He's very interested that we put the mosquito net on C's crib every night. If not, he trails around with it saying, "Skeeto baby!"

29 January 1966: Christopher was with us at Provincial Synod in Blantyre. It only took him a day to realise that if he opened his mouth, somebody would shove something into it. Basil enjoyed himself with his cousins in Zomba and wasn't in the slightest bit upset at being away from home or us.

24 February 1966: Last night Christopher didn't settle and Jane went in at 3.00 a.m. to give him some sustenance and found him crawling with army ants. One in a hundred is bigger than the rest and gives a nasty nip – the others are harmless, they just crawl over you. This morning the whole house is being drenched with dieldrin.

Last week we were down on the Lower River to see a Catholic hospital with Art and Nan Johnson and the boys. On the way back, we came to a river in full flood because of a storm in the hills. We waited half-an-hour for it to fall but as it was still rising, we turned back – but a smaller river we had already crossed had risen two feet. The villagers were most sympathetic and gave us a room in a new house being built for the court president. The ten of us squeezed in. Basil thoroughly enjoyed himself and trotted off the next morning to see a cow being milked and the pigs, piglets, ducks, pigeons, dogs and cats which had kept up a chorus through the night. He was especially taken by the sow and her litter just underneath our window.

17 May 1966: Basil is well into the cheeky stage. At dinner he offered me chunks of pineapple with a sweet smile, but when I got to my plate, popped them into his own mouth.

5 June 1966: Government has just said that European children may not attend Malawian schools so the boys will not be allowed to attend Malosa Secondary School. But Blantyre is too far for them to travel. We have problems.

24 July 1966: In spite of warnings from Art Johnson about terrible diseases that can be caught from sand-pits, we have had one built. Basil and the gardener's little boy, Chikonde, spend hours in it. Last weekend it kept the boys and the Crofton family quiet for the whole day – well worth the masses of sand when they undress.

31 August 1966: Christopher now snakes along the floor at a tremendous pace. He went through the agonizing days when he could stand up but not sit down and bellowed until he collapsed. Now he bobs up and down very

happily. Basil plays all day with Chikonde – good that he has a playmate and that he is the younger and therefore by no means gets his own way all the time.

17 October 1966: Christopher now pushes a chair around the khonde at great speed and doesn't often fall over. The two of them get on well together. Basil seizes every opportunity of feeding Christopher. We have to be careful he's not jamming a worm down C's ever open mouth.

21 October 1966: The humiliation when we found Basil age two and a half knew more Chichewa than we did – his one-upmanship revenge for his parents' spelling out in English words they didn't want him to understand!

8 January 1967: (On our return, following time in Birmingham initiating the new Diocesan link and a brief holiday in Spain before picking up the ship in Trieste to take us to Beira). The boys are still slightly confused about having two look-alike mummies. Basil asked Brigid, "Mummy, where's Mummy?" Christopher shoots all over the garden on all fours and has stood for a record 5 seconds without holding on to anything.

28 January 1967: We leave in five minutes for Nkhotakota, taking Basil on his first long trip since he was a little baby. Christopher is doing everything except walking. He has an extraordinary crawl with legs straight and body up in the air like a baboon. He can get about as fast as an adult so perhaps doesn't feel the need to walk. He is enormously strong physically. The khonde chairs he climbs on to by just putting one foot on the seat and hauling himself up. He will stay with Brigid and Mel and their children in Zomba while we are away.

6 June 1967: Basil has now had four nasty attacks of asthma which leave him and Jane exhausted. Each time they last for two or three days of gasping for breath. We are lucky in having a good doctor at hand, Art Johnson, or it would have been frightening.

Christopher has been walking for some months now. He is a tough little thing. He has had a stye in one eye which gives it a drooping look, like a prize-fighter who has been worsted, but it doesn't seem to worry him. He has a passion for motor-cars and the only two words he can pronounce are "car" and "lolly". We are planning to build a simple guest-house for diocesan staff on the lake shore at Kaphiridzinja, near where we spent our honeymoon. None of the staff can afford expensive holidays and it would be a great boon for everyone.

24 June 1967: So grateful to Felix for the prescriptions. None of them are available in Malawi but Jane's father has tracked them down in Salisbury.

Basil began a cold ten days ago and we immediately gave him antihistamines and tranquillisers so that he only wheezed for half an hour and avoided an asthma session. Christopher is a solid little fellow and struts about all over the place, usually in the direction of the water taps!

28 July 1967: Felix's medicines are doing Basil a power of good and have stopped him going into spasm.

5 October 1967: Christopher says quite a few words now and thumps Basil if he doesn't approve so they're beginning to be companions for each other! Basil climbed up a ladder and was walking around on the roof the other day – a bit shattering but we're pleased he's developing self-confidence while Christopher can climb out of his cot, wreck the cupboard drawers and climb back again without anyone knowing.

26 October 1967: 6.30 Mass in the little chapel in our house. Query: is it a reason against the westward position that one's first-born sprawls on the steps leading into the chapel and makes faces at his father?

12.15 – Lunch interrupted by screams from Christopher who has discovered a nest of stinging ants on the lawn. Remove clothes and ants and comfort with Maltesers.

4.00 – Basil lays out sweetcorn plantation, properly contoured. Donald says, "Stamp firmly on the seed, then fill the furrows with water." Basil fills furrows with water, then stamps. Both have mud-bath followed by conventional variety.

6.30 – Donald reads to Basil and Christopher about animals of Africa. Basil has them divided up into good and bad. Leopards are good because they eat baboons who are bad because they steal our bananas.

6.40 – Come to fish-eagle in the book. "There's my good eagle that brought me my chambo!" This refers back to a Sunday breakfast on the lake shore when a thoughtful fish-eagle delivered an enormous bream on the ground beside Basil.

14 December 1967: (Jane) Basil and Christopher always have a good half hour with Donald reading to them before they go to bed – not sure who enjoys it most, him or them!

Story time with Beatrix Potter

29 March 1968: Christopher, who had an operation for a hernia two weeks ago, spent Saturday afternoon rolling down the grass slope in front of the house, interspersed with fights with Basil for possession of the tricycle they were given at Christmas. The stitches still had to be taken out in spite of all this and he is as chubby as ever. Sorry, no photos of the children, my camera was pinched by a passing white guest.

22 April 1968: Christopher has developed another hernia now on the other side! While we were in Zomba, Basil joined Nigel in going to the Nursery School. He bellowed to begin with but by the end of the week quite enjoying it. Continued to go after our return to Malosa, with the Leak and Lane children. It is now the middle of the school holidays and Basil keeps asking when he will be back at school again. Christopher has developed a splendid lisp – we try to get him to say words beginning with "s" just to hear it! He's a wonderful comic.

Excerpts from letters to my mother:

> Basil and Christopher are growing frantically – busy on outward bound courses in the garden at the moment – they have swings, a slide and rope-ladders rigged up under the trees.
>
> The garden is thriving again – the delicate little coral creeper on the front khonde off again, the yesterday-today-and-tomorrow bush covered with mauve, lilac and white flowers in turn, and the pale blue plumbago we thought had died come back to life again. We have several boxes full of flamboyant tree seedlings, ready for planting at the lake shore diocesan cottage.
>
> For our Christmas letter, we fitted the close-up lens and recorded just one of the days of our life we happened to be together:
>
> 04.30: D struggles out of bed to tape-record an eagle-owl snoring in the big tree outside the bedroom – act of reparation for two mornings ago when the machine wouldn't work and he missed a ground hornbill, a huge, grotesque bird like a turkey, unusual in these parts.
>
> 06.30: Mass in the little chapel at the end of our house. We use the 1964 Liturgy which is having a hard time recovering from the title attached to it A Liturgy for Africa, which has made Africans unhappy – "Why only for Africa?"
>
> 07.15: Breakfast. Tot up the different birds seen yesterday in the garden: thirty-two, but J cheats by adding four more heard but not

seen. Christopher joins in the fun: "bird" – rush for glasses to find he is pointing at a plate bought in Athens with a stork on it.

18.00: D plans a vernacular course for expatriates, including self. Overhears Basil having an argument with playmate Sayikonde, our gardener's son. Decides instead to take Basil on as tutor.

Sayikonde, Basil and Jane on the Yamaha

While I was at the Lambeth Conference we solved the problem of intercommunication between Jane and myself with a tape-machine. Donald was certainly the only member of Lambeth who could lighten the views of the Archbishop of Sydney on women by plugging in what he hoped would be mistaken for a hearing-aid and listening to his son and heir rendering "Baa-baa black sheep!"

I arrived back in Blantyre five hours late, just as the welcome-home party was dispersing. The five-hour wait was amply justified in Basil's eyes by me arriving in a real super VC10 jet instead of a dirty old Viscount. It was a great joy to find that Basil, who had been plagued with asthma since he was a small baby, was now a different boy, thanks to new medication prescribed by a remote control specialist in London.

No snail ever crept more unwillingly to nursery school in Zomba than Basil when he began at Eastertime. Now he was going off as if he intended to enjoy it. Christopher – just on three – was enjoying himself rolling down the grass slope in front of the house and trying to catch pied wagtails. We felt they would be a little sad when the day finally came when he realised that a chap of his size and shape would never catch one.

An early birthday party on the front lawn

We have man-eating lions at present who leave paw-marks round the orange trees at the bottom of the garden. Jane says she will never forget the roar that vibrated through her from near the back of the house in the middle of the night. Hunters and traps containing a live goat, have been trying to catch them but they continue to rove uncomfortably close to the house. When Jane asked the night-shift telephonist who runs our wind-up mini-exchange, why he had not been on duty, she found it difficult to question his explanation, "I was on my way to take over the midnight shift, but I met a lion on the path and thought I'd better go home." There was no challenging the regular chant of the little gang who were Basil and Christopher's constant companions, "Mrs Arden, there's a lion in your garden!"

Once again, Michaelmas, our wedding anniversary, found us at opposite ends of Malawi. I was on the hippie-deck (the focsle head) of the *Ilala*, wondering which of the happenings of a packed year were too boring (or too lurid) to find their way into our Christmas letter. The captain didn't allow lights on the focsle head and you could dodge the mwera (the south-east trade winds) only by getting right inside your sleeping-bag. So making notes was out. At dawn, when the anchor chain clattered through the hawse-pipe a few inches from my right ear, I could recall only a few things strung together by the letter "B" that I had thought of before dropping off to sleep:

Bees – the swarm that invaded Soche church where I had gone for their Easter Eucharist. Smoking them out with a burning car-tyre expelled the people but not the bees.

Burglars – On President Banda's birthday, the police-catch over the past years is set free. Two came our way, one in the bedroom who beat Jane to the door by a short head while I slept, and a belated one who was still burgling when – unhappily for him – Elias, an athletic man who was cooking for us, came on duty.

Bush-baby – An entrancing little chap, all ears and bushy tail, silhouetted just after sunset on the roof of Lilongwe church.

Birds, boys and berries – We had a row of mulberry trees that grew exuberantly in the soak-away of the septic-tank. Any dark object seen in them about July was either a purple-crested turaco, a great purple-black bird with surprising pillar-box red underwings or it was Basil, Christopher and their friends, faces also a dark purple.

The new attraction at Kaphridizinja, the diocesan lake shore cottage, was a four-foot crocodile, whose home base was half-a-mile from our beach.

Boys with cousin Nigel gorging on Zomba Mountain raspberries

Playing Bau with good friend David Kacholola

The Fisheries Officer was keen on the balance of nature and wouldn't allow crocodiles to be exterminated. They were, we understood, being trained not to eat the wealthiest of the tourists whom Malawi was trying to coax to the lake, though they had recently taken one of our builders.

Basil, who has made so much progress in conquering his asthma as to be a different boy, is taking swimming lessons. Part I is apparently, "How to swim", Part II "How to remain on top." He has done only Part I to date, and operates like a whale, surfacing occasionally to blow.

Discovering a chameleon

Kaphiridzinja, the Diocesan lake shore cottage, like our garden at Malosa, has turned out to be a bird-paradise. Up to now, we have listed – as total amateurs – eighty-six species, and there are probably more to be identified. After sunset one evening recently, we watched for five minutes the display-flight of a pennant-winged nightjar, silhouetted against a vermilion sky. The nightjar migrates here from the Sudan and in the breeding season grows two-foot streamers from the tip of each wing. As he operates after dark you could bird-watch for a lifetime without seeing such a magnificent sight.

Endless games of football were played in the front garden

For a wonderful ten-day holiday, Mel (my brother-in-law) lent us the Mirror dinghy he had made in his garage. I have an agreement with Jane that I will not tell you anything about the time she tipped me into the middle of the lake if she does not say anything about the time I tipped upside-down with an apprehensive visiting missionary nurse on board.

Close to where we met for Synod is the school where our two may have to go as boarders in a couple of years' time. Our hearts bleed at the thought of exporting these two small shrimps (Christopher is still 3!) five hundred miles to be schooled.

Family with Gunde and Elias – 1973
(Pets: Tigger, Ginger, Chips (nose) and Chambo)

Developing a Malawian church

A vision for Malawian leadership

Two weeks after arriving in Malawi in November 1961, I wrote to the Swaziland staff that "the next bishop must be an African." My first visit to Central and Northern Malawi – where four-fifths of Anglicans lived – made this an immediate need, not only for a second bishop, but for one living in the centre of the country. I was based in the south of the country. The obvious place was Nkhotakota, where Arthur Frazer Sim had in a single year, 1895, built the first school for 100 pupils, baptised the first Christian, a murderer just before being hanged, and died of malaria.

The first African priest – Padre Abdullah – was ordained by Bishop John Hine of Likoma in 1898. In the following year he said that our aim was building up an African Church – not admitting Africans to an English Mission but a "Church of the people of the land." But he was transferred to Zanzibar after two years, then to Northern Rhodesia and the vision faded.

The Presbyterian Synod of Blantyre of the CCAP (Church of Central Africa Presbyterian) in the south and Livingstonia in the north, had a more consistent picture of African leadership, especially in recent years. At Blantyre, Jonathan Sangaya, partly Ngoni, partly Yao by birth, became General Secretary (virtually bishop) just as I arrived. He was nine years older than me, a teacher who had worked in Ethiopia in World War II and was ordained in 1952. He had had a year's training for the post in Scotland, and had previously been assistant to an Iona Community General Secretary. In the same headquarters were a number of Scots missionaries, including Tom Colvin – an imaginative hymn-writer and politically aware minister to whom Malawi today owes the Christian Service Committee and other ecumenical initiatives. Jonathan continued in his post until his death in 1979. His enthusiasm and ours were identical and we did much together, including the founding of Chilema Lay Training Centre, the Christian Health Association of Malawi (CHAM) and the joint theological college at Zomba.

A bishop in Nkhotakota (a mainly Muslim community) would be virtually on his own, in a town renowned for its political problems. He would have to be tough, capable and imaginative. And able to spend weeks away from home in a part of the country that had few passable roads, where most congregations could be reached only by push-bike or on foot.

My thoughts went back to that seminar in Canada on Roland Allen. Was there a layman in the diocese who already had the vocation and the required training and gifts? I thought of Alec Rubadiri, the first African Assistant District Commissioner, a lay member of the Diocesan Standing Committee, who had gone to spend a year at Exeter University. I wrote to a friend, Jack Dobson, also at Exeter. Yes, the priesthood was something he would think and pray about. Alec wrote later to say, yes, he had made up his mind and was offering himself for the priesthood. Sadly, by the time he returned to Malawi he was already a sick man, but continued reading theology in hospital, where he died in April 1964. I said at his funeral that, "I came to see him in hospital, not so much to give him help as to learn what faith, courage and dedication mean."

Almost daily I faced the problem: how could I, as an expatriate, new to the country, not knowing a word of the two languages used in the areas where we worked, be midwife to an African Church?

I took the problem to my fellow bishops in the Province, who were in what are now Zimbabwe, Zambia and Botswana. They were unanimous that it would be right to have a suffragan (assistant) bishop, but only as a stepping-stone to the creation of a new diocese.

Ordaining Deacons in 1963
Left to Right: Edward Nanganga, Archdeacon Habil Chipembere,
George Mchakama, Nathaniel Aipa

Winds of change

6 July 1964 was Independence Day, Nyasaland was reborn as a self-governing member of the Commonwealth and renamed Malawi. We had the privilege of attending a dinner with the Duke of Edinburgh and the Governor before proceeding to the newly built Kamuzu Stadium to witness, with thousands of others, the lowering of the Union Jack and raising of the tricolour flag of Malawi – red for the blood that had been shed in the struggle for independence, green for new life and black for Africa, on which was superimposed the rising sun for the dawn of a new life.

The proposal to appoint a Suffragan Bishop was put to our Diocesan Synod in August 1964, seventy members were present and for the first time laity outnumbered clergy. It was also the first time that Catholic and Presbyterian observers attended. The idea was received with enthusiasm. Some wanted two new bishops, some three. Everyone accepted the wishes of the Province that the appointment of a suffragan must be seen as a stepping stone to the creation of a new diocese. Only a few realised the implications – offices, staff, housing, transport and finance.

Other actions of this creative Synod made it possible for the divorced to be readmitted to communion, accepted the new idea of "voluntary clergy" and ensured that there would be women in future synods by giving the Mothers' Union two seats. We also invited Presbyterians and the Churches of Christ to take part in formal talks about reunion.

Most people seemed to take it for granted that Habil Chipembere would be the first to be consecrated, followed perhaps by Dunstan Choo, who had been born on Chizumulu Island and was about to be appointed Archdeacon of Likoma. Dunstan had spent a lifetime in the Transvaal as a layman, priest and archdeacon.

The only choice for a bishop among the clergy of the diocese was Habil Chipembere, Archdeacon of Nyasa and based at Malindi. He had been an army chaplain in East Africa and India and a member of the Legislative Council while his son, Henry, was in prison with Kamuzu Banda in Gwelo in Southern Rhodesia. He was loved and respected but already in his sixties and I sensed he was looking forward to retirement rather than pastoral responsibility for the whole of the Northern and Central Regions. Henry had returned to Nyasaland in 1960, but three months later was imprisoned in Zomba, where both Bishop Frank Thorne and I visited him.

It was agreed to appoint a Diocesan Elective Committee with power to nominate a Malawian or other names to the Provincial Elective Assembly for a decision.

Nobody was aware that the day after the Committee met Orton Chirwa would be telling the Governor General that if Dr Banda did not step down as President, all the cabinet would resign.

By the time the Committee met again, Habil Chipembere was in exile on Likoma Island, this as a result of his son Henry, a prominent cabinet minister, being part of the opposition to Dr Banda. We met with no clear idea of whom God was pointing to or who should be recommended. Before long the members were unanimous in nominating Josiah Mtekateka to the Provincial Elective Assembly. Josiah was Archdeacon in South West Tanganyika diocese. He had been born on Likoma Island 61 years earlier, but had spent almost all his ministry in Tanzania.

Archdeacon Josiah Mtekateka

Touring the diocese with the Archbishop

While the political earthquakes of October 1964 were happening in Zomba, I was mostly incommunicado, accompanying our Archbishop on his first visit to Malawi. Apart from brief meetings in Blantyre and my inauguration, no archbishop had visited Malawi since the Province of Central Africa was formed in 1955. Now Oliver Green-Wilkinson had set aside ten days and wanted to see the diocese as it really was. We sailed in *Boatie Paul* – in a previous existence a Dutch canal boat – to Likoma Island where Alban Chilalika, one of the most promising of all our new priests, was to be ordained and Dunstan Choo instituted as the first Malawian Archdeacon of Likoma.

After Likoma we spent a day on Chizumulu Island, ten miles to the west of Likoma, where Dunstan was born and then sailed the twenty miles across the lake to visit the congregations on the lake shore south of Nkhata Bay.

At dawn, as we landed at the little village of Kapando, a message came that the local leaders of the Presbyterian Livingstonia Synod would like to visit us. Our surprise was great when after lunch there arrived, not just the local leaders but four ministers and forty church elders from fifty miles around. An impromptu meeting was held under a great tree.

The UMCA history records that "In the early part of 1881, Mr Johnson sought help from the Scottish Mission station at Livingstonia. His hands were ulcerated, and these good Samaritans nursed him and sent him away well." I said that we had been working alongside each other for two-thirds of a century, yet we had hardly ever worshipped together or made any attempt to plan jointly how the gospel could take root in the north. Oliver and I thanked them most sincerely for taking the initiative to meet with us. It was a good meeting and we agreed we would work together more closely in the future.

We then sailed south. Disaster struck after sixty miles as we approached Liwaladzi. A passenger from Likoma said he knew the coast well and the sandbanks had shifted. We should head straight for the village, not up the small inlet. The crew took his advice – and then, a hundred yards from the shore, we ground into the sand, jamming the propeller and buckling the rudder. The reception party of church elders stripped off their clothes, waded out to us and carried Oliver ashore to the cheering crowd awaiting us. After this we walked about ten miles to the Bua river, crossed by canoe and then continued by car to Nkhotakota.

This all happened on the day that – 250 miles further south – the government finally broke up, with four ministers sacked by Banda and three more resigning. All left the country.

We went through Nkhotakota and on to Sani, six miles south. This had been the village where Leonard Kamungu began his brief work as the first African priest in Malawi. He was ordained in Likoma Cathedral on 18 April 1909 and posted to Sani. There was an old man who still remembered the fire of his sermons and the sadness they felt at his early death. He had volunteered to go with a small group to Northern Rhodesia. They reached Msoro on 8 January 1911; in May 1912, twenty-four Wakunda people were baptised, "The first fruits of my work," Leonard said. On 27 February 1913, he died. It was thought that he had been poisoned by the chief, afraid that these Christians might steal his authority. What I knew for certain is that fifty-one years later I met this old man whose faith was still sustained by his vivid memories of Leonard Kamungu.

I reached home for a relatively quiet ten days. For five months we had been without a diocesan secretary or treasurer, so there was no shortage of letters to be answered and account books to be made good. But reinforcements were on the way and one week later we received Laurence Lees to be the new head of Malosa Secondary School, bringing skills learned in Pakistan. Jeff Schiffmayer, whom I had met as a student at Nashotah House seminary in Illinois in temperatures of thirty-four degrees below zero, and David Hammond from Texas, to be both secretary and treasurer.

A week later a youth gang – for no obvious reason – burned down the girls' dormitory and two houses at St Michael's Teacher Training College at Malindi, presumably because Anglicans were perceived as being too friendly to Henry Chipembere, son of the Archdeacon, who was hiding in the hills behind Malindi.

Senior leadership

Habil Chipembere had been the only African amongst the four archdeacons. Now he was gone, never to return. At village level pastoral care depended largely on teachers, trained not only to teach but also to take charge of one or more village congregations. They preached on Sunday, took classes for the young, prayed with the sick and buried the dead. The priest, who had no transport, might appear every two months, as he had ten to twenty "out-stations" to look after.

With independence, the system collapsed like a pack of cards. Teachers became employees of the government and looking after a church was not part of their contract. There was an urgent need for archdeacons who could train clergy, new and old, to operate in a changed environment. We prayed for a solution, but none was in sight.

Then two unexpected letters arrived – answers to our prayers. One came from a priest I had known in the 1940s in Pretoria, Dunstan Choo. Born on Chizumulu Island, seven miles west of Likoma and a quarter of its size, he had worked on the Northern Transvaal mines as a layman and was ordained in Pretoria in 1946, when we first met, and now was an archdeacon.

Dunstan's letter said he wanted to give the last year of his priesthood to God in the land of his birth. I wrote back to say we should be delighted to have him as the first mainland priest of the Northern Region but pointed out the snags: a salary one-fifth of what he earned in Pretoria; a push-bike instead of a car in a mountainous region the size of Wales; no more than a token pension and no assistant priest for at least two years.

Archdeacon Dunstan Choo

He wrote back simply, "I have prayed about this and am coming." He began work in February 1963 at Chilambwe, near Nkhata Bay where there was a small congregation. He also had the care of Mzuzu, with a more embryonic group, and a few house-churches that appeared and disappeared as civil servants were moved around.

Dunstan did a magnificent job as the first Anglican priest ever to live on the mainland of the Northern Province. He also opened a clinic in his kitchen, later staffed by his daughter Joyce Nyirenda, a trained nurse. Forty-two years later, Chilambwe Health Centre still serves the fishing people south of Nkhata Bay.

Six months later I was able to report:

> Fr Choo's churchwarden at Nkhata Bay is paying his bus-fares when he travels. He is also paying for work to be done on the church, and finding from his own income, £1 a month for catechists wherever his priest may require them.

I was delighted when the Diocesan Standing Committee approved my suggestions that Dunstan should be the new Archdeacon of Likoma, when Gerald Hadow moved to South West Tanganyika in October 1964.

The second letter was from Sheldon Jalasi, whose story was parallel to that of Dunstan. He came from Likoma Island, trained as a teacher and then went to work in Northern Rhodesia, where he was ordained and worked on the Copperbelt and in Lusaka. There he was made a canon and given an MBE. He too wanted to serve his final years in the land of his birth. He became Archdeacon of Nkhotakota, which had become vacant when Guy Carleton left for the Caribbean.

Archdeacon Sheldon Jalasi

The job was challenging. Fr Oswald Chisa, the priest-in-charge, was a sick man and retired shortly afterwards. On a recent visit I had been met on arrival by the new MP, who called me into an office and said, "I just wanted to tell you that if you do or say anything that might affect my political standing in Nkhotakota, you mustn't be surprised if you find your student midwives' hostel is in flames."

This didn't seem to worry Sheldon and in July 1964 I was able to induct him as Archdeacon. Cyprian Liwewe, who had just succeeded Oswald Chisa as priest-in-charge wrote:

> The Church of All Saints was filled to capacity, with some outside. People were gathered beneath the great fig-tree under which Dr David Livingstone sat a century ago. Under this same old tree the new Archdeacon blessed his people.

In 1965 the Diocesan Standing Committee created a new Archdeaconry of Ntchisi, covering all the Central Region, except for the lake shore strip. The gospel was first preached here in 1907 by Petro Kilekwa and nurtured by him as teacher, deacon and priest for the next fifteen years. It was the fastest growing area in Malawi. I had confirmed three-hundred at Madanjala on my first visit. Jane drew the plans for the first house we had ever had that was designed for a married archdeacon. When she and I sat in the house in 2005 it had no cracks or termites to show for its forty years.

Sheldon often travelled with Bishop Josiah and together they took far-reaching decisions. Dancing Nyau was a traditional custom among the Achewa of the Ntchisi area. Most missionaries frowned on it as a symptom of heathenism. Josiah writes of a visit to Malomo, where the priest was Dunstan Ainani, who in 1981 followed me as Bishop in Southern Malawi:

> Fr Ainani tells me these people are regarded as heathens because they were Nyau dancers. He told them there was nothing wrong in Nyau. After a long and fruitful discussion, they asked if they could become Christians. Malomo people are very happy and ready to make bricks for their priest's house.

With no Anglican teacher training college in the Central Region, ecumenical relations were vital. I was delighted to receive a letter from an Anglican student at the Catholic St John Bosco college at Champira saying:

> For the many years since this College started, no Anglican priest or layman has ever visited us. On 13 June both Archdeacon Jalasi and Fr James Lunda came. Both the Chaplain and the Principal paid tribute to the priests who have come this month, including Fr Lloyd Chikoko, who came seventy miles on foot from his parish of Dwambazi.

After five years in Ntchisi, Sheldon returned to Chipata, in Zambia, just across the border. Bishop Josiah wrote of him, "He did very excellent work in Ntchisi. All Secondary Schools and Young Pioneers of Ntchisi and Dowa Districts miss his pastoral care and cheerfulness." The churchwarden at Chipata was more concise, "He bounces round like a rubber ball."

Ordaining Priests 1964, Malindi
Left to Right: Yonathan Chambombe, Michael Kamaliza, Robert Chikoma,
Josiah Mteketeka preached

Searching for a suffragan bishop

On 6 December 1964 the Diocesan Elective Committee unanimously nominated Josiah as suffragan bishop. Clearly intending that he should become bishop of a new diocese as soon as funds could be found for buildings and staff. I wrote to Josiah at once. He took my letter to Bishop John Poole-Hughes who then told him for the first time that the clergy of SW Tanganyika had told him they too wanted Josiah as their suffragan bishop. "Why didn't you tell me?" he asked. "I was asking the government. As you are not a citizen of Tanzania I was afraid you might not be acceptable." Josiah agreed to go into retreat for three days of prayer. He then made up his mind – it would be Malawi. Bishop John was genuinely sorry and gave him the cross and ring he had bought for him. Joseph Mlele became suffragan of SW Tanganyika three months after Josiah's consecration.

On 27 May 1965, Ascension Day, Josiah Mtekateka[1] was consecrated

---

[1] Bishop Josiah's early years were recorded in a booklet written and published by Dr Denis M'Passou in 1979 entitled *Josiah Mtekateka – from Priest's Dog-boy to Bishop*. This is included in the chapter on his life at https://donaldardensreflections.org/ (As the cost of using the internet in Malawi is so high, a book containing both Josiah's early life and Donald's appreciation is being published in Malawi.)

bishop in Likoma Cathedral before a congregation of 5,000 inside and outside the building. Those present included two Catholic bishops from the regions where Josiah would be working, Jobidon of Mzuzu and Fady of Lilongwe, both French; the heads of three Presbyterian synods; Sir Glyn Jones, the Governor General, bishops from the Province headed by Archbishop Oliver Green-Wilkinson. Bishop Frank Thorne had come from Tanzania to take Josiah's retreat. The address at the consecration was given by Cecil Alderson, Bishop of Mashonaland in Southern Rhodesia. He spoke in Chinyanja, though he had probably hardly heard a word of the language in the thirty years that had gone by since he was briefly a missionary on Likoma Island in the early 1930s.

Consecration of Josiah Mtekateka
Archbishop Oliver Green-Wilkinson, Bishop Josiah Mtekateka,
Bishop Donald Arden

Josiah stayed three months with us, based at Malosa. After which we spent five weeks travelling together 900 miles in the Central and Northern Regions. Between us we confirmed 1,104 teenagers and adults. The people were delighted for the first time to have a bishop born and bred among them. At some of the new congregations the services had to be held out of doors as they could not fit into the buildings. At others there were eager faces of boys peering in at the windows. We were even able to show George Carlisle from Texas a parish bigger than any in his home state; we spent ten days in it and still did not visit all its congregations. The needs were overwhelming; half the children were sitting under mango trees instead of being in classrooms.

A health centre was 100 miles from the nearest doctor. Most of the clergy had no room in which people could speak to them in private. Despite this the church was vibrant and growing. In four parishes we confirmed between them more than there had been in Nyasaland ten years earlier. In the most lively parishes, three quarters of those confirmed were adults. I had never seen this before in my 21 years in Africa. So many goats were given to Josiah that we had to set up sub-stations for them, goat-pens where they could find bed and breakfast till he could come and collect them.

Josiah sharing his Christian faith

On 21st September, St Matthews Day I celebrated the Eucharist in the little church of Nkhunga, north of Nkhotakota, in which we had been sleeping the night before, to celebrate the 25th anniversary of my ordination as a priest in 1940. A minister of the Synod of Livingstonia and the paramount chief had come to visit us the evening before so we invited them to receive communion with us. I felt it made a new start for the next 25 years of my ministry in an increasingly no-Christian world which would have to be more ecumenical. We finally got back to Nkhotakota on Friday but had to leave two hours later for four days in Chia Parish which is always invigorating. We began with a brand new congregation in a forest then another congregation only three years old inland from Chia Lagoon, 45 confirmed, nearly all adults. Half the congregation was outside peering through the window slits.

Chongoni

Then on to Chongoni, the only permanent church built since I came to Malawi and almost the only one in the diocese, apart from the "European" ones in the townships and Soche. I celebrated facing the people, as it has a

Donald, Alice and Josiah

Leslie (Josiah's son), Alice and Josiah, 2005

Josiah Mtekateka's grave beside St Paul's Cathedral, Blantyre

proper free standing alter, dedicated to St Christopher. They had brought in benches from the school but put them all on the men's side of the church. I said, "Perhaps I have come to the wrong building. Is this the new mosque?" They took the hint and shared the benches out 50:50.

We slept by the lagoon and the first sound when we woke up was of bombs being dropped on a lake shore village in Mozambique, 32 miles across the lake. It reminded me of the London blitz. In the afternoon we went on to Salima. About 250 people, Roman Catholics, CCAP, Muslims and Anglicans, had come for a confirmation in a tiny church that could not have held 60, so we headed out of doors in a dust-storm that had been blowing for two days and had already drowned one fisherman.

Josiah was 62 when he became Bishop and I did not expect him to be able to cope with this demanding job for more than a few years. In an area twice the size of Wales there were no tarred roads, other than a couple of streets in Lilongwe and a mile or so in Mzuzu, built to take Elizabeth, the Queen Mother from the airstrip to her house for the night. From Nkhotakota, where Josiah was to be based, if you headed south, you would inevitably meet a washed-away bridge; if you went north, you came to the Bua River with only a canoe for crossing. It you went west, you met a mudslide in the rainy season. And east was the lake where there was only *Ilala* going north one week and south the next. The diocesan headquarters was just a block of three small rooms, now the primary school office. With no complaints and huge courage, Josiah kept up a vibrant ministry until Peter Nyanja succeeded him thirteen years later.

While Bishop Josiah and I were away at Lambeth for four months in 1968, the Diocese, for the first time, was cared for by a Malawian Vicar General, Mathias Msekawanthu. And Malosa Secondary School, our next-door neighbour, now had a Malawian head, Frank Mkomawanthu, one of our candidates for the voluntary ministry. But there was still far to go before Bishop Hine's 75-year old dream of a wholly African-led diocese was to come true.

Josiah wrote:

> I was one of many to attend the Lambeth Conference for the first time. It was exhausting but very interesting especially for the opportunity of meeting and getting to know my brother bishops. Before the Conference I was one of five who made a pilgrimage to Holy Island and Lindisfarne. We had to walk barefooted for two and a half miles when we arrived.
>
> At the Queen's Garden Party there were some who stood all the time but had no luck in speaking to the Queen. I was one of those fortunate enough to reach the Queen and shake hands with her and later with Princess Margaret who was with Donald Coggan, the Archbishop of York.
>
> After the Lambeth Conference Donald and I spent two weeks in Birmingham staying with Bishop George Sinker, the Provost of the cathedral. We visited many places, trying to thank them for all they have done and describing the work of the church in Malawi. In Birmingham for the first time I took part in consecrating another bishop, Paul Burrough, their chaplain for overseas people whom the diocese of Mashonaland had elected as their new bishop. Three days after arriving I conducted a confirmation in one of the Birmingham churches.

There is more about the Lambeth Conference in the section Inspiration from the wider Christian Community.

Learning Chichewa

I began a course to learn Chichewa at the Roman Catholic White Fathers' language school in Lilongwe. Speaking Chichewa was one of the conditions set when I was elected in 1961. The real reason is to avoid the patronising eye of Basil, now five and a half, when I have to ask him to translate for me. It's a little like being back at my theological college at Mirfield. But there are considerable differences.

It is co-educational – eleven fathers or brothers and nine sisters. Eight nationalities are represented. A fellow student, who has just looked in to repair a lock as I write, tells me he began life in Poland, continued at seven in a concentration camp in Siberia, did his schooling in Tanzania and trained as an electrician in England.

We are definitely post-Vatican II. At Sunday lunch this morning the little Breton father, who is bursar, appeared in a clerical collar. This caused an outburst of applause and cries of, "Have a good leave, father!" Some of our more conservative Anglican clergy would have been surprised to see the co-celebrant accompanying the Kyrie at Mass on an African drum, or the nun at the south end of the altar playing spirituals on a guitar.

The 1968 Provincial synod held at Marendellas (now Marondera) was lively and encouraging, with a genuine African feel about it. A tense moment in a debate about whether the Province could continue in view of the political tensions between Ian Smith's Rhodesia and Kenneth Kaunda's Zambia, was relieved when one of the African laymen said, "I came here fearing apartheid but I find myself sleeping in the same room as the white Dean of Bulawayo."

In a letter I wrote to my brother Felix relating to Africanisation:

> I feel like a stranded whale, left on the beach by the outgoing Colonial tide. In independent Africa I shall soon be the only white Bishop other than in Northern Uganda.

Archdeaconry Councils

Early in 1966 the Diocesan Standing Committee (DSC) gave flesh to a proposal from the Pastoral Committee that we should set up Archdeaconry Councils. The idea appealed to me as the cost and travelling time in the 1960s of bringing clergy and lay people 400 miles from the north to attend synods meant these could be held only at two-year intervals. This was far too rarely to support lonely people doing a lonely job. The DSC listed for guidance some of the special areas where Archdeaconry Councils could help, such as circulating literature, stewardship, the training and deployment of Lay Leaders, co-operation with other churches and election of a representative to the DSC.

The success of the first two that I attended convinced me that this was the way forward. All the clergy were involved together with a number of lay people. I was astonished at the range of issues raised: the work of Elders, church gardens as a means of self-support, polygamy, Sunday Schools, the ordination of catechists after a one-year course at Chilema, the proposed new People's Prayer Book, outreach to Islam.

More and more I wondered if dioceses should be the size of archdeaconries, instead of the vast units we had inherited. When Frank Thorne became Bishop of Nyasaland in 1936 the diocese included the present dioceses of Ruvuma, SW Tanganyika, Niassa (in Mozambique), Eastern Zambia and the present Malawi, with seven languages used for the liturgy. In the early church, a diocese was just a single city and the villages that surrounded it. It is sad that today's structures often result in the setting up of a diocesan administration that is so financially demanding.

Anglican Council of Malawi

Beginnings

The Anglian Council of Malawi (ACM) was created in 1972 following the division of Malawi into two dioceses, with Josiah Mtekateka bishop of the new diocese of Lake Malawi and I bishop of the new diocese of Southern Malawi.

Unlike the Zambian Anglican Council, ACM had very few teeth to it. It controlled the Pension and Provident Funds, and various other trust funds. If money was given for the building of a particular hospital or school and it was not possible to begin work immediately, the trustees safeguarded the money. The trustees were registered under Malawi's Incorporation Act and became the legal owners of all church land.

Purpose

Its purpose was best summed up in the first object of its constitution:

> To undertake on behalf of the two dioceses, and with the authority of their respective synods, such work as can only be done together, or can best be done together.

Training of ordinands

Anglican Council of Malawi (ACM) looked after the training of ordinands. Seven years could elapse between the time an ordinand was chosen and the time he was ordained. After such a long time-gap no one could say which diocese would be in most need of a priest. All ordinands were therefore trained under the umbrella of ACM who then decided to send them to the dioceses in proportion to their needs.

Publishing

Since it would be expensive and confusing to have different prayerbooks used in different parts of Malawi, it was the job of ACM to look after publishing.

Consultative

Apart from these functions ACM was a consultative body which meant it was a place where representatives from the two dioceses could exchange views and reach agreement. It had no power to compel either diocese to do anything, including no power over the annual budget of each diocese.

Officers

In order not to waste money, each diocese sent only its bishop, an elected priest, an elected layman and its diocesan secretary. A ninth man was to be chosen jointly to avoid a deadlock. The first elected office holders were:
  Chairman – Revd Douglas Yeppe (DSM)
  Secretary – Miss Doreen White (DLM)
  Treasurer – Mr Wesley Mauwa (DSM)
Minutes were sent to all members of both Diocesan Standing Committees.

Josiah elected Diocesan Bishop

On 15 June 1971 the Provincial Standing Committee met in Lilongwe for the first time. Josiah was elected as the Diocesan Bishop of the newborn Diocese of Lake Malawi by 38 to nil. I wrote in *Ecclesia*:

> His new diocese has more work going on than the whole of Malawi had in 1962, largely because of his tireless visiting while a Suffragan (assistant) Bishop.

In the 1960s only 9 of the 73 voters on the Provincial Standing Committee were "people of the land". Now the province could be said to have come of age.

We also discussed a resolution at the Lambeth Conference of 1968 that families where husband and wife belonged to different churches should be free as far as the Anglican partner was concerned, to receive communion in either the wife's church or that of her husband. At Lambeth this had been passed by a grudging 351 votes to 75. At Lilongwe the vote was unanimous.

It was at this meeting I was elected to be the fourth Archbishop of the Province of Central Africa (Botswana, Zambia, Zimbabwe, Malawi). I was installed the next morning in St Peter's, Lilongwe.

The last action of the standing committee and one which was deeply appreciated was to recommend to all the dioceses that they should try to raise at least £166 to avoid cuts in Malawi clergy salaries. They added that they were wholly convinced that Malawi was doing everything in its power to increase its internal income and to reduce its expenditure in order to cope with the extraordinary drop in income from overseas it had been forced to absorb.

I ended my report to the diocese:

> Before the meeting began, we read much in the newspapers about tensions and breakaways in the province. When we got there, we found only the Holy Spirit teaching us with some success how to speak the truth in love.

New Diocese of Lake Malawi 1971

The independent diocese of Lake Malawi was born on 1 October 1971 in a celebration at Nkhotokota attended by all the great and good – Bishop and Mrs Lawrence Brown from Birmingham; the Bishop of Ruvuma from Josiah's former diocese in Tanzania and a team of 15 from Texas led by Bishop Scott Field Bailey who came with a pectoral cross made from material which had been to the moon and back.

Josiah was 62 when he became Bishop and I did not expect him to be able to cope with this demanding job for more than a few years. In the huge area for which he was responsible there were no tarred roads, other than a couple of streets in old Lilongwe and a mile or so in Mzuzu, built to take Elizabeth, the Queen Mother, from the airstrip to her house for the night. From Nkhotokota, where Josiah was based, if you headed south, you would inevitably meet a washed-away bridge; if you went north, you came to the Bua river with only a canoe for crossing. If you went west, you met a mudslide in the rainy season. And east was the lake, where, after *Boatie Paul* was wrecked, there was only *Ilala* going north one week and south the other.

The Bishop's house was an elderly house and the diocesan headquarters a block of three small rooms, now used as the primary school office.

Things improved in 1971 when the Diocese of Lake Malawi was formed and got a little better over the years as funds arrived from Texas. With no complaints and huge courage, Josiah kept up a vibrant ministry until Peter Nyanja succeeded him over thirteen years later.

At the end of 1971, I wrote:

> The new Diocese of Lake Malawi, incorporating the Northern and Central Regions, goes ahead steadily but Bishop Josiah has no chaplain and no graduate priest in his diocese. At the age of sixty-seven he continues to cover great distances on foot and is now preparing to take on the nightmare of running a diocese with more work, as measured by confirmations, adult baptisms, schools and health centres, than I faced in 1961, with a fraction of the skilled staff I inherited.

Malawi traditional religion

I found little in traditional religion that was incompatible with Christianity. I was encouraged by the *African Ecclesiastical Review* (AFER), an East African Catholic periodical to which Adrian Hastings contributed and which often reported the imaginative use of traditional music and dance.

No African language with which I am familiar even has a word for "religion". The existence of a supreme Being is normal, at least in Southern and Central Africa. There are customs, such as polygamy, that all churches reject, though many churches would – correctly in my view – say that a polygamist being baptized as a Christian, would be right to keep a second or third wife, if the only alternative for her would be destitution. The current tension about homosexuality shows how difficult it is, even for Western Christians, to balance traditional attitudes with modern psychology.

The closest parallel is the difference between the Old and New Testament ethics. There we have guidance from Jesus, himself for example. "You have heard it was said by men of old times ... but I say to you ..." The African Church still has the Spirit to guide it. I see Africa's traditional religion as their Old Testament – full of positive ethics, but as Jesus showed, to be used with discretion.

Music

My father tried but with limited success to transfer his love of music to me. The attraction of South Australian sunshine proved too strong and I got no further than my one composition, "The March of the Tin Soldiers." In Pretoria I did my best with the bass part of hymns because South Africa has a strong musical tradition and every adult male is expected to sing tenor or bass. If there was a blackboard in a classroom, a quarter of it would be taken up by the hymn of the week in tonic sol-fa. Unexpectedly, because the Anglican Church in Malawi had, at that time, no strong musical tradition, African music became one of our first footsteps towards becoming an African Church.

Mindolo

The All Africa Conference of Churches in April 1963 highlighted the need for African church music. As a result, Mindolo Ecumenical Centre on the Zambia copper belt announced a month's course in developing African liturgical music. Victor Chunga, who taught in Chididi school, south of Nkhotakota, applied and represented us. In the 1890s the Synod of Livingstonia CCAP had developed African church music to a high degree, by adapting traditional music for use in church and by encouraging African composers. This reflected their Angoni links with Zululand and the foresight of the first Scottish missionaries. These tunes had spread to other CCAP synods and to other churches through funerals.

Victor Chunga wrote delightedly from Mindolo of his first exposure to an ecumenical gathering:

> Central Africa is being born afresh with mutual racial understanding. The Holy Ghost is really working in people's minds to reach the goalpost of religious reunion. Christian friends, regardless of the churches they come from, have come to find out methods of improving African church music.

Victor spoke to our next diocesan synod and told us how he had been asking elderly people to sing their old tunes to him so that he could find suitable words to fit the tune. Christians, he said, should not despise their cultural inheritance.

In 1964, Victor took Maxwell Maputwa, a fellow teacher, with him to another Music Workshop at Mindolo. They told *Ecclesia*:

> We have been working on the tunes originally collected by Canon Hicks at Nkope for the new diocesan hymnbook. These can be arranged and harmonised in tonic-sol-fa.

Missa Malawi

Our setting for the mass, using African tunes, has so impressed the music director and other members of the course, that parts of it were performed at Luanshya Church. This became known as "Missa Malawi".

A lay member of Chombo church responded:

> How impressive it was to hear "Missa Malawi" sung in our church! Young children sang as if they were singing their own traditional songs. We should all co-operate with Mr Chunga and invite him to our parishes.

Victor Chunga wrote in *Ecclesia*:

> As I looked at the leaves of a mango tree, I noticed each one was different. The same is true of human beings. New experiences happen in every generation: the Church grows in changing. Music is one of the chief ways of expressing our feelings. Researching African music is hard and needs a lot of people to help with suggestions and criticisms.

George Merikebu, joined the debate:

> Psalm 150 says, "Praise him with the trumpet: praise him upon the harp." This answers my long wrong belief that to play an instrument in church is against God. So why not drums?"

Chilema

Richard Baxter of the Iona Community and a minister of Blantyre Synod CCAP, a lover of Malawi music, became the first warden of Chilema ecumenical lay training centre. In 1966 he announced an international music workshop.

Kungoni Centre of Culture

Twenty miles from us a young Canadian White Father called Claude Boucher, was doing creative things in liturgy. John Leake, the priest who was looking after the imaginative Anglican programme at the Chilema Ecumenical Lay Training Centre, invited me to go with him to Claude's parish centre north of Balaka for the pre-Christmas mass for his outstations. It was a revelation – Malawian music, liturgical dance, drums – the lot. I praised it in *Ecclesia* and sent Claude a copy.

He asked me in return to write to his African bishop, who was angry with him and had threatened to expel him. His bishop relented, but a few months later changed his mind and sent him back to Canada. I am glad to say that Claude was invited back a few years later by another diocese and founded the Kungoni Centre of Culture and Art at Mua, where he still works. Mua is famous within Malawi and internationally for its imaginative carvings, often by young men with little formal education.

Claude Boucher

By 1970 even tiny congregations would have their own youth choir. The resistance to drums lingered in larger and older congregations. We were delighted to hear the magnificent drumming in Likoma Cathedral itself during its centenary in 2005.

Liturgy

A brief visit to Liuli Cathedral in South-West Tanzania in 1962 opened my eyes. This was the people of God celebrating the eucharist together, not a priest "saying Mass". The altar had been moved from the remote end of the chancel to be just in front of the people and the celebrant faced them. Worship seemed to have come alive. In a large building packed with people I could hear every word from my place at the back. The Spirit of the Second Vatican Council seemed to have reached the Anglican Church in this remote corner of Africa, even though the Council had not yet met.

Liturgically, in Nyasaland, we were still in the doldrums. The printing press on Likoma Island, that had done wonderful work for over eighty years, was closing down and could never be reopened, partly because we could not afford it, partly because a press on a remote island could never expect the flow of commercial orders needed to keep skilled staff busy. Its method of typesetting – letters picked out of hundreds of little boxes with a pair of tweezers – belonged to the age of Caxton. It had a glorious past and had produced tens of thousands of prayer-books, hymnbooks, school readers, catechisms, and guides to marriage in two editions. The green edition was for the Mothers' Union in general, the red edition was given to brides only, a few days before their wedding. All in four or five different languages. But it had no future.

Provincial comments

The Province expected us to abandon the rather fine UMCA liturgy for the Eucharist and change to the old and uninspired South African form. This meant our vibrant and relevant liturgy would have to go. Instead of prayer for the rich to share with the poor; and for Jesus, who was a refugee in Egypt to be with our migrant workers in the Rand gold-mines; and for the Jesus who questioned the teachers in the Temple to give wisdom to our teachers – we were expected to go back to the long and boring Prayer for the Church Militant here on earth. It seemed to me a case of "Backward, Christian soldiers..."

There were also problems of language. Likoma Island spoke the Nyanja of Mozambique. This was perhaps as different from the standard Nyanja of Nyasaland as Robbie Burns's Scots is from standard English. This in itself was no problem to Africans who are born linguists. Children of six or seven at Broederstroom, which I used to visit once a month in the 1940s, spoke their own language, Ndebele, which they brought with them when they arrived from Matabeleland in the 1650s; Tswana, which everyone around them spoke; English and Afrikaans, the two official languages; and Zulu, in which I read the services. However, they had trouble in understanding the Xhosa-speaking headmaster I appointed. Xhosa-speakers, certainly in the 1940s, had a strong linguistic loyalty and tended to take it for granted that others would understand their language.

Chilikoma

The problem was that "Chilikoma" – as other Malawians called it, the language of Likoma Island – had imported many Swahili theological words. Swahili is not a true Bantu language. It grew up over a thousand or more years as a means of communication with Africans of many different tongues along the 1,500 miles of Indian Ocean coastline between Mozambique and Somaliland. Its grammatical framework is Bantu, but 25 percent of its vocabulary is Arabic. Malawi had few contacts with Arabs, apart from slave-traders, and has never used Swahili. UMCA missionaries inherited a tradition based on Zanzibar Island and its Swahili speakers. Thus a number of strange Arabic words had become UMCA-speak for key theological words – *Mtakatifu* for "Holy Spirit", *mazabau* for "altar" and many more.

This gave UMCA a foreign flavour and was a serious barrier to evangelism. When I first went to Salima, on the western lake shore, to take a confirmation, I had problems in finding the church. Nobody had ever heard of an Anglican church. I tried "UMCA", "Church of England" pretended to put on a mitre ... no response. Half a dozen went into committee and then came out beaming – "Is it the Church of Likoma?" Yes, they all knew that, a quarter of a mile out of town. Even in Soche, the first new urban township in Blantyre, 400 miles from Likoma, the congregation was mostly made up of Likomans who could understand the language.

One spark of hope was at Nkhotakota where Fr Oswald Chisa and Archdeacon Guy Carleton had battled with the "Chilikoma" problem. Working together they had published a hymnbook in standard Nyanja/Chewa. Oswald Chisa had been detained before my arrival for being over zealous in the cause of independence but subsequently released as he was far from fit.

People's Prayer Book

On a hot afternoon at Mponda's in January 1966, the People's Prayer Book and hymnbook was conceived. I noted in *Ecclesia* that the previous prayerbook had sold 3,000 copies in ten years, and that in those ten years, 20,000 people had been confirmed. Few of them would ever see in print the promises they had made at their confirmation or their wedding.

The problems were many and acute. Did we submit to the Province and accept the Provincial Prayerbook? Could we ask our people to buy a book that would cost a month's earnings or a quarter of their harvest? How could we escape from the English and German hymn tunes droned out at a snail's pace in most churches? How could we bring to life the many saints whose lives we celebrated but about whom we knew very little? Which of the frequently changing spelling systems for Chichewa should we use.

Eventually decisions were made. We could select ruthlessly and put into the hands of the people the minimum number for worship. The hymns would have printed tunes, even though few except those who had worked in South Africa knew tonic sol-fa. Then perhaps Anglicans might learn to sing as well as Presbyterians. We would also print some of the lively Malawian tunes that set the whole church echoing. We would borrow from Livingstonia some of their magnificent Tumbuka tunes. We would choose only the best bits from thirty-one psalms so that laypeople who did not have time for the daily prayers could use one on each day of the month. Each psalm would have its key thought printed as an antiphon to be said or sung after each verse. Even those who had not been to school or whose eyesight had failed, could join in.

Gradually the book grew. A manuscript was presented to synod. They didn't like it and sent the Liturgical Committee on a round of archdeaconry conferences. Agreement was reached and in 1968 we were ready to print when all kinds of setbacks appeared. Devaluation of the Kwacha upset the estimates. Nkhoma Press had to buy new type to set the sol-fa on their linotype machines. Twice the approved spelling of Chichewa was changed. The printer went on long leave.

Mapemphero

At last, in August 1971, *Ecclesia* was able to announce:

> MAPEMPHERO NDI YIMBO ZA EKELZIA is now published! 12,000 copies have been printed. As soon as they are sold, the revolving fund can produce an edition in ChiYao.

In addition to the services found in prayerbooks throughout the world and thirty-one psalms, Maphemphero also included features which in 1971 were still unusual, such as Sunday readings on a two-year cycle, obviating the need for circulating to all lay leaders the readings for the year, thirty-one canticles, again with a chorus and a congregational Service of Penitence, services for baptism and confirmation, marriage, burial and compline.

Also included were a brief biographies of each of the forty-four saints commemorated, including many African saints and martyrs – to name only the local ones: David Livingstone and Bishop Charles Mackenzie, who led the way; Fr Arthur Fraser Sim who baptised the first Christian in Nkhotakota on the lake shore, opened the first school and died there in 1886 all within a year; Leonard Kamungu, the Malawian priest who died, perhaps as a martyr, a few months after being the first to bring the gospel to Zambia; Bernard Mizeki, born in Mozambique, attended a Christian school in Cape Town, became a catechist in Mashonaland (Zimbabwe), martyred for his faith; and William Percival Johnson, the founder of all the seven dioceses that border Lake Malawi.

Islam

Yao-speakers in Malawi are approximately ten percent of the population and most of them are Muslims. The two main Muslim centres are Nkhotakota, a port on the western lake shore in the Central Region with a population of 30,000 and the southern lake shore where Chief Mponda was the senior Yao Chief in Malawi. His court was within 200 yards of the mission station. Many of the children at our school would go on to the

Quran school where they would read in Arabic with a Muslim teacher. The only priest in Nyasaland who could meet these requirements (apart from a handful of recently ordained) was Petro Kilekwa. But he had retired 12 years before I came on the scene (see Appendix).

I wrote to my contacts in Nairobi and was delighted to hear of a short course being run in Mombasa in 1966 by the Christian Council of Kenya, who offered us two places. I consulted with Bishop Josiah on whom to send, and he at once said, "Me and Joseph Chikokota", naming a young priest from Malindi, where the congregation was really a group of Christians who had migrated from Likoma Island (such as the Chipemberes) in a totally Islamic area.

The Mombasa course was a great success and both came back full of new things they had learned. Josiah wrote in *Ecclesia*:

> None of us had visited a mosque before. The people praying made different actions during their prayers, kneeling and prostrating their faces and noses onto the mat, repeating likewise three times. Then they pointed one finger indicating they believe in one God only. Then they looked right and left, showing they wished God's blessings to their fellow Muslims. Then all stood and prayed together with hands raised. When they had finished they sat around in classes learning their Laws. That day the Sheikh was teaching his students about the dividing of dead people's property. All the teaching came from the Quran.
>
> It was a very interesting visit for us. We saw many boys who came to worship. This to me is a challenge. Our Christian boys do not take part in worship during the week, only on Sundays.

A few months later, John Liomba, who was teaching at Msusa, in Joseph Chikokota's parish, a wholly Muslim area in the hills behind Malindi, reported:

> Thirty-six catechumens, male and female, big and small, were baptised by the Revd Joseph Chikokota. It was interesting to observe the age contrasts. The youngest boy was Wilfred, aged 8, the oldest lady, Beatrice, in her late 70s. The priest and his servers walked side by side with the Godparents to and from the New Jordan brook, half a mile from the church. If all adult baptisms were done this way, none would have a wrong picture of the tremendous work of St John the Baptist.

It was impossible to resist Joseph when he came to ask if he could accept the offer of a place on a nine-month course on Islam in Nigeria. We all learned from his Question and Answer articles in *Ecclesia*.

A few years later I received a letter from Douglas Yeppe, one of our younger priests, saying:

> In December 1972 I was invited by a Muslim teacher to attend their mosque on Friday. I accepted their invitation, washed my hands and feet and dressed myself like a Muslim. I was then asked to preach a short sermon, which I did. Again on 26 May, Dennis Kalino, Catechist Madota and myself were invited to the Islamic festival of Siyalah. I was also asked to preach. I was amazed to see the Sheikh emphasising his sermons by quoting Christ's teachings.

Political turmoil around Independence

I came back to Malawi at the beginning of August from leading a retreat for clergy in Southern Rhodesia to find the government was torn in half by disagreements between Banda and his cabinet. The three most powerful ministers were Henry Chipembere, then away in Canada and the only Anglican, Orton Chirwa, who had sponsored my appointment, and Kanyama Chiume.

There were three main reasons why the ministers were rebelling.

1. The rebel ministers wanted strong links with mainland China, whilst Banda insisted on developing relations with Taiwan.

2. In addition they objected to Banda's friendly relations with Apartheid South Africa and Portuguese East Africa (Mozambique).

3. They were also not happy with the slow pace of Africanisation of the civil service and other issues.

In Henry's absence they presented Banda with a list of issues on which they disagreed with him. They were also frustrated with Banda's reliance on Cecilia Kadzamira and the Tembo family, and riled by his repeated reference to them in public speeches as "my children".

President Banda

Treatment of dissident ministers

After a week of discussions, often positive, Banda turned them out of his office saying, so that everyone could hear, "You will not make a Nyerere out of me. You can shoot me. I will not be Nyererized" – the reference being of course to the gentle and unassuming Julius Nyerere of Tanzania.

Orton was beaten up several times by Banda's supporters after he met with Banda. The Governor General Sir Glyn Jones subsequently wrote to

Orton to say that Banda had agreed only to an acting appointment as a judge, provided he first made a public declaration of loyalty to him and his political disassociation from the other ministers. But Orton had had enough. He left Malawi for Zambia, hidden in the engine-room of a boat from Fort Johnston to Nkhata Bay, and then on to Tanzania. He was the last of the ministers to leave Malawi, all the others, except Chipembere, were already in Tanzania or Zambia.

Henry Chipembere had been the closest to Banda, as he was the only minister to have shared fourteen months in prison with him at Gwelo, in Southern Rhodesia. Much of the detailed planning for the independent Malawi was done between them. He was also the last to be set free in Nyasaland. Sir Robert Armitage, the previous Governor, had prosecuted him for incitement to violence, for which he was sentenced to three years in Zomba prison. I visited him there – something which Banda never did – and we became friends.

Henry came back from Canada on the 8th September and addressed public meetings in Fort Johnston (Mangochi), Blantyre and elsewhere supporting the rebel ministers. Banda banned all public meetings without police permission and issued orders to the police, "If necessary people must be shot and I mean that the Police must shoot to kill." On the same day a meeting in Soche addressed by Henry was broken up by gangs of pro-Banda Malawi Youth.

Two days later there was a general strike of all African civil servants in Zomba. On 30th September 1964 Henry was issued with an order confining him to a four-mile radius of his house in Malindi. Henry saw this as an opportunity to form his own "army" of over four hundred men in the uninhabited forest area which they called "Zambia", between the lake shore and the Mozambique border. The army was in sections commanded by "generals", one of whom was George Ndomondo, whom I ordained a priest in 1975 and in 2010 was still doing Yao translation work. His eventful life is described in *The Life of George Ndomondo* (George died in 2015).[1]

---

[1] Copies of this book can be requested from the Secretary of Malawi Association for Christian Support, founded 1993, http://malawimacs.org/

Armed rebellion

The staff at our lake shore centres were well aware of what was going on and kept me informed. At about 9.00 p.m. on 12th February 1965, Henry and some two hundred men headed for Fort Johnston. Here they attacked the police station and made away with the guns belonging to the police. While this was going on, the District Commissioner, who had been spending the evening with one of our missionary nurses, was greeted by a hail of bullets as he returned to his house. Without stopping to gather details, he drove the forty miles to the Malawi Railways dockyard at Monkey Bay to send a wireless message – telephone lines having been cut – to the army and police headquarters, to tell them of the armed attack.

Henry and his now better armed men, headed sixty miles south for Zomba, the capital. This involved crossing the Shire River at Liwonde on the ferry powered by a diesel engine. The ferry was on their side of the 75m wide and fast flowing river but, unhappily for them, the engine had broken down. Despite energetic exhortations to the mechanic, the engine remained silent. When, after some hours, the army began to arrive on the other side of the river, Henry had no option but to retreat with his men to the wild no-man's land north of Malindi. Here he remained with an "army" of three to four hundred men, where the Malawi Army could neither find them nor defeat them.

In March 1965 Henry wrote to Banda through the Governor General, Sir Glyn Jones:

> On grounds of principle I will not leave the country. That would be an act of desertion or betrayal of our supporters in gaol... If I did not have support I would be in my grave now. But the villagers themselves hide me, feed me and stand guard around the village to warn me.

He asked Glyn Jones to mediate and seek an amnesty for his men who were "languishing in gaol, exile and the forest". Banda's response was to make the death sentence mandatory, and to abolish the constitutional right of appeal to the British Privy Council. The results were described by Henry in another letter back to Glyn Jones:

> The security forces are perpetrating unheard of brutalities... Rape, burning of houses, shooting, beating of men, women and children, looting of homes, stores and gardens, indiscriminate arrests etc. are the order of the day.

Colin Baker, to whose *Revolt of the Ministers* I am indebted for much detail previously unknown, adds:

> It could have been worse. When the Commander of the Malawi Army was instructed to carry out the campaign, he told his officers to take a drum corps with them and make plenty of noise to warn the inhabitants of their imminent arrival and give them a chance to escape.

Diabetes did what Banda was unable to do. In the bush, Henry received medication for his diabetes from various friends but was unable to cope with this long-standing problem. Chiume says he was almost dying of diabetes. With Banda's full consent he was smuggled to America via London. I was able to play a part in making this possible. I met him some years later in Los Angeles, where he died in 1975.

Chipemberes sail to Likoma for safety

I had hardly been at home and had seen little of Basil since he was born in April 1964. We had to cancel our holiday, so in October Jane and I and six-month old Basil were spending a few nights on nearby Zomba Mountain. We took with us the few architects' plans that we could lay hands on. There was not an architect left in the country, apart from those in the Public Works Department, and for the first time there was a little money for the clergy houses, health centres and schools that were so desperately needed. This space would enable us to sketch out plans for buildings that could be afforded.

In the small hours of Saturday morning there was a telephone call from Sir Glyn Jones, the Governor General. President Banda and he were both worried about the safety of Catherine, Henry Chipembere's wife, her children and of his father Habil, the Archdeacon of South Nyasa. Would I go at once to Mponda's, where Habil was now living and persuade him to go to Likoma Island, and then to Malindi to persuade Catherine to go with him. A large Fisheries boat was on standby at Mponda's and John Bolt the District Commissioner would accompany them to Likoma.

Habil Chipembere

We drove down the mountain, left baby Basil with the Croftons and headed for Mponda's, seventy-five miles away. Habil and his wife listened to the message and, with obvious sadness, agreed. But how could their daughter-in-law Catherine be persuaded? She was in hiding near Malindi, ten miles north-east on the other side of the Lake. We agreed that I would stay with Habil and sail on the government Fisheries boat with them to Malindi to pick up Catherine and the children. Jane would go by car and take on the harder task of persuading her to go, knowing that she might never see her husband Henry again. He was officially a bandit, having broken the rules of his confinement to Malindi, and the army was out searching for him.

On arrival at Malindi mission, Jane was told to drive four miles north to the village where Henry and Catherine had their house. There she was asked to leave the car and walk some distance to the house and wait. People were polite but suspicious. Eventually Catherine, looking rather dishevelled, emerged from the bush and sat and listened to Jane's message and, after many reassurances, agreed to go to Likoma. She went off into the bush again to gather her three young children and a few belongings. After some time, she returned and walked with Jane to the car. By this time a threatening crowd of several hundred people had gathered. The spokesman for the group, John Liomba, said they did not trust what was happening but Catherine was able to persuade them that she wanted to go. Jane then drove Catherine and the children to the mission on the lake shore at Malindi. Several years later John was ordained as a voluntary priest.

Henry and Catherine Chipembere in happier times

When the Fisheries boat reached Malindi, I was served with an ultimatum. Either Archdeacon Habil came ashore or I would never see Jane again.

Habil parried this threat – he was highly respected, both as a much-loved Archdeacon and as an active representative of the Malawi Congress Party.

It was dark by the time Catherine and Jane arrived at Malindi, from where it was just possible to see the silhouette of the Fisheries boat with only her guiding light showing. It took several trips in a small dinghy to ferry Catherine, her children, belongings and Jane out to the boat. Jane asked Catherine if there was anything she wanted. She thought for a moment and then said, "Shoes for the children." Jane found some paper and, as the boat rose and fell in the swell, drew outlines of the children's feet so as to know the sizes.

After giving God's blessing to Habil, his wife, Catherine and the children, we boarded the dinghy and watched the lights of the Fisheries boat disappear into the distance. Apart from a brief meeting in Zambia some years later, it was the last I saw of Habil, who I had once thought would be the first African bishop in Malawi. He had been ordained before World War II, in which he was an army chaplain and served in India. At the UMCA centenary in London in 1957 he had been presented to the Queen and made a five minute speech of thanks for those who had brought the gospel to Nyasaland.

It was now 10.00 p.m. and, after a bite of food with Francis Bell, the wonderful mission engineer based at Malindi, we headed back the eighty-five miles to Zomba. A few miles down the road, we were surprised to see a fire ahead and realised that the bridge over the Lusalumwe river was burning. A small group of people watching it said the bridge had been set on fire to prevent us leaving Malindi. They were still uncertain as to whether the Fisheries boat was a trap to capture Catherine and her children.

We returned to Malindi. The never-at-a-loss Francis showed us a small, little-used track running close to the lake shore that would bypass the fire. We started off again. Before reaching Mangochi, we were surprised to see the lights of a vehicle heading towards us. This was the police who had been instructed by their HQ in Zomba to find out what had happened to us. We eventually fell into bed in Zomba at 3.30 a.m.

The Church's role

In April 1965, Habil Chipemebere wrote to me to say that, owing to inflammatory speeches by visitors to Likoma, Catherine and he no longer felt safe. After months of discussion, Banda agreed to transport them with an escort of Young Pioneers to Mbamba Bay in Tanzania, but only on condition that he leave Malawi for ever. Habil was profoundly distressed because his three daughters were all married to Malawians. He ended his letter, "If I cannot return back to this country then I shall bow my head with tears under the Prime Minister's feet and obey his orders." I saw Habil only once more, in Zambia – a dear and much respected friend who had married Jane and me and baptised Basil. He died some years later in Tanzania.

For the next decade, Malindi – the most important and, almost the oldest mainland Anglican centre – was under a heavy political cloud. This resulted in the internment of many leading Anglican laymen and the closure of the seventy year-old St Michael's Teacher Training College.

It was some time before the full impact of the Banda-Chipembere conflict was felt. From now on Banda was the undisputed ruler. The Young Pioneers became a quasi-army, not the spearhead of modern agriculture, trained by Israelis, as they were first presented to the country. Ministers were hired and fired according to whim.

The churches did what they could to restrain the more evil aspects of policies that often appeared progressive to outside observers, who praised Malawi as an island of peace compared with the Congo, Mozambique and South Africa. There was truth in this but the price of living in a police state was high. Many Malawians were incarcerated under appalling conditions of solitary confinement, some for eight years and more. Expatriates were declared to be prohibited immigrants, and "P.I."ed with 24 hours to leave the country, including one of our missionaries.

The heads of churches met informally, sometimes in our house, to exchange information and to bring what pressure we could. Often this was done through Blantyre Synod and its General Secretary Jonathan Sangaya since most of the ministers belonged to the CCAP. Victor Smith, a wise senior missionary of the Churches of Christ, which in England is part of the United Reformed Church, was our secretary and was once asked to convey our feelings to Banda. Once, when Victor Smith accompanied Jonathan to his meeting with Banda, the meeting was interrupted by the Secretary of the Malawi Congress Party bringing a list of people to be detained for Banda to sign. Banda agreed to all the names except one. "We want them all." "No, not that one." "We want them all." "Oh, very well."

After the MCP Secretary had left, Banda turned to them and said, "Some people think it's easy to be a President."

Trying to reinstate the Scouts and Guides

Soon after independence President Banda banned Scouts and Guides. The reason for this banning was the serious mistake made a few years earlier when the then Commissioner, Dorothy Peterkins, withdrew the warrant of a promising Malawian guider, Grace Rubadiri, for taking part in political rallies.

Jane, who had been running a Guide Company and a Sea Ranger Crew for a number of years, succeeded her as Commissioner. She and the Deputy Commissioner, Jean Potter, were granted an interview with President Banda to make the case for lifting the ban. The President appeared sympathetic but, despite the support of the Government Minister, Aleke Banda, who was a keen Scout, they were subsequently told that the ban would remain.

Postscript

Catherine returned to Malawi when Banda's rule came to an end in 1994 and was elected MP for Mangochi East, where her husband Henry had been the first MP. She married Clement Marama, our lay representative to the 1963 Toronto Conference – they retired to live on Likoma Island.

In 1981, Orton, who was teaching law in a Zambian university, and Vera Chirwa unwisely decided to revisit Malawi. At the Chipata border, they were arrested by Malawi police and then held separately in Zomba prison, manacled to iron bars for long periods. Their son, Fumbasi, was detained incommunicado without charge for over two years. Orton and Vera were tried before a Traditional Court on charges of treason in May 1983. They were not permitted to call witnesses for a defence and were both sentenced to death. In response to an international outcry, the sentence was commuted to life imprisonment. Although both were in Zomba prison, they were not allowed to see each other until September 1992, when a delegation of British lawyers was given access to them. Orton, "nearly deaf and almost blind from untreated cataracts, and often in leg irons" died the next month. Vera was not allowed out of prison to attend his funeral.

By this time Vera was "the longest serving African prisoner known to Amnesty International". She was released from gaol three months later. She has spent the rest of her life fighting for women's rights in Malawi. The autobiography of this brave and amazing lady entitled *Vera Chirwa: Fearless Fighter* was published by Amnesty International in 2007.

If it had not been for Orton's speaking up for me, I probably should not have been allowed to enter Malawi – certainly not to function as a bishop after independence.

Companion dioceses

Over the years, relationships were formed with other dioceses, known as companions.

Texas

Bishop Stephen Bayne, the first Chief Executive of the Anglican Communion, initiated MRI (Mutual Responsibility and Interdependence) in 1962 and suggested to John Hine Bishop of Texas that Nyasaland might be a possible partner. In January 1963 we stayed with Bishop John, in Texas, who had taken an uncompromising position on racial equality.

Diocesan Convention

We arrived just as their Convention began. John's stance on racial issues had provoked stormy opposition. I was on the floor with convention members and found myself in the centre of a small group of very angry laymen advancing on John and chanting, "You Communist! You Communist!" After that, I wondered how people would react to the proposal that the dioceses of Texas and Nyasaland enter into a companion relationship. After introducing the motion John invited others and me to speak. Following after some discussion there was a unanimous vote for a companion diocese partnership for the next three years.

First time

I believe this was the first time that any American diocese had formed a companionship outside the "Jurisdiction". Such links were for three years and could be renewed once only. It brought an immediate grant, backed and doubled by ECUSA (Episcopal Church of USA) headquarters in New York, which enabled us to wipe off past debts and to move the Diocesan Office from Mponda's to Malosa.

The three years grew to twelve and, in an unofficial way, the friendship still existed 40 years later. The real credit for the companionship getting off to a good start goes to a priest, George Carlisle, secretary to the link, and to Milton Richardson, the Suffragan Bishop who made Malawi his special cause, and who later became Diocesan Bishop. They both visited Malawi.

Renewing the link

The renewing of the companion diocese link coincided with the creation of the new Diocese of Lake Malawi in 1971 comprising the Central and Northern Regions, and the ECUSA allowed a new link to be formed with them. Somehow, this continued until the early 1980s. The Diocese of Texas underwrote the building of a new diocesan centre in Lilongwe, which had become the capital of Malawi in 1972. They rightly felt that the diocesan bishop should not have his headquarters one hundred and twenty miles from the capital.

Birmingham

Our link with Birmingham, where Leonard Wilson had been Bishop since 1953 was a creative one for both dioceses. Most valuable of all was the wisdom and experience and the new ideas that poured out of Leonard whose deep personal faith was often at odds with authority. In 1953, when the question of a Central Africa Federation was at the forefront of colonial policy, he chaired a meeting at which Dr Hastings Banda and Michael Scott, a doughty if sometimes erratic champion of African rights, had been the main speakers. Geoffrey Fisher, then Archbishop of Canterbury, rapped him over the knuckles for doing so. Leonard's interest in Nyasaland continued from then on.

As a result of Leonard's interest in Nyasaland, John Parslow a priest born in Birmingham arrived at St Paul's church in Blantyre in 1960. John had an instinctive love for everyone and always responded gracefully when I asked him to move to parishes that needed special care and understanding. He died in Malawi in 1995 after thirty-five years of dedicated service there.

Leonard's daughter Susan Cole-King attended her father's meeting with Dr Banda in 1953 and later met him in London when he was practising there as a doctor. These meetings resulted in Susan training as a doctor and arriving in Malawi with her family in 1964 to work in the government health service. Susan and her family often stayed with us at Malosa.

Bishop Wilson visits Malawi

Leonard and his wife Mary visited Malawi in early 1965 to stay with Susan. Leonard was wondering whether to establish a companion diocese partnership between Birmingham and Malawi and asked me to show him around the diocese. Together we visited several of the lake shore centres.

While they were with us informal discussions were held with members of the Diocesan Standing Committee about a possible companion diocese partnership.

Soon afterwards came an invitation to stay with him and Mary. We stayed with them for two weeks of almost non-stop meetings, visiting schools and colleges in the daytime and spending each evening with a parish or deanery meeting.

Partnership agreed

In June 1966 the Birmingham Diocesan Conference unanimously agreed to form a companion diocese partnership with Malawi and set up a committee to develop the partnership.

One immediate result of our partnership was a grant of £5,000 from Birmingham to SPCK, publishers throughout the world, to set up a CLAIM (Christian Literature Association in Malawi), a Christian book distribution network in Malawi known as Mabuku (books). The Catholics had two printing presses in the southern Region alone; CCAP one in the central Region and ourselves had nothing. Maxwell Zingani, our Literature Secretary, had devised a box which displayed whatever we had – mostly New Testaments and Bibles – which I took with me wherever I went. My driver – often a Muslim – was an enthusiastic salesman. But we had little to offer. Now there was a challenge to set up Christian bookshops in the major centres and to find authors who could speak to literate young people. This was followed by another £5,000 to build a church at Biwi – a traditional housing area on the southern edge of Lilongwe, which was to be the new capital of Malawi.

Leonard Brown succeeded Leonard Wilson as bishop and was equally involved in the Malawi link and equally forward looking. *Ecclesia* reprinted part of a letter to his diocese, suggesting topics for house-groups, their answers to be passed on to Synod members: Do you wish to see women as priests and bishops? Should divorcees be entitled to remarry in church? At what age should children be admitted to communion? Is confirmation essential at that stage? Can the Church still afford full-time paid clergy? How should voluntary priests be trained? These were new and relevant questions for both sides of the partnership.

Strengths of partnership

The lasting strength of the ongoing partnership has been developing personal relationships with Malawians visiting Birmingham, several studying at the ecumenical Selly Oak Colleges and people from Birmingham visiting and coming to work in Malawi, including John Workman in 1980 as treasurer of the Anglican Council in Malawi. Forty-two years later it is stronger than ever. [*Editor*: celebrations were held in 2016 for the 50th anniversary.]

Province of Central Africa CAPA

Council of Anglican Provinces of Africa (CAPA)

The Province of Central Africa was formed in 1955 and linked the dioceses of Mashonaland and Matabeleland in Southern Rhodesia (Zimbabwe), Northern Rhodesia (Zambia) and Nyasaland (Malawi). To Malawians this sounded like "the stupid Federation", to use Dr Banda's phrase, under another name.

Bishop Frank Thorne in Nyasaland, who had for years made his anti-Federation views known to the Legislative Assembly in Zomba, embarked on a long correspondence with cabinet ministers in Britain and Salisbury in an unsuccessful attempt to get the African view considered. In 1959 he wrote to Roy Welensky, the Federal Prime Minister:

> Government in Central Africa depends on the consent and goodwill of the governed and I am afraid that in this county at any rate your Government does not enjoy this as far as the African population is concerned.

The Archbishop of Canterbury, Michael Ramsay, gave his public approval to Frank Thorne's opinions but it was the rebellion of Malawi's African people that finally broke up the Federation. When I arrived in Malawi in 1961, Federation was dead in all but name.

Visit by Archbishop 1964

I invited Archbishop Oliver Green-Wilkinson, Bishop of Zambia since 1961, to spend a week or two in Malawi to meet some of the people who had never seen an archbishop. He accepted at once and in May 1964 we arrived on Likoma Island on *Boatie Paul*, our Dutch canal barge. It is hard to imagine how she came to be sailing on a lake which in 1946 had swamped the *Viphya*, a brand new steamer and drowned 350 passengers and crew. The crew were well aware of *Paul*'s limitations and we trusted them.

Provincial Synod 1966

Oliver as archbishop was supportive and challenging. In January 1966 Provincial Synod met in Blantyre, Malawi. It was a tense moment. Ian Smith, Prime Minister of Rhodesia, had two months earlier declared UDI – a unilateral declaration of independence from Britain – claiming that he was defending Christian values.

Most of the delegates to the Synod from Rhodesia were white, most of those from Zambia and Malawi were black. Oliver opened synod by saying:

> We meet today for the first time in Malawi, divided by sharp political differences. It is certain we cannot all be right, it is possible that we are all wrong. It is probable that God can find something of good to use in what each one of us offers. Jesus came as one who serves. We must come as servants, stripped of status and honour but freed to put first our task to tell people the good news about Jesus Christ, the servant.

Rhodesia

The big issue in Rhodesia then, and in Zimbabwe now, was and is land distribution. In 1908 a Missionary Conference said the soil of "Native Reserves" was poor and they should be enlarged. In 1917, the Native Reserves Commission recommended to Britain that five and a half million acres should be added – but also that six and a half million "most suitable for European farming" should be removed. Obediently, an Order in Council was issued in London in 1920 to enforce this division.

Arthur Shearly Cripps – a missionary and a poet extensively quoted in the *Oxford Book of Mystical Verse* had arrived in Rhodesia in 1901. He admired and imitated Francis, the Poor Man of Assisi, and identified with the Africans of Rhodesia. He gave his clothes to the cold, ate little but sadza (maize-meal porridge) and made long journeys on foot to fetch medicines for the sick.

Cripps, backed by John White, a Methodist missionary, published a blistering attack on the Administration in a pamphlet, *A Million Acres*. He had no support from his bishop, who wrote to the *London Times*: "Natives in this country are dealt with in that spirit of even-handed justice for which the flag of England stands." The African majority was powerless. In 1923 government was placed in the hands of its white population.

Bishop Edward Paget, Bishop of Mashonaland 1952-1957, was the dominant figure for the next 30 years and became the first Archbishop when the Province was formed in 1955. He faced a racial issue even before his enthronement. It had not occurred to the cathedral authorities to invite Africans to the service. Paget heard about this and ordered them to send invitations. If they did not, the enthronement would be transferred to a downtown African church. Later, he wrote that in his early years, "It was thought strange that I stayed as the guest of an African priest. I received unstamped and anonymous letters of abuse."

However, Paget believed in working through the Establishment, described by Guy Clutton-Brock, who was later deported, as "Bishops, politicians and generals who all met in the colonialist Salisbury Club. The bishop had ever one foot in the Establishment and one in the kingdom of God."

In the late 1950s the situation altered. After the war, the white population had grown from 53,000 to 223,000, many of whom, mostly artisans, now felt threatened by African advancement. Independence had already come in Ghana and nearer home in Zambia and Malawi. Joshua Nkomo's African National Congress caused alarm. In 1959 the Whitehead government declared a State of Emergency and imprisoned leading nationalists without trial. Gonville ffrench-Beytagh, Dean of Salisbury, asked Synod to support a motion asserting that government action was based on "other than Christian principles," but his own churchwarden moved an amendment stressing Paul's teaching that, "the powers that be are ordained by God," and accepting without question the need for imprisoning people.

Some of the clergy supported Bishop Cecil Alderson but only a minority of the laity, including some very able people. Sir Robert Tredgold, a Presbyterian and the grandson of the pioneer missionary John Moffatt, resigned as Chief Justice in protest against the legislation he was expected to enforce. Many members of the Christian Action Group against discriminatory laws were detained or deported, including the Clutton-Brocks.

Kenneth Skelton had been the outspoken Bishop of Matabeleland from 1962 to 1970. In 1964, when UDI was threatened, he said in a sermon, "The Church might have to say its people were under no obligation to obey a government which took such illegal action." The sermon earned him the title of "Red Skelton" in a section of the white community. He also questioned the disparity in clergy salaries within the church itself.

Jeffrey Fenwick, who worked in Rhodesia for twenty years and who was totally in sympathy with his views, says of Kenneth, "His was a lonely voice. His exhortations could often be dismissed as the eccentric views of a left-wing individual and would have carried more weight had he worked more closely with some of the liberal-minded lay people in Matabeleland, who were always ahead of the Salisbury establishment."

Kenneth's wife found the ostracism hard to bear and for this and other family problems, he returned to England where, as Bishop of Lichfield, he masterminded the revolution in marriage laws which have allowed thousands of couples to remain as communicants after a second marriage.

Mark Wood followed Kenneth as Bishop of Matabeleland in January 1971. He was an articulate Welshman and we had been contemporaries at Mirfield. He had worked in the Johannesburg townships for ten years, originally as a member of the "old students" team. Following his marriage, they moved to Rhodesia and Mark was the outspoken Dean of Salisbury Cathedral when he was elected bishop. I had high hopes and was not disappointed. In his charge to synod in 1973 he said:

> Despite detention and deportation I thank God that more and more people, both black and white, are willing to make their political views known. Rhodesia needs more politics, not less. Lay members of the Church most certainly should engage in politics. I denounce terrorism as unchristian; in the same breath I also denounce as hypocrites those who denounce terrorism but are unwilling to do something about the injustices and grievances which cause it.
>
> When will people learn to talk to each other and see each other's point of view before the breaking-point of resorting to violence is reached? Leave your colour outside this synod – and your status and your sex too – and as Christ's body, the Church, let us try to see things through Christ's eyes.

Here from Bishop Mark's last Synod charge is one of those things that was not easily said in Rhodesia, and even less easily accepted:

> If white people are to stay on in Rhodesia, it can only be in a multi-racial society. White privilege cannot be maintained for ever, or even much longer. And even if it could, we could not organize the Church on that basis.

Declaration of Independence 1965

Ian Smith became Prime Minister in 1964 and in November 1965 declared "UDI" – claiming that in doing so he was defending "Christian values". The Governor, Sir Humphrey Gibbs, an Anglican layman, refused to co-operate. From then on either Humphrey or his wife were in Government House twenty-four hours a day, since laying hands on them personally would be high treason against the Queen. Whenever the bishops met in Salisbury we would spend an evening with them.

The churches were united in opposition. On the closure of Vatican II in

1965 Donald Lamont, the Catholic Bishop of Umtali, came straight from the airport to Government House to show his solidarity with the Churches which had stated: "We do not recognise the present regime as the legal authority of Rhodesia."

Provincial Synod 1968

The 1968 Provincial synod held in Rhodesia at Marendellas (now Marondera), was lively and encouraging, with a genuine African feel about it. A tense moment in a debate about whether the Province could continue in view of the political tensions between Ian Smith's Rhodesia and Kenneth Kaunda's Zambia, was relieved when one of the African laymen said, "I came here fearing apartheid but I find myself sleeping in the same room as the white Dean of Bulawayo (FROM MALAWIAN CHURCH LEARNING CHICHEWA).

Church and State in Rhodesia

Relations between Church and State in Rhodesia quickly got worse. In June 1970 I wrote:

> There was such a moment in South Africa fourteen years ago. Government wanted to make a law to stop black and white worshipping together. Archbishop Clayton wrote to the government to say that if the law was passed his clergy would go to prison rather than obey it. As he signed it he had a heart attack. His body was found the next morning beside the desk on which the letter lay. The law was dropped.
>
> Now the same issue has arisen in Rhodesia. Bishop Paul Burrough has written to the government to say, "The Churches cannot exercise Christian charity to all 'by permission'. If permission was withheld, all their institutions would become useless bricks and mortar."
>
> Bishop Kenneth Skelton of Matabeleland has written of "The specious lie that our government is upholding Christian standards by its racial policies." Magnificently said, but was this just the lone voice of a political bishop out of touch with his own people, as some have said? The answer came the next day when his Diocesan Synod carried by 98 votes to 8 a resolution moved by a white layman endorsing the statement of the church leaders.

Archbishop's last visit

In May 1970 Oliver, accompanied by his sister Prudence, who was showing the first stages of the Parkinson's Disease from which she subsequently suffered for many years, made another visitation, this time of the southern lake shore, including Chief Mponda, the senior Yao Chief. They visited all seven institutions at Likwenu/Malosa and went on to Blantyre where they called on Revd Jonathan Sangaya, General Secretary of the CCAP Blantyre Synod, the Catholic Archbishop Chiona and the ecumenical Christian Service Committee. I wrote:

> The last day was a marathon – Mass and a sermon at St Paul's; 143 candidates to confirm at Matope; a tour of Matope Hospital and the new maternity unit for which Chief Symon and his people have given so generously and back to Malosa after two hundred miles of driving, mostly on gravel roads, just in time to address the students at Malosa Secondary School. It is visits like this that makes "Oliver bishopu wathu wamkulu" – Oliver our Archbishop – step out of the pages of Mapemhero and come to life.

Death of Archbishop and funeral

Three months later came the terrible news that Oliver had been killed on 26 August when a tyre burst on his car. He was returning to Lusaka after saying good-bye to the staff of St Francis Hospital, Katete, preparatory to his move to the Copper-belt in central Zambia and handing over of Lusaka and the whole of southern Zambia to Bishop Filemon Mataka.

Bishop Josiah Mtetateka and I were present at his funeral in the new Lusaka Cathedral. In my address I said:

> When St Francis knew he was going to die, he said, "Welcome, my sister Death." The man we know and love as "Oliver" was also baptised with the name "Francis". He was a member of the Third Order of Franciscans. The last thing he did was to say good-bye to the staff and patients St Francis Hospital, Katete. In that same hospital he died a few hours later and his ashes will rest in the outdoor Chapel of St Francis in the grounds of this Cathedral.
>
> The things that made St Francis loved and remembered are those for which Oliver was loved and will be remembered – his simplicity of life; his burning love for Christ and for all who God created; his sense of fun; his surrender even of the happiness of marriage.
>
> A clue to his life and influence is in the simple wooden coffin in which he lies among us now. They wanted to take his body out and put it in a splendid shiny coffin with silver handles but his sister said,

"No. He wanted to be a bishop of the people. Let him be buried as a man of the people."

During the war Oliver was a Desert Rat in North Africa, he fought in Italy and on the Normandy beaches and was decorated for bravery. He was a citizen of Zambia and a personal friend of your great President. He agonised over all the tensions of race and politics and poverty that are part of the life of everyone in Africa today. He had a fiery love for his nation of Zambia, but of that President Kaunda will speak in this Cathedral on Saturday.

Another clue is in the simple iron shepherd's crook he carried when he visited us in Malawi. At a lake shore village he was given a live sheep and he demonstrated with zest how a shepherd's crook is used. His work as Archbishop involved him in the life of five countries – Congo, Botswana, Rhodesia, Zambia and Malawi – as different as any in the world. There are tensions, political and racial, in and between some of these countries. More than once Oliver found himself under cross-fire. But he understood that the healing oil of personal friendship has a magical power, and this was his greatest gift.

He had an immense circle of friends. They were not just friends in name but those for whom you would find him praying on his knees in his chapel before sunrise. They were of different races, of different faiths, of different political convictions. He saw his task as the building of unity. This wish he carried as a team ministry with his sister Prudence, for whom our love and prayers go out today.

When Francis of Assisi was dying, he called the Brothers together and asked them to recite his hymn in praise of Brother Sun and Sister Moon and all who suffer. Then he added some new lines. I cannot think of any better way to express what this follower of St Francis has to say to us today:

> Be praised, my Lord, because of Sister Death
> From whom no one living can escape.
> Happy are those found doing your will.
> Praise and bless the Lord, and give him thanks
> And serve him with great humility.

Provincial meetings Lilongwe 1971

"Daddy, why are you always at meetings?" our first born complained. Sometimes I wondered, but the Provincial meetings in Lilongwe in June

1971 made history and changed my life. For the first time in the sixteen years it had been in existence, its Standing Committee had an African majority. Between 1963 and 1969 only nine of its 73 voting seats had been occupied by Africans. Now it had come of age.

Its first act was to create a new diocese of Lake Malawi, consisting of Northern and Central regions, which held half of the population of the country and nearly two-thirds of its Anglicans. The next was the election of Josiah Mtetateka as its founding bishop by a vote of thirty-eight to nil. Measured by annual confirmations and baptisms, his new diocese was growing faster than any Anglican work in the Province, including Southern Malawi where I was bishop.

The Province welcomed the recommendation of the 1968 Lambeth Conference that if there was no Anglican church nearby, and on special ecumenical occasions, Anglicans should be free to receive communion in other churches. At Lambeth the bishops had agreed to this by a majority of 351 votes to 75. At Lilongwe the vote was unanimous.

Much thought was given to the training of clergy. Until 1957 all Malawian clergy had been trained in the vernacular at St Andrew's College, Makulawe on Likoma Island, most recently by Leonard Viner. From then on they had been sent to the new Provincial Seminary at St John's Lusaka, of which John Weller was head. There were no boarding facilities for wives or children and there were constant requests for ordinands to be brought home to meet family crises, a long and expensive journey. Every diocese wanted its new priests to be trained alongside those from other churches and those heading for other professions, with their families, in their own countries. This was a tall order at a time when grants for theological training were focussed on "properly staffed" ecumenical colleges.

No theological college existed in Malawi that met these requirements. For the coming year some of the Malawi ordinands, with their tutor Rodney Hunter, were quietly absorbed into the Catholic major seminary at Kachebere. The border between Zambia and Malawi ran through the centre of the seminary. This worked well until the new Malawian Catholic bishops, all trained before Vatican II to regard Anglicans as protestant heretics, realised that their future priests were being trained dogmatic theology by Rodney Hunter. They put an end to the arrangement. Several years later, George Ndomondo, now released from detention for his part in the Chipembere rebellion, joined Nkhoma Seminary, linked to the Cape

Province Dutch Reformed Church and at the other end of the Catholic-Protestant spectrum.

The final solution was a joint CCAP-Anglican theological college adjoining the university's Chancellor College in Zomba.

Lastly they elected me as archbishop and installed me in St Peter's Lilongwe the next morning. The Province was a complex animal.

Province

In the four countries contained in the Province were Zambia, Malawi, Botswana and Zimbabwe. Zimbabwe had Mashonaland based on Harare (then called Salisbury) with Paul Burrough as bishop, and Matabeleland centred on Bulawayo in the south-west, where Mark Wood had just taken over as bishop from Kenneth Skelton. Zambia was being divided into three and later four dioceses, while Malawi remained with Lake Malawi and Southern Malawi. Botswana was just about to elect its first bishop.

Botswana was by far the wealthiest, having discovered diamonds and other minerals in the 1970s and was the only country in sub-Saharan Africa to have a "developing economy" equal to that of Brazil. Zambia was benefiting from a copper boom, while the two Zimbabwean dioceses were the most developed. Malawi was by far the poorest of the four countries and survived economically only by exporting the more adventurous of its young men to work on mines and farms in Zimbabwe, Zambia and South Africa.

Zambia visit

I began my new job with a three-week visit to Zambia. I stayed with Canon George Hewitt who had begun his work as a missionary in the year I was born (1916) and I paid homage at the grave of Leonard Kamungu, the first Malawian priest and a member of the missionary team which brought the gospel to Zambia. St Francis' Hospital, Katete, had been founded by the priest-doctor Francis Trefusis in 1946, formerly a missionary in Nyasaland and had now been developed by James Cairns into a fine hospital. I was interviewed on radio and TV at the fine inter-church multi-media centre in Lusaka. I had lunch with President Kenneth Kaunda, who asked for the church to criticise him when he went off the rails, a request one could not imagine President Kamuzu Banda making.

At Kitwe on the copperbelt, I asked an inter-racial congregation to put themselves into the shoes of two sets of parents, one in Zimbabwe whose only son had been called up to serve the security forces and the other in

Zambia where an only son had joined the freedom-fighters. I asked them to hold them both in their prayers. Outside the church afterwards a very angry white woman came to me brandishing her sunshade and saying, "I never thought I would live to hear a bishop calling terrorists freedom-fighters."

I met six frustrated Franciscan monks at an old rural centre where most of the people had left for the copperbelt. If they had been posted to one of the burgeoning urban centres, I have no doubt they might still be there today. I met an inspiring voluntary priest who was "Father Kampango" on Sunday and "R.Phiri – Tailor" from Monday to Saturday.

Provincial Synod 1972

Provincial synod met in Lusaka. The theme of my charge was the one word "Sent". I asked the delegates from seven dioceses to confront the hard fact that our population was growing by 500,000 each year and our membership by only 1,000, saying:

> We clergy see ourselves as chaplains to those from the well-springs of the missionary pioneers – Penhalonga, Msoro or Likoma Island – rather than as messengers. We have been too anxious to exclude. One man was brought to me recently who had been cut off from the sacraments for twenty-five years. His fault? That fifteen years before he was baptised, he had married a Muslim wife from whom he rightly refused to be parted and with whom he had lived faithfully for forty years.
>
> As the church in Central Africa we must reflect a continent where most are young, where half are female and where 98% are black. It would have been hard to guess any of these things from the Provincial Synod which met here ten years ago. Perhaps the man who described us as "Unyoung, uncoloured and unpoor" was looking through the window. It still has, God forgive it, a white Archbishop.
>
> We must shed the rigidity and the Englishness we brought to Africa. We need a church where the young feel accepted instead of being criticised; a church that is self-supporting right down to the local unit; a church that is self-propagating because every member has accepted his or her commission to show that God cares and therefore his family cares."

Alston Mazingaliwa, Diocesan Secretary of Lake Malawi, said in his report:

> I will never forget the synod Eucharist. There was a youth choir, with drums, visekese (reed and seed rattles) and other African instruments.

I asked myself, "Are these young people sinning against God? Is the Church in Zambia sinning by accepting the use of drums in church? The time has come for we Africans to worship God in our own culture."

Provincial Synod 1976

Provincial Synod meant getting together representatives from Zambia, Rhodesia, Botswana and Malawi, of which the first two were in a state of undeclared war. After three failed attempts we succeeded in holding it in Botswana. It was the most African synod of the twenty-year history of the Province. Even the disappearance of my suitcase in Johannesburg with all my robes and papers was relieved by the tongue-in-cheek telex sent by Malawi Airways to all the airports in Southern Africa – ARCHBISHOP IRATE AND WITHOUT CLOTHES.

Among the important motions agreed to at the Synod were those relating to marriage and the ordination of women. The Synod agreed that a non-Christian man with more than one wife may be received into the church with his believing wives and children and in due course be confirmed and receive communion, provided the local community gives its willing consent and only within a context where the church's teaching on monogamy is strictly recognised. This had been forbidden by the Lambeth Conference of 1888 and had caused much heart-burning especially where we were working in Muslim communities.

On the question of the ordination of women, the Synod agreed to ordaining women as deacons but another motion to ordain women as priests was defeated.

Diocese of Lake Malawi visit 1977

Lake Malawi diocese had not had a proper "visitation" from me for the eleven years that Josiah had been in charge, first as suffragan and then as diocesan bishop. October found us, together with Canon Lloyd Chikoko, at Imani on the Central region lake shore. My diary records:

> Wednesday. Woke up in church. Shaved by feel, followed by hot and cold shower by emptying the two pots of water over self in the grass bathroom specially built for us. Mattins, mass and confirmation in a grass lean-to specially built as the church could not hold the crowd expected. Twenty-two confirmed. Three years ago there was one christian in the village – a young widow.

The rest is her work, helped by Canon Chikoko, aged 62, who travels on foot a parish fifty miles by twenty. He nearly died of cholera a year ago and now has a hand in plaster, broken when he fell ten foot over a river bank at midnight, having lost his way in search of a new village. Now he has 53 congregations in his parish, all but seven of them newly created in the past five years.

As we end, a rabid dog scatters the congregation but is quickly dealt with by the newly-confirmed who are almost all young men and their wives.

We go on to Siyasiya. Of the 52 confirmed, three are village headmen. One old man, formerly a Muslim, tells me of his fighting in German East Africa in World War I, where he learned enough Swahili to become an interpreter in the Cape Town courts.

The day ends at Mkokoka with chicken roasted in the coals of a wood fire and a concert of hymns to traditional Malawian tunes, magnificently sung by the young men's choir, while I struggled to read the words by the light of an African full moon.

Thursday. Wake at 5.30 and realize the beauty of their new church, plastered in two coloured earths, charcoal grey below and beige above. Outside the lovely call of the black-headed bush-shrike. Realize with a shock that the 62-year-old canon and the 73-year-old bishop Josiah have long since risen, washed and packed up their beds and that the servers are laying out vestments...

A young woman reads the first lessons with her baby on her back. "She preaches a very good sermon too", Canon Chikoko whispers in my ear.

On the way we stop to greet old Canon Jameson Mwenda, who retired many years ago. Every room in the house and every patch of shade in the yard is filled by a milling crowd of a hundred mothers and children. Knowing his firm views on morality, we ask if this is a wedding celebration for a second wife. No, just that the District Council wanted somewhere to start an Under-5 clinic, so he offered his house.

Provincial visit 1979

Jane was elected Provincial President of the Mothers' Union in 1978, so we made a joint visit to Rhodesia and Botswana in January 1979.

Diocese of Mashonaland

Bishop Paul Burrough had arranged an outline programme for our visit.

Shabani – a "hot" area, where we visited Noel Williams, a gently-spoken dumpy, iron-fisted saint and a Mirfield father. He had a long-standing arrangement to travel on a motor-bike to an isolated congregation. The District Commissioner said he must not go as it was too dangerous. "Nonsense," says Noel, "I've promised and I shall be there." After a long argument he agreed to walk, considered safer, and the DC said he would collect him in a reinforced Land Rover at noon. At 4.00 a.m. Noel set off by himself through the bush. Twelve noon came and went but no DC's Land Rover. So Noel started walking back at 1.00 p.m. All the way he could see members of his congregation criss-crossing through the trees and calling to one another, making sure no guerrilla aimed a gun at him. Next day the DC explained that he had not come to collect him "to see what happened!" For the next year guerrillas and security forces allowed him to go unmolested, something that would not have happened had be been collected in the DC's Land Rover.

Jane writes:

> It was intended that Donald and I should meet people at a township church, but there had been shooting there the night before and I was disappointed at not being allowed to go. Donald went alone to the confirmation. Just before the communion in the church where I was worshipping I heard six or eight rounds of automatic rifle fire. I had visions of Donald lying in a pool of blood at the altar steps. But all was well and he appeared for a late lunch.

Garfield Todd was a New Zealander, Churches of Christ missionary, Prime Minister in the 1950s, adviser to Joshua Nkomo, and held in detention on his ranch by Ian Smith. He lived twelve miles outside Shabani, where we went to see him. The week before he had had metal meshing fixed to his windows, having received letters threatening assassination from members of the white community. He and his wife Grace had lived in Rhodesia for forty-four years and were wonderful examples of Christian witness. It was good to hear him say that on his rare visits to Bulawayo many whites came up to him to wish him well.

Gwanda – Police insisted we should have an armed escort, so for 120 miles we followed a Land Rover with four automatic rifles sticking out of it, held by two black policemen. Keeping up with guns that would shoot to kill was a sobering experience.

We met the Enrolling Member of the Mothers' Union who was from Malawi. She told us that her fifteen-year-old son had disappeared the week before, possibly to Mozambique. Last year another son of seventeen had joined guerrillas in Zambia. She had been intending to take the fifteen-year-old to Malawi. She was desolate at leaving it too late. Lunch at a hotel with whites of the congregation, one of them wearing a gun.

Comments received: a miscellany –

* The war is tearing me in half. I have a son fighting for the security forces and another for "The Boys". What happens when they meet?

* The "Keeps" in Tribal Trust Lands (fenced-in cages with no protection from sun or rain) are like concentration camps. It is mostly young people who are put there – no buildings, no lavatories, men and women together, very little food or water. They stay for months.

* Planting of crops is forbidden by guerrillas in some places, by security forces in others. Long curfews make care of crops and cattle almost impossible.

* A chief had been killed by guerrillas. The District Commissioner supervised the burning down of 53 village houses until a white man intervened to stop him.

* The referendum by whites on 30 January might have happened on Mars as far as Africans were concerned. But it did show eighty percent of whites ready to live under a majority government.

* Many Africans commented on the pressure they were under for following "the white man's religion".

* All big government services take place in Salisbury Cathedral, giving the impression that this is the state church, unsympathetic to the African struggle for independence.

Consecration of Peter Hatendi

The consecration of Peter Hatendi as suffragan and later diocesan bishop of Mashonaland was moving and memorable. The choirmaster to the largely white choir had said the choir could not sing on Friday nights so one of the clergy gathered a choir from various township churches. The result was a packed cathedral resounding to triumphant Shona music, accompanied by drums, kudu horns and rattles. The conductor, paralysed from polio, was sitting cross-legged on a high stool. Many church leaders were there, including Bishop Muzorewa of the African Methodist Episcopal Church and Archbishop Chakaipa of the Catholic Church.

Matebeleland

Matabeleland is on the dry south-western side of Rhodesia, far poorer than Mashonaland with its capital of Salisbury, now Harare. The Ndbele used to call Salisbury "Bambazonke" – "Grab all". Robert Mercer, who had been deported from South Africa in 1970 for his stand against apartheid, the bishop living in Bulawayo had arranged an interesting visit.

At Kwekwe we were taken to a supper party for clergy and their wives by a priest carrying a gun. As we reached the house after several miles on earth roads he said, "We made it!" It is much easier to plant landmines on earth roads than on tarred ones. He was just voicing what most people feel when they get to the end of an earth road.

As we travelled we noticed a number of good things happening:

The Guild of St Agnes

This for girls who had left school but not yet married. I found them building a new house for their priest, learning baby-care, taking Mattins and Evensong when the priest was away on ulendo, playing the drums in church, teaching the Sunday School, being the choir, learning and teaching in Literacy classes and beating the school team at netball. Two young organisers move about the diocese stimulating new groups and providing ideas. Malawi, please copy!

Urban ministry

This is carried out by a team of five priests, four black and one white, of whom the leader is Archdeacon Jonathan Siyachitema. He will be the guest of our two dioceses in Malawi for a fortnight next month, learning something of Malawi before going to Canada as our Provincial representative at their planning conference. I hope our urban team will pick his brains when he is with us.

Worship

A church where candlesticks are carved out of wood, two African women kneeling with pots on their heads, which are the sockets for the candles. Why, I wonder, do we beg for ugly brass cast-offs from churches in England when we have the finest hardwoods in the world?

Music

Throughout Rhodesia drums are a normal accompaniment to singing. The singing puts us in the shade, partly because hymns in Malawi are pitched at the level a normal male can't reach.

Crops

Matabeleland is not the most fertile part of Rhodesia. Much of it is flat, dry thorn bush country, better suited for cows than for human beings. Yet the Gokwe "Tribal Trust Land" last year exported crops equal in value to the total tea exports of Malawi. This is what good co-operation between the races can do.

As we flew back to Malawi it was easy to see the boundaries of the Tribal Trust Lands – over-crowded, over-grazed and eroded. Ian Smith had recently agreed that there were at least three million acres of unused, good quality European-owned land. Re-allocation of land needs to be dealt with as a matter of urgency, together with an intensive programme of agricultural training and an ongoing transfer of skills.

Botswana

Botswana was pleasantly relaxed. Following the resignation of Bishop Shannon Mallory, the election of Khotso Makhulu as the new bishop had gone smoothly, though we were a little sad that the only woman on elective assembly was Ruth Khama, the wife of the President, Seretse Khama. The vast wealth of the new diamond, nickel, coal and copper mines shows itself in better resourced services.

The Mothers' Union were doing wonderful work throughout the country, especially in the more remote areas.

Dean of Cathedral detained

The shadow of South Africa loomed large as was shown by the detention of Michael Molale, the dean of Gaberone Cathedral. He had been helping refugees from South Africa and was changing planes at Jan Smuts (OR Tambo) airport in Johannesburg. When passing through customs he was arrested and taken to the Vorster Square police station opposite the cathedral, notorious for people "falling out of the window". He was questioned for twenty-four hours non-stop and was surprised to see photostats of letters he had sent to Europe (all overseas mail from Botswana goes through Johannesburg) and to have quoted to him conversations in his own sitting-room. On the same floor were forty-eight children, most of them had been in solitary confinement. Their only way of knowing who was still alive was to pass a song from one to another at 5.30 p.m. each day –

> By the blood of the Lamb
> And our own blood
> By the blood of the Lamb
> We shall be free.

Michael sang this to us to a haunting Zulu tune.

Michael's wife, Joyce, became worried when Michael did not telephone and got in touch with friends in Johannesburg who told their lawyers. They issued a statement to the international media, saying that the Dean of Gaberone Cathedral was being held by South African police. He was released the next day, after fourteen hours of solitary confinement.

Council of Anglican Provinces of Africa (CAPA)

In 1979 we had the privilege of inviting to Malawi the archbishops of the eleven Anglican Provinces of Africa for the first meeting of the Council of Anglican Provinces of Africa (CAPA) which was held at Chilema Lay Training Centre. Archbishop Festo Olang of Kenya was its Chairman and I its Secretary.

The aims of CAPA were to develop links and understanding between the Provinces. One of its first greatest achievements was to set up training courses for newly appointed bishops in Africa. The Council has since gone from strength to strength.

Travelling by Bishop Josiah Mtekateka

United States – 1968

Josiah wrote:

> In the United States I first of all stayed with Mr and Mrs Chindongo in Washington DC. She is my daughter. She is leaving Washington for Malawi because her husband is to enter Harvard University for three years to obtain his degree in Fine Arts.
>
> When I arrived in Houston, Texas I was met by Bishop Milton Richardson, George Carlisle and others including the Mayor of Houston who gave me the key of the city. The garage which George Carlisle uses said, "You are not going to take a bishop round in your car, I am going to let you have mine – a Thunderbird which has never been used." In my last week one of George's parishioners wagged her finger at us. I asked George what she was doing. He said, "Don't you understand? She is saying 'You, a clergyman, supposed to be a poor man, driving a Thunderbird!"
>
> At Waco I met Braz Walker. As the result of polio, he can move neither his feet nor his hands but he can type with his tongue, he had some sort of machine and showed me how he types. He is very interested in Lake Malawi fish and gave me a book with pictures of Malawi fish. In his room there were three tanks where he kept live fish. What struck me was the happiness he had, his face filled with joy. Really he is a wonderful man."

Nursing Sisters of St John the Divine (NSSJD) (Nkhotakota 1970-1974)

For many years people had longed to have an Anglican Community of Sisters working in Malawi.

While in England in 1968 for the Lambeth Conference of bishops from around the world, Josiah and I visited the NSSJD sisters in London and won their hearts with Josiah's description of our longing for a Community and the need for training midwives. In December 1968 we heard that the Nursing Sisters were having a week of special prayer to find out whether they were called to work in Malawi.

In February 1969 we heard, "After a week of prayer the NSSJD Sisters have accepted Bishop Josiah's invitation to establish a house at Nkhotakota, to take over the midwifery training school and to provide training for African novices for the community.

Josiah offered his own house for the use of the Sisters. The Mother Superior is Margaret Faith who worked as a UMCA nurse in Masasi Diocese in Tanzania.

> The first three Sisters will be Sister Mary who worked for 20 years in Namibia and Sisters Janet and Christine.
>
> It is a great adventure of faith and it is wonderful that their skill and dedication will now be used to assist our girls in Malawi.
>
> Their chief purpose is to make it possible for Malawian girls to serve God as Sisters. The Community accepts novices – trainees – only if they are trained nurses. To form a training school for Sisters we need a group of 3 or 4 young Malawian women. The Catholic Church in Lilongwe Diocese has over 130 African Sisters.
>
> Please pray that by 1980 there will be Malawian Sisters of St John the Divine who are also qualified nurses.

Bishop John How ACC with Sisters Mary, Christine, Janet, Margaret with Bishop Josiah

Bishop Josiah describes the Sisters' contribution:

> We have had three ordinations where six men were made priests and one made Deacon. They were all held in churches which have had no chance of witnessing an ordination. At one of them the Reverend Mother of NSSJD was with us. She insisted on staying with us all the time under the hot sun of Africa. She also visited Likoma.
>
> Sister Mary spoke at the Clergy Conference of the way God calls a person and how everyone feels that vocation in their heart. Of course, anyone can join any job they like but without God calling then

it just cannot work at all. She urged the clergy to explain this well to their people and to pray to God that He may guide them.

In November 1972 Sister Christine, who had been Sister Tutor at St Anne's Training School, was replaced by Sister Pamela who took over her job as Matron. Before joining the Community Sister Pamela worked for 15 years at the Charles Johnson Hospital in Zululand where she was Matron. Sister Janet had to leave for England because of health reasons and was replaced by Marion Palmer, a trained midwifery tutor sent by USPG.

In September 1974 Bishop Josiah reported:

"We are sorry to lose the two members of NSSJD who have just returned to their Mother House. Sister Pamela has been Matron at St Anne's and Sister Mary has been responsible for the Community House and was also Bursar of St Anne's Hospital. We thank them for their work."

NSSJD leave for England

At the end of the year Bishop Josiah wrote in *Ecclesia*:

The Sisters found they could not fill the gap after the ones who had left because of illness. There used to be three and when two went back to the UK they could only be replaced by one.

Although they only stayed in the Diocese for four years there has been a great improvement at St Anne's Hospital. During their time work has increased as a result of the extensions. The Sisters were always cheerful and we thank them for their kindness in caring for visitors and for all they have done in this Diocese.

I hope they will still pray for a religious community to be founded in our Dioceses. Sister Mary has left one who is in her first training as a midwife. She has been giving her instructions of the work of a novice. I do not lose hope, let us keep on praying, God will call them and make provision when the time comes.

Editor note: *Call The Midwife* later became a popular TV programme in the UK and covered the work of NSSJD.

Nkhotakota – early days 1894

The Revd Arthur Fraser Sim was the first priest at Nkhotakota arriving in the middle of 1894 building himself a small house and a church. He built the first school which by March 1895 had 100 pupils. In September of the same year Bishop Chauncy Maples was drowned in the lake near Nkhotakota, Arthur Sim took his funeral, the body was placed in a grave in front of the altar in the church. A few months later Arthur Sim died of blackwater fever aged 34, his grave is outside the east end of the church. A large new church was dedicated to All Saints on 25 April 1902 and is now the Cathedral for the Diocese of Lake Malawi.

Unity amongst Christians

In Pretoria I hardly ever met, even casually, any priest or minister of any other Christian Church, except at the big Kilnerton Methodist Mission. In Swaziland our only real contacts were with the Methodists at Matspha I used to visit to see Anglican secondary school students. Arthur Matthews, the minister in charge, resigned to become an Anglican priest. "You have a bishop as a father. We have only a Board," he gave as his main reason. It served me as a model which I wish I had followed more faithfully.

In Nyasaland, Presbyterians and Catholics vastly outnumbered Anglicans. The largest Church, known as CCAP – the Church of Central Africa Presbyterian – was made up of three synods.

Presbyterians

Livingstonia Synod in the north had been created by Robert Lawes, a human dynamo and a doctor of medicine, theology and law. He came to Nyasaland in 1885 and returned to Scotland 52 years later. By 1922, although the area served was thinly populated, Livingstonia had 768 schools with 40,000 pupils. Lawes was a personal friend of William Percival Johnson the tireless UMCA archdeacon based on Likoma Island. In more recent years there had been little contact with UMCA.

Nkhoma Synod in the Central Region was the offspring of the Dutch Reformed Church of the Western Cape and still in the missionary age with an Afrikaans medium school. Their medical work was superb. Dr Blignaut was one of the third generation of doctors of that name and Nkhoma hospital was renowned for its eye surgery.

Blantyre Synod in the south was our natural partner with the diocesan office first at Mponda's and then at Malosa. Jonathan Sangaya, a wonderful man, had been appointed General Secretary in 1960, with similar authority to an Anglican bishop. He remained in that post until his death in 1978. The Synod was reinforced by members of the Iona Community, three of whom, Richard Baxter, Hamish Hepburn and Ken Pattison were our neighbours when serving at Chilema Lay Training Centre.

In my enthronement address I said, "We who brought the gospel to Africa are deeply conscious of our sin and folly in bringing it in broken parts. The prayer of Christ the High Priest still goes on: 'May they be one that the world may believe'.'" I said that in India all the major churches, other than Catholics, had pledged themselves to seek visible unity and thanked God for the wise leadership of Pope John XXIII, who was urging his people to open their bibles and listen to the Holy Spirit.

Catholics

This raised the eyebrows of a few white lay people but it also brought an invitation to meet Fr van Asdonck, Secretary to the Catholic Episcopal Conference. He lent me *The Council, Reform and Reunion* by Hans Küng, then a little-known Swiss theologian. The seventy-seven year-old caretaker Pope, as he had been seen, was calling together the Second Vatican Council in October 1962 to be a new Pentecost which would renew the life of the Church and bring about reunion. "Only when the Church appears healthily modernised and rejuvenated can we say to these separate brethren: 'Look, brothers, this is the Church of Christ. Come! The way lies open'."

Hans Küng listed his hopes – Mass in the vernacular; better preaching, bible-study by lay people; reform of marriage laws – among many others.

We had similar needs. Most Anglican churches, except at Nkhotakota, used the dialect used on Likoma Island. Rural parishes had up to fifteen "outstations" where all preaching and pastoral care was given by laymen, generous but untrained. Few people had a copy of the bible, or of the New Testament; if they had one, there were no guides available. The marriage laws showed no mercy to the many mothers whose husbands had gone off to work in other countries and had never come back. If they found another man to support their orphaned children, they were excommunicated and left in limbo.

Later, I asked Fr van Asdonck why he and others were so involved in reunion.

> Most of us were in the underground during the war. We never asked questions about each other. If we were tortured, we had nothing to reveal. When peace was declared we threw off our inhibitions. I disclosed for the first time that I was a Catholic priest and learned that my half-section was a Protestant engineer. We both said, "We believe in the same God. Let's work together to rebuild our community."

Soon afterwards I put this new relationship to the test. An Anglican student at a Catholic secondary school had just been told that he would not be allowed to sit for his final exams there unless he was re-baptised. I sent his letter on to Bishop Fady, the French Catholic Bishop of Lilongwe. His reply came by return of post. The student would write his exams. The head of the school had been moved. Would I please let him know of any similar incident in the future.

When we returned from the United States in 1963, I was delighted to know that the Catholic Diocese of Zomba had agreed to be a junior partner in Chilema Lay Training Centre, along with the Churches of Christ. The latter is now part of the United Reformed Church in England, though it retains its identity in Malawi as a Church founded with the reunion of Christendom as its major aim. The Diocese of Zomba withdrew from Chilema two years after its opening, not through any disagreement but because following Vatican II, the founding of catechetical centres throughout Africa had become a major target.

Chilema Ecumenical Lay Training Centre

Meanwhile the Revd John Leake and Alison, who I had met in York, had arrived with their children in 1963 to help staff Chilema for the next eight years. After John's sudden death from asthma in 1974, two years after their return to England, Justus Kishindo, the Chairman of Chilema, wrote movingly:

> In 1965 Chilema opened its doors with Richard Baxter (of Blantyre Synod and the Iona Community) as Warden and John as his assistant. He and Richard made a very good team – Richard would pour out ideas and John would put them into action. During the three years that John was later Warden, one could always think of Chilema as John Leake and John as Chilema. He was quiet and shy but also kind and loveable. He always respected people as people and it was this which made him popular with students and visitors.

In January 1965 twenty Malawian students, some from Karonga, four hundred miles to the north, came to Chilema on the first ecumenical work-camp ever held in Malawi. They painted the new buildings, planted 100 flamboyant trees, cleaned up rubble and met for study sessions on "Service". On the Saturday they hiked up the Domasi valley, where villagers sold them apples, a fruit some had never seen. On Sunday there was a united Eucharist led by John Leake in the outdoor chapel at Chilema, a vast fig-tree that had partly fallen over and then re-rooted itself. It seemed a fitting symbol of what we were being called to do and be.

It is often the impromptu that is the most memorable. At a Saturday meeting of official representatives of the four churches involved in Chilema, the invited speaker failed to turn up. We had no programme – someone suggested that the representatives of the four churches should first meet separately and list the things they felt to be essential in a future united church. Then we came together, and each church read out its list. Anglicans, trained in the Anglo-Catholic traditions of UMCA, wanted (for example) the sacrament of absolution, and so did the Catholics. No problem! Presbyterians wanted synodical structures at every level. No problem! The Churches of Christ wanted the reunion process to be ongoing until every denomination in Malawi was involved. No problem! And in the room were the heads of all the four churches that sponsored Chilema.

Unity spreads

The drive towards unity spread throughout the country, even in the Central Region, where Josiah Mtekateka was bishop and where Nkhoma Synod with its South African Dutch Reformed tradition had not been on speaking terms with Roman Catholics. Maxwell Zingani describes the Week of Prayer for Unity at a Catholic church in the Central Region in 1970:

> The introductory prayers and blessing were taken by the Roman Catholic Father. The first sermon was preached by a Presbyterian minister, Rev. Magombo, who said it was a new experience for him, a Presbyterian minister, to preach in a Roman Catholic church. He asked for everyone to pray hard for the guidance of the Holy Spirit that our prayers for the unity of the all churches, in Malawi and in the world, might be fruitful. The second sermon by an Anglican priest, Canon James Mwenda. Hymns were conducted by Fr Dunstan Ainani. These were Anglican, Presbyterian and Roman Catholic hymns. They were beautifully sung.

In 1972 many expatriate Catholic bishops in Africa were replaced by Africans. This should have added strength to the ecumenical movement, but this was not so. To be senior enough to be a bishop meant that you had learned your theology in the 1950s and expatriate bishops, who had absorbed new insights by attending Vatican II were replaced by priests who had learned their hard-line theology in pre-Vatican days. Now they in turn have moved and the new leaders of all churches are being trained in theological colleges and seminaries in Zomba enabling students to be in contact with each other. There is hope.

Laity

The church in Africa, especially in rural areas, is a lay church, where most worship, teaching and pastoral care is given voluntarily by a lay person in Malawi. In UMCA (Universities Mission to Central Africa) days at the end of the nineteenth and first half of the twentieth centuries, the situation was partially met in the diocese by training and appointing teacher-catechists to look after both school and congregation. This came to a sudden end with independence in 1964. Teachers were now paid and appointed by government. Taking charge of a church was not part of the contract.

My personal questions about clergy and laity were older and deeper. I have always thought of Jesus as a carpenter and the twelve, as far as we know their trades, as fishermen and a tax-collector, Simon the Zealot, one of those who wanted to rid Judea of Roman rule by violence. Mediaeval painters might dress them up in court robes, but this was distorting the facts, however brilliant the artist.

The Quaker blood in my veins perhaps prompted the second theme of my enthronement "charge" in Likoma Cathedral in 1962:

> I read with envy of the Diocese of Masasi in Tanzania where 900 members of the Brotherhood of St Andrew are week by week and without pay, teaching, preaching, praying with people and training choirs.

In 1965 Chilema Lay Training Centre held its first conference: "Christian Laypeople in Malawi". Half the lay participants were Presbyterian, half Anglican. Following a silent retreat on Maundy Thursday and Good Friday morning, Tom Colvin, a gifted and bold member of the Iona Community, opened a series of discussions on "God's Frozen People". "These", says the report, "proved so absorbing that delegates needed considerable persuasion to break off for meals." We ended on Easter morning with a joint Easter Eucharist in the open-air chapel, in the shade of a vast fig-tree, the top branches of which flowed over to touch the ground. Nothing like this had ever happened in the eighty years both churches had been working in Malawi.

We were fortunate in three wonderfully gifted laymen who joined the diocesan staff. The team of three – Justus Kishindo, Maxwell Zingani and Maxwell Maputwa – were the main agents for turning dreams, which they shared, into reality over the following years. Justus Kishindo was the son of a priest in Mozambique and, like Maxwell Zingani, a teacher. There the resemblance ended. They were the closest friends. I greatly valued their speaking the truth in love. Justus would make an appointment for an evening after dark and then Maxwell and he would come up to my office and tell me in the nicest possible way that I had put my foot in it. They were always right, but bishops in UMCA days had been above criticism, especially from lay people.

Justus Kishindo

Justus Kishindo was the son of a priest in Mozambique and an experienced teacher and headmaster. One of the first things I did in 1962 was to appoint him Education Secretary. He lost no time in convening an Education Sub-committee including representatives from the forty-five primary schools, Principal of Malosa Secondary School and Archdeacon Chipembere. Later in the year he was one of the diocesan representatives to Provincial Synod in Lusaka.

In January 1964 Justus began a year of studies in Birmingham from where he wrote:

> Life at Woodbrooke College is not an idle one. There is so much to learn in a short time. The huge College and Selly Oak Colleges libraries with their thousands of volumes on every subject made my desire for reading greater than ever. Whenever I am free from lectures or other college duties, I sit there for hours reading. The thing that impresses me most at this college is its friendly and Christian atmosphere. There seems to be no class distinction between teacher and taught. Everyone seems to be a friend of the other.

Donald, Bob Thupa, Justus Kishindo

Justus was a caring, thoughtful man who several times wrote moving obituaries in *Ecclesia*, the diocesan newsletter. One was of his goddaughter, young Joy Zingani, killed in a road accident:

> Being Joy's godfather words fail me. Her tragic death has been a stunning blow. Standing by her deathbed and seeing her little body lying cold and motionless, I burst into tears and cried loudly like a woman for minutes. To the Zingani family such a sudden and untimely death is just immeasurable. But it is my sincere hope that, as the Archbishop said in his sermon, hope of seeing their little "Joy" in the next world is great in their mind. May the risen Lord rest her little soul.

John Leake was a priest and assistant warden of Chilema Ecumenical Centre, following his sudden death in August 1974, Justus wrote in *Ecclesia*,

> I came to know John intimately soon after I was elected Chairman of Chilema's Board towards the end of 1965. From that time John and I became close friends, our friendship culminated in my becoming Martin Leake's godfather. It is difficult to think of Chilema, of which he became Warden in 1969, without thinking of him also. He was quiet and shy, kind and also loveable, popular with staff, students and visitors. John, Alison and their three children returned to England in 1972.
>
> John's sudden death from a heart attack is premature and a shock for Alison and the children. There is nothing more shocking than to lose a lifelong partner and, for the children to realise they can no longer talk to their beloved Daddy is something they will not be able to understand for some time. May he rest in peace!

Justus was appointed Diocesan Secretary in 1975 and worked tirelessly visiting and encouraging people in parishes. He strongly supported a spiritual renewal campaign and followed that by taking part in a stewardship programme. Extracts from an interview for *Ecclesia*:

> What do you do in the parishes? First I discuss with the people about church council responsibilities. We also discuss self-reliance both from the administrative and from the financial point of view.
>
> Do you think the situation will keep on improving now you have taught them? My experience as a teacher has taught me that no student will master anything without drilling. This programme needs repetition to sink into people's minds.

Justus was highly regarded by everyone who knew him. He was Chairman of the Board of Chilema Lay Training Centre as well as Chairman of the Anglican Council of Malawi. Justus retired in 1980, having served the church in Malawi devotedly for thirty-nine years. He was a quiet, gentle man with immense wisdom, cared for by his wife Grace, especially during his severe migraine attacks. His family of ten children have continued to serve Malawi in a number of distinguished careers.

Maxwell Zingani

Maxwell, like Justus, was the son of a priest from Mozambique, who was teaching at the primary school at Mponda's when, without being prompted, he started Mponda's Christian Stewardship. I have no idea where his ideas came from, but they were good. To be a member of a team you need to have sympathy, to belong to a united home and to be willing to meet twice a week. There you first prayed and then went out to visit Christians and Muslims. Mponda's was a large Muslim village and Chief Mponda's forebears had been deeply involved in the slave trade up to the 1890s. Archdeacon Habil Chipembere backed the campaign, saying that it showed what being a Christian meant.

The Province had been a little edgy about our link with Texas and in our last month in California we floated the idea of a Province-to-Province link between Province VIII, the Pacific Province and the Province of Central Africa. Our bishops accepted this idea and each diocese was asked to find someone to join a team to visit America. Our Diocesan Standing Committee chose Maxwell. In January 1965 the team set off on a two-month speaking tour, which took Maxwell to nine States, including Alaska. One of his messages was that the USA and Africa had complementary gifts – America had the gift of resources, Africa the gift of sympathy.

Back home, Maxwell was appointed a full-time member of the diocesan team, responsible for stewardship, literature and publicity, which included being editor of *Ecclesia* and later also for youth. He was tireless in visiting parishes throughout the diocese, encouraging each to elect effective councils, which should include a good number of women.

His sharing in the All Africa Conference of Churches in the Ivory Coast in 1969 was a major experience in his life. The presence of the Catholic Archbishop of West Africa, a doughty fighter for the openness of Vatican II, astonished him. "Despite our differences, we could talk, eat and pray together in brotherhood." When he came back church unity was near the top of his agenda.

In the Central Region, the CCAP (Church of Central Africa Presbyterian) synod had a different tradition to that of Blantyre, which had been influenced by a team of dedicated missionaries belonging to the ecumenical Iona Community. Nkhoma Synod in the Central Region had been planted by missionaries of the South Africa Dutch Reformed Church who had grave doubts about Roman Catholics. Maxwell wrote in *Ecclesia*:

> Rev Magombo of Nkhoma Synod CCAP said it was new for him to preach in a Roman Catholic church. Please pray hard for the guidance of the Holy Spirit that all the churches in Malawi may be one.

Stephen Makandanje, the Malawian priest I had known in Swaziland, visited Malawi for the first time since 1975. Maxwell was obviously moved by Stephen and I ordained him as a voluntary priest in 1979 just before he retired. The last page of the last number of *Ecclesia/Mpingo*, of which he had previously been editor, tells the story of his retiring to the little Muslim village of Chigonera, between Monkey Bay and Mtakataka where he and his wife Rhoda farmed and where we visited them in 2005.

> When I retired to Chigonera we were four families totalling 15 people. They were planning to build a church. I joined them and the walls were finished but we had no grass to thatch it with till the next season. But only half would turn up for Sunday worship. So I started visiting and to my joy found another 10. Chigonera is predominantly Muslim. As I go round I talk to people to find out if they would accept Christ and join either the Roman Catholic or the Anglican church. We are now 70 Christians in All Saints church.

Maxwell goes on to describe how other congregations began at Matapan'ombe, Kapiri, and Golomoti and how "Canon Martin Malasa (a retired priest who came from a Moslem family) although of ill health, is 'a big light'. Six people came to see us and told us he is their spiritual and physical father and adviser." Maxwell went on to start a branch of the Mothers' Union and a choir. A few years later, when a group from England was staying at the nearby Kaphiridzinja lake shore cottage, Maxwell brought his choir, who were excellent.

Maxwell was a gifted speaker with a great command of Chichewa and English, who captivated those listening to him through his vigour and sincerity. This made him an excellent interpreter and when the Archbishop of Canterbury, Robert Runcie, visited Malawi in the late 1980s, Maxwell was brought down to Blantyre to interpret for him.

Maxwell served the Diocese with creativity and dedication for fourteen years looking after stewardship, literature and publicity. In 1969 he represented the Diocese at a conference of the All Africa Conferences of Churches in the Ivory coast which convinced him of the importance of working together with other Christians, which he did with his usual energy. Stephen Makandanje visited Malawi in 1975 and Maxwell was obviously moved by meeting him. Just before he retired in 1979 I ordained Maxwell as a voluntary priest.

Maxwell Maputwa

The third of the trio was Maxwell Maputwa who came at the beginning of 1964 from being headmaster of the vast primary school at Nkhotakota to teach at Malosa Secondary School. African music was a special interest and after a short course at Mindolo Ecumenical Training Centre in Zambia, he set out to find and popularise the Malawian hymns sung to traditional tunes which had been collected by Canon Hicks at Nkope.

In January 1966 Maxwell was asked to assist Majorie Francis, who was starting a chain of Sunday Schools. This was a vast operation involving training volunteers all over the diocese and keeping them supplied month by month with lessons in Nyanja and Yao. Maxwell then went for further training at the College of the Ascension at Selly Oak, Birmingham, and in April 1968 came back with a Diploma in Education to take over from Marjorie.

From then on the two Maxwells worked hand-in-hand running joint courses in stewardship and religious education. Barnaba Chipanda, one of the liveliest and most dedicated young priests, reported on one such course for the churches on Likoma and Chizumulu islands:

> Mr Maputwa said we must take a keen interest in our children. They were our future hope. He told us of Our Lord's teaching about young children and showed us how to use visual aids and bible pictures and how to make our own apparatus and lesson notes.

Maxwell wrote about a visit to The Bar, a Muslim village on a sandbank at Mponda's where Lake Malawi runs into the Shire River:

> After the service I asked them how they survived as a church. They said they believed in practical Christianity. I asked what they meant. They gave two examples:
>
> * the church elder said they went with their catechist to build a house

for a Muslim leper who was not being looked after by his own family. He was living in the new house.

* the women went to cultivate the garden of an old Muslim woman, too old to do it herself. They said, "We're now looking round to see if there is anyone else we can help."

The catechist told me that every week he receives Muslims who wish to become Christians because they see Christians here showing love and sympathy to anyone in need.

Maxwell had the ability to recruit and inspire new volunteers. In 1973, after the division of the two dioceses, he reported that in almost every parish in Southern Malawi, lay people were visiting Sunday Schools and were using their own bicycles:

In one parish in Mangochi the volunteer is a woman day-school teacher. She leaves her own children at home and cycles to various Sunday Schools, I found her cycling from Mponda's to Mpinganjira, a distance of ten miles. I asked her, "How do you like work?" She replied and said, "It's a call, and I am happy to respond. I very much enjoy it."

In 1978, Maxwell was appointed Education Secretary-General of the Christian Council of Malawi, releasing his enthusiasm into a wider sphere but involving a move to Lilongwe. When I had the privilege of ordaining him as a voluntary deacon in April, many prominent Presbyterians took part. David Onaika took his place as Religious Education Adviser for the Southern Diocese. David was a former catechist of great ability, one of a group sent to Chilema for a year's training to prepare them for priesthood.

In October 1979, Maxwell was sent to Jerusalem on a ten week course at St George's College. Our monthly news sheet *Ecclesia* had by then been renamed *Mpingo* and printed Maxwell's vivid account of nine days in the Sinai desert, part of which I quote:

There was to be no recorded music, no radio and no contact with the rest of the world for nine days. We left behind money and important documents. It was an act of faith; we trusted in the experience and competence of the staff. We were beginning to understand the faith the Israelites needed to leave the security of slavery in Egypt and to venture into a new land. It is so easy for us to find false security by becoming slaves to so many things of minor importance.

Maxwell was ordained as a voluntary priest by Bishop Peter Nyanja on 22

July 1979 in St Mary's church at Biwi, where he was to serve the people of this traditional housing area of Lilongwe. To the great loss of the church in Malawi, Maxwell died in 1987.

Mothers' Union

Editors: A Christian organisation, the Mothers' Union (MU) has been going internationally since 1876. It works to end poverty, inequality and injustice by working at grassroots level in communities bringing hope and practical support. In 2024, there are 13,000 members in Malawi. Donald said of those he worked with:

Margaret Woodley retired in 1968 after thirty years' service initially as a nurse at Nkhotakota, and from 1953 leading the Mothers' Union throughout the diocese. I was always grateful for her wisdom and experience.

Helene Jones followed Margaret, she describes Easter morning at Matope:

> When ninety adults are baptised at one service, people walk eighteen miles to make their Easter Communion and women come round the houses at 4.00 a.m. singing the Good News, it leaves a lasting impression. After the Easter ceremonies, the people took the remains of the Paschal Fire into their homes to rekindle their cooking fires, this, for me, was most touching.

Helene was enthusiastic and did a great job with the MU, also running courses for clergy wives. For a successful one in Nkhotakota she was joined by Joyce Nyirenda a midwife at St Anne's Hospital who later succeeded her. Helene retired in 1971 after a time of ill health.

Joyce Nyirenda, a daughter of Archdeacon Choo (see "Developing a Malawian Church"), wrote in 1971:

> As the Mothers' Union Worker I joined the Christian Education Team of the Diocese of Southern Malawi in April, we went round the diocese training councillors, church elders, Sunday School teachers and members of the Mothers' Union. I must say I have been impressed by this training team.

Joyce was a good encourager, she continues:

> One encouraging thing is that younger women are showing great interest in the Mothers' Union. May I ask that wherever this happens, these ladies should not be delayed. If they are not received they lose interest and change their mind. In the past new members waited for

a long time and as a result they have been discouraged. Area Leaders should inform the priest about new members and ask him to do something. My appeal is that Area Leaders should be helped so that they may do their work properly.

May I ask that every PCC sees to it that they consider the Mothers' Union group to be just as important as church elders and councillors and that they should help by seeing that each congregation has a strong and active group.

Joyce was one of five representatives from Malawi, and the only Anglican, to a Women's Leadership Training Seminar for Eastern and Central Africa held in Uganda in April 1972, attended by 75 women. After the seminar she stayed on to visit MU branches and wrote:

I have seen that there is not much difference, except they have more workers. I noticed members are very interested in their work, making many crafts. Their organisations are very good, with committees and presidents in all branches.

Joyce continued working in the diocese until 1978 when she moved to the Diocese of Lake Malawi continuing her work with the MU, living at Chinteche where she also helped at the clinic.

Elizabeth Ngoma became the MU Worker for urban parishes in and around Blantyre in March 1975, while Joyce covered the rest of the Diocese working from Mponda's.

Elizabeth wrote of the MU at Christ the King church in Soche:

We meet on Saturdays and have a number of things on our weekly programme. They often visit the sick at Queen Elizabeth Hospital and in homes, hold discussions, learn sewing and cooking, tidying up the church and its surroundings. I visited all parishes at least twice a year, especially in the remote areas.

Before joining the Diocese, Elizabeth was a primary school teacher in a government school in Blantyre, prior to that she was a social worker in Zimbabwe, where she joined the MU.

Elizabeth attended a Pan African six-month Women's Leadership course at Mindolo Ecumenical Foundation in Zambia, from where she wrote:

We are 14 women from nine African countries, all of us are interested in serving our sisters better. Our subjects included community leadership, planning programmes, economics, bible study, office practice. My room mate is Mary from Sierra Leone, an expert in tie and dying cloth, which I am interested to learn.

The monthly diocesan paper *Ecclesia* reported on a four-day Women's Leadership course held in April 1976 attended by twenty-five women from different parts of the Diocese run by Elizabeth. Subjects included human relations, child care, vegetable growing, the role of women in the church, sick visiting. Mrs Malango Banda was Chairman and Mrs Chikoko Secretary. The closing ceremony came up with some wonderful activities from the women on their role in the church. During the Mass the only man, the priest, conducted the service but the rest was done by the women, Mrs Ngoma preached while Mrs Chikoko administered the chalice.

The girls of St Agnes Guild and MU members were thanked for taking care of the participants during the course and the Archbishop was thanked for encouraging women by giving licenses to two women to administer the chalice.

With the growth in numbers and workload Alice Chilinkwambe was appointed a MU Worker for the urban areas in July 1977 and Elizabeth moved to live at Malosa the headquarters of the Diocese and wrote:

Peter and Elizabeth Ngoma, 2005

> I met so many challenges, looking after women's work throughout the Diocese, representing women at many diocesan meetings, member of the Boards of Malosa and St Michael's Secondary Schools and Chilema Training Centre.

In September Elizabeth was joined by Joyce Nyirenda and Alice Chilinkwambe in running a very successful seven day MU conference at Chilema Ecumenical Training Centre. In the same year Elizabeth chaired the committee of the WWDP (Women's World Day of Prayer) in Blantyre and was elected to the Christian Council of Malawi, the first woman member of the Council.

As Chairman of the WWDP Elizabeth attended an international conference in Lusaka in April 1978 attended by eighty representatives from forty-five countries. The conference was opened by the President Dr Kenneth Kaunda. Elizabeth wrote: "I was highly impressed with what was discussed at the meeting, we made plans in advance up to 1984."

For further development it was possible to arrange for Elizabeth to go to Birmingham in September 1978 for a year's course on Mission, Social Studies and theology at the Selly Oak colleges. While there the MU asked her to join delegates from Central Africa to attend the Worldwide Conference in Brisbane, Australia where she was able to meet my brother Felix.

True to form, in 1980 Elizabeth organised a creative five-day MU conference at Malosa Secondary School that I enjoyed opening. It included a retreat and biblical sessions led by my successor, Bishop Dunstan Ainani. The report added:

> There were a number of other topics such as health education, home economics, pastoral care and a visit to St Luke's hospital where we cheered the sick with hymns and prayers. We had forty-five from both rural and urban parishes, including working-class members (people in paid employment). A new Executive was elected at the Annual Council meeting with Georgina Chikoko as Chair, Elizabeth Secretary and Alice Chilinkwambe Vice Secretary.

Elizabeth retired as MU Worker in 1988. She and her husband Peter went on to found a flourishing primary school in Bangwe township in Blantyre.

[*Editor*: Elizabeth celebrated her ninetieth birthday in January 2023.]

Alice Chilinkwambe MU Worker for urban areas wrote enthusiastically of a conference she organised in Matope Parish in November 1977:

> Since we had our courses at Chilema last year the women are rushing in doing their duty to God side by side just like men. Four women of the CCAP (Church of Central Africa Presbyterian) preached the word of God.
>
> Fr Dunstan Ainani celebrated the closing Mass which was well organised by MU members, who read two lessons and for the first time the chalice was administered by a woman who possessed the Bishop's licence. Both men and women Christians were happy to see and receive the Holy Communion from one in the Christian family without any hesitation. Praise the Lord.

Alice made the most of a five-month Leadership course at Mindolo Ecumenical Centre in Zambia in 1978, a three-month Women's Home-making course at Magomero and continued excellent work in the urban areas.

The Voluntary Ministry

The idea of a voluntary ministry had been with me from Swaziland days. On my first visit on a Vespa scooter to Hlatikhulu I was astonished to find a large church, serving an African congregation near the hospital. This was led by *Stephen Makandanje*, a Yao-speaker from the far south of Malawi. He had become a Christian during his medical apprenticeship and had then walked the 1,000 miles south to Hlatikhulu, where he found work as a Medical Assistant. In 1915 no Swazis in that area had heard of the Anglican Church, though there was a small whites-only chaplaincy. So Stephen asked to be put on night-duty and in two years, working single-handed, built a church for a hundred people, moulding and burning bricks and begging money for cement, doors and windows. He then set out to fill it.

As mentioned earlier, he refused. But when asked if he would be ordained without payment, he accepted. Bishop Tom Savage accepted him for ordination but thought normal training was not appropriate, so Stephen lived with us for a year as part of our Usuthu team.

When I first heard of Roland Allen, who coined the name "voluntary ministry" his ideas, enfleshed in Stephen's ministry, seemed to provide a solution to one of our greatest problems: how Malawian clergy could minister with confidence to the growing numbers of professional and business people in our urban congregations. Until the 1970s these were still being served by expatriate clergy. The idea of Voluntary Ministry was fine – but how could candidates be selected and trained?

In 1966, quite unexpectedly, a letter came from *Gerry Hotblack*. Gerry had had three careers. As a professional soldier had served in the front-line in World War One and in officer-selection and training in WW2; as a teacher he became deputy-head of Blundell's, a well-known public school in Devon, now he was an apple-grower. He had stayed with us in Swaziland. His letter said that he was currently a voluntary priest and that he and his daughter, Joan, who had retired from being an accountant in Kenya, would like to come and see what the possibilities were of being voluntary missionaries in Malawi.

They came, and a day or two later said:

> This is where we should like to work if you would have us. Voluntarily of course. Could you think of building us a house, naturally at our expense? It will belong to the Diocese when we retire or die. But first we must talk to our family.

A little later, a letter came to say they had made up their minds and we would find a tree up the hill from the diocesan office, with string round it to mark the site where they would like to live. It took time to find the tree, but like all Gerry's plans, this one worked. They arrived in 1967 and stayed for the next seven years.

The house was designed by Jane and built by one of her teams at the Building Department. As well as being the parish priest at a distance of Mulanje and Thyolo, Gerry set up a scheme, modelled on officer selection in the British army, for the selection and training of clergy. On his eightieth birthday in February 1971, *Ecclesia* noted that he was "as busy as ever as priest, gardener and adviser; he and his daughter Joan continue to keep Malosa alive!"

Gerry retired in 1972 when he and Joan went to live with relatives in Harare.

Frank Mkomawanthu had been Headmaster of Malosa Secondary School, Principal of an Education College in Blantyre, held senior posts in the Ministry of Education and was always an active member of every parish where he lived. I had the privilege of ordaining him priest in St Paul's Blantyre in 1978.

In May 1971, the *Requirements for Voluntary Priests* were published. Sometimes this was referred to as the "Tent-Making Ministry", from the way that St Paul maintained himself. A Voluntary Priest must have a secure job, a solid record of voluntary work as a layman, willingness to undertake a fairly tough three-year course of private reading, and strong recommendations from the congregations where he lived and where he worked, from the interviewing panel and from the Diocesan Standing Committee. There was some understandable unease among the stipendiary clergy, most of whom had made great sacrifices of money and time in order to be ordained, but generally the plan was accepted.

In 1976 I wrote in a small booklet for USPG entitled, *Out of Africa Something New*:

> The tent-making ministry appeals to the African sense of history: this is how the Church began. It reflects the African sense of the unity of life and evades the false split between sacred and secular. It helps a congregation to grow and to throw up its own leaders. It encourages true ministry, which is serving and not ruling.

It was good that the idea of voluntary priests was also being widely taken up in Britain, often under the clumsy title of "The Non-stipendiary Ministry", now being replaced by more positive names such as "Self-supporting". Perhaps the best title of all is its original one, "The Tent-making Ministry".

Inspiration from the wider Christian community

Editors: The Diocese gained from international contacts as it became more self-reliant. This section summarises some of them.

Donald and Josiah at Lambeth 1968

Lambeth Conference

As mentioned earlier, Bishop Josiah Mtekateka and I headed for London in August 1968 for what for both of us was our first Lambeth Conference, chaired by the loveable, holy and wise Archbishop of Canterbury, Michael Ramsey. We arrived full of fears. Would the moves towards unity in our brash young Province be slapped down? Would we appear foolish in the eyes of the young and concerned?

The first few days didn't help. The mediaeval pageantry, the trumpets, the scarlet and white – what had this to say to the Black ghettoes of apartheid in South Africa?

The group of sixteen for which I had opted, dealt with the laity and I had been made secretary. Could we meet with laypeople who could tell us what their problems were? Security said, "No!" We had been provided with one layman and one laywoman from among the consultants in case we wanted to see what they looked like. We circumnavigated this obstruction. Our first witness, a merchant banker, told us that at forty-seven he was the oldest member in his firm. A quick calculation on the first names in *Who's Who* at Lambeth showed an average age of sixty-two.

There were more hopeful signs. Only one bishop appeared in old fashioned leg gaiters on the first day, and he not again. Most of us lunched in one of the then popular pancake bars – there were no central dining arrangements. Bishop Neil Russell's motion calling for radical reassessment of titles and forms of honour was carried by applause without dissent.

Michael Ramsey's opening sermon foreshadowed themes that would recur again and again. God was a God of compassion, concerned about all human life, not just our religious activities and concerns; our faith would be tested in what we did about peace, race and poverty; Anglicanism was not a separate encampment but a bright and unself-conscious colour in the Christian rainbow; unity did not mean combining churches as they are now, it meant radically transforming them.

In my report to our diocese I wrote:

> Christ requires those who exercise leadership in the Church to be servants of all. We bishops have often obscured this truth. What we do and how we do it should remind people of Jesus the Servant.
>
> There is nothing new in this. Bonhoeffer in a Nazi prison, Fr Damien on his leper island, St Francis with his begging bowl, all tell us about Christ, the Man for Others.
>
> Many of us still think of hospitals and schools as things done for us by kind friends in the West. We have to learn that these are done by us for our neighbours, most of whom are Muslims or of African Traditional religion.
>
> Our group on the laity said in their report that the Church's task was to challenge all that cramped fullness of life. We called for active support for all who struggled for a fuller and better life for humanity, including Marxists and Humanists whom many Christians saw as public enemies. We called for dialogue with those whose expertise in psychology, economics, journalism and the social sciences could lead to fullness of life – irrespective of their faith or lack of faith.
>
> We were encouraged to develop the ministry of voluntary priests which Stephen Makadanje had exemplified in Swaziland and Gerry Hotblack in Malawi. Lambeth said, "Go ahead. This is consistent with scripture and the early Church. There is no evidence that recruitment to full-time ministry has been affected."

The ordination of women priests? Surely, some said, this was alien to the patriarchal structure of much of Africa? Yet the bishops from our neighbouring Province of East Africa (Kenya and Tanzania) told us they had twenty women in training to be deacons and that as Taizé priests they could be a way of restoring a full sacramental life to dioceses where twenty or thirty congregations shared one priest.

I spent a week-end at Taizé on my way back from Lambeth. It is a small rural village in Burgundy, France and an inspiring place to be. A living example of reconciliation and unity with this wording over the entrance:

All you who enter here be reconciled
The father with his son
The husband with his wife
The believer with the unbeliever
The christian with his separated brother

The ecumenical community of ninety Brothers was founded in 1940 by Brother Roger Schultz. Most of the Brothers were scattered all over the world, working together in pairs in Africa, South America, USA and elsewhere.

When at Taizé I was deeply saddened to hear of the death of Christopher Lacey. I knew that he was seriously ill with a gastric ulcer but never dreamed that it could be fatal. There is more on Christopher Lacey in the Appendix.

People joining the Taizé Community in prayer

Uganda and Kenya

From Taizé, I flew to Uganda where Archbishop Erica Sabiti, whom I had met at the Lambeth Conference, was extremely generous and we visited some of the work that was going on.

The Church in Uganda was almost wholly African and vast numbers attended. The Church Missionary Society had been led by prophets such as John Taylor and had been preparing for African independence for twenty years. Young clergy had been trained for leadership, large churches had been built in strategic places which could become cathedrals. There was now only one white bishop out of ten and only a handful of missionaries.

There were, of course, plenty of problems. The clergy were paid by their congregations, nominally twelve pounds a month but half were not receiving that. Anglicanism had come in one form only and almost everywhere prayer books used the old 1662 format translated into the local language despite the efforts of Leslie Brown, the last white Archbishop, to introduce a new liturgy based on the lively South Indian rite which he had devised.

From Uganda, I went on to Kenya on the invitation of Bishop Obadiah Kariuki, a veteran of the Mau-Mau struggle, who had taken part in my consecration seven years earlier. I had never seen a church so alive or growing so fast. Here, also, the clergy were paid by their own congregations, but at twenty-five pounds per month. I was told that they all received their money, though this may not have been true in less developed areas.

Health in Nyasaland, 1899-1996

Soon after arriving in Nyasaland I called on the Director of Medical Services. He had just received his budget from the Federal Government in Salisbury, Southern Rhodesia. Nyasaland was at this time an unwilling member of the Central Africa Federation of Southern/Northern Rhodesia and Nyasaland. Harold Macmillan had seen the Federation as a way of dealing with the poverty of Nyasaland without having to spend very much money. The Director threw the papers onto his desk. "I am expected to provide medical services for the whole of this country of three million people on the same budget as that of Salisbury Hospital in Southern Rhodesia."

This unequal division of Federal funds for health in 1958 are quoted in Michael and Elspeth King's *Story of Medicine and Disease in Malawi*:

Population	Health expend.	African admissions	Govt Hospitals
Nyasaland	2.8m	£ 715,000	64,000
S.Rhodesia	2.7m	£3,655,000	475,000

The figures illuminate the reasons for my predecessor, Bishop Frank Thorne's opposition to the proposed Federation, which was British policy throughout the era of Harold Wilson's and Harold Macmillan's governments.

Malaria

In 1897, Ronald Ross proved the connection between malaria and mosquitoes. He wrote:

I find thy cunning seeds O million murdering death.

A few years later he passed my mother for service as a nurse in Malaya, despite "a dicky heart", as she used to call it, from teenage rheumatic fever. In Malawi, sixty-five years later, we were fortunate with malaria. For twenty years, two paludrine a day and one daraprim a week gave all four of the Arden family total protection, but by the time we left in 1981, malaria was developing resistance to anti-malarials. For Malawians, this was not an option as it destroyed the immunity which protected most adults from the severe outcomes of malaria.

When our son Chris went back in 1988 to finalise his medical studies he confirmed the increasing resistance to chloroquine and other drugs.

By the age of five, most Malawians have developed sufficient immunity to make malaria a major nuisance but not a life-and-death issue, except for the very young and pregnant women, for whom it can be lethal. "Perma-nets" – permanently impregnated nets – and the spraying of internal walls with DDT are today the only defence.

The first UMCA (Universities Mission to Central Africa) doctor, Robert Howard reported on arrival on Likoma in 1899:

> In the past six years, twelve missionaries have died and six were invalided home.

Usually this was the result of "blackwater fever", an advanced stage of malaria. As a versatile builder, carpenter and harbour-master, he built Nkhotakota Hospital in 1902, followed by Malindi Hospital in 1908.

Nurse Kathleen Minter describes Nkhotakota Hospital in 1899:

> It was many months before anyone would come for treatment. My first patient was a slave wife who had fallen in the fire, burning her arms and knees badly. She had been lying there for five days. No one around would help her. Neema, our one-legged cook, is the first African here to wear a wooden leg.

A footnote: Robert Howard and Kathleen Minter married in 1910 and were exiled to Zanzibar for breaking the rules of UMCA by "committing matrimony".

Medical Assistants

Editor: From the beginning (1890s), the mission trained local people to work alongside the doctors in order that they could practise independently. Malawi had so few qualified doctors that Medical Assistants were and are essential for delivery of the health service.

Dr Howard realised the urgent need to train African staff and in 1900 asked Edward Nemeleyani to take up medical work. Edward was awarded the Order of the Epiphany (an award given to lay people in the Province of Central Africa, Botswana, Malawi, Zambia, Zimbabwe) for outstanding service just before I arrived.

Edward Nemelayani and Swinny Mtiesa were the first Medical Assistants to take charge of a hospital, Edward at Nkope, Swinny at Malindi, which is where I found him in 1961. Edward died in 1968 after sixty years of devoted service.

Swinny Mtiesa began his training at the UMCA Hospital at Liuli in Tanzania, followed by four years at the Scottish Mission Hospital in Blantyre, the predecessor of the present Queen Elizabeth Hospital.

Following the Chipembere rebellion in 1965, people in and around Malindi were arrested and detained without trial. Swinny, one the gentlest of people, was taken into political detention, where he remained for many years. A large number were held for years, some in solitary confinement, under appalling conditions. When speaking with people after their release, I used to marvel at their lack of resentment and bitterness over what they had been through. Swinny personified this generous spirit.

Soon after his return to the hospital in Malindi, Swinny realised that his eyesight was failing so travelled the one hundred and twenty miles to see the Israeli eye specialist at the Queen Elizabeth Hospital in Blantyre. After careful examination, he was advised to return to Malindi and learn Braille as he would soon have no sight. A disappointed Swinny returned to the people and hospital he loved, wondering how long he would be able to continue to serve them. A man of deep faith, anchored in prayer, who began and ended each day in the hospital with prayers with staff and patients, Swinny prayed for guidance and help.

A few months later he had a dream. He should return to the Queen Elizabeth Hospital so that his eyesight could be cured by an American doctor. Not knowing why but sure that he should follow his dream, Swinny went to Blantyre. When he arrived at the hospital, the Sister in charge of the crowded ward, who respected his many years of work as a Medical Assistant, put him in a private room.

The next day, while Swinny was lying on his bed, he heard the voice of a visiting eye-specialist asking, in an American accent, "Who's in this room?" He was told that Swinny was beyond treatment. The visiting consultant said he would like to see him anyway. After examining Swinny and listening to his story, the consultant said to him, "I can't promise anything but I did read in a recent journal that massive doses of vitamin B12 occasionally help people with your condition. Let's try it." Swinny was not only cured but continued working for many more years.

Late one night, I was staying with Swinny at Matope, where he was in charge of the Health Centre – a hot, humid place beside the Shire River with very active, king-sized mosquitoes. There was a rap at the door. Some miles away, a family had gone down with cholera, then a new illness to us. Swinny left at once and popped around to a friend with a pick-up truck. Half an

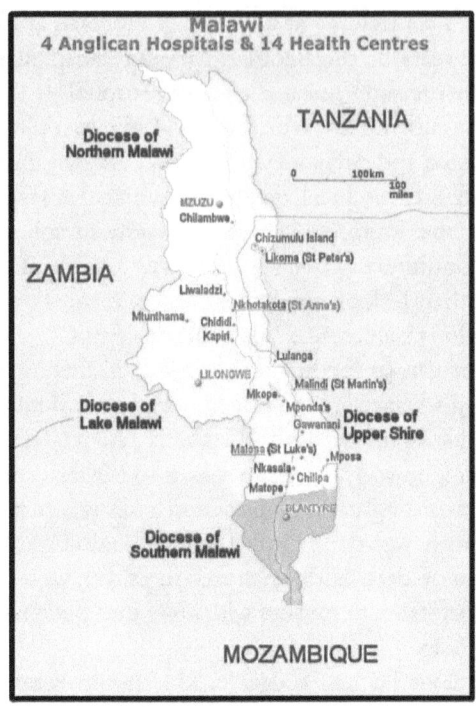

hour later, he returned with half a dozen adults and children writhing in agony. He set up saline drips and I went to bed. At sunrise the family was laughing and chattering on the ground beside the pick-up.

The following year, I met a Muslim man whose problems had defeated the government hospitals in Zomba and Blantyre. He was saying that Jesus had cured him through Swinny's hands and now he was visiting all the Muslim homes in the Matope area with a Chichewa Bible New Testament saying, "This will tell you about Isa (the Arabic name for Jesus) who has healed me."

While at Matope, Swinny's diagnostic skills appeared on the front page of a national newspaper in the shape of a glass jar containing 988 worms. A man had travelled to see Swinny from Blantyre, where people had been unable to diagnose his problem. The worms were his reward. Each time we have returned to Malawi, we have visited this saintly man, though in 2005 he was nearly blind and very old.

A few months after returning to Nyasaland from our fundraising tour of the States we were desperate for a doctor to help build a hospital to replace the one built in 1913, which was higher up the hill at Mkuli. St Luke's Hospital was to be nearer the main road at Malosa.

I said to Jane, "Do you remember a doctor at Houston Cathedral saying he would consider work in Nyasaland? A slightly built man I think?"

This led to *Art and Nan Johnson* (she was a nurse) and their three children coming to St Luke's early in 1965. I think Art was the biggest man I have ever met, with a generosity to match. Nan was only slightly smaller. They arrived with a huge metal container packed with everything for an operating theatre, laboratory and much else for the hospital they would help to plan and build.

The metal container was so large and so heavy that a slipway had to be dug into the ground so that the lorry carrying it could reverse down into it and the container manhandled off with wooden poles. The container is still at St Luke's, housing the standby diesel generator.

By the time they returned to the States in 1968, St Luke's consisted of an operating theatre, laboratory, and male and female wards. They were a wonderful pair and poured out their energy, expertise and love on everything and everyone.

Art and Nan Johnson were so impressed with Swinny Mtiesa's medical work that they invited him to visit them in Texas in 1969.

Training Midwives

The systematic training of Malawian midwives in the Diocese was later than that of medical assistants. It began with Margaret Woodley at Nkhotakota in 1941 at St Anne's Hospital, which has always specialised in children and maternity care. The UMCA history quotes Margaret:

> The Midwives Training School began with five pupils. I had arranged the official opening for 26 August at 11.00 a.m. but at 10.30 there was great excitement, "Come quickly, we are going to open the school with a baby!"

Three hundred and forty-seven babies were born in the hospital in 1946 and the Training School provided a steady stream of midwives. In 1963, I wrote to my brother Felix, a paediatrician in charge of the Children's Hospital in Brisbane:

> We have two UMCA fully-trained nurse-midwife tutors overseeing nurse-midwives in eleven hospitals and health centres dealing with 500,000 outpatient attendances a year.

In July 1970, a new Student Midwives' Hostel, designed and built by USPG missionary Michael Ryan, was opened by the Netherlands Ambassador, whose government, together with the Beit Trust, had given the funds. Japanese nurses, under a scheme similar to VSO (Voluntary Service Overseas) joined the training staff in 1973. For a number of years until his death in August 1979, Dr George Kunkwenzu, a dedicated Christian and much-loved doctor, was in charge of St Anne's and its Training School.

Christian Health Association of Malawi

Clearly, we needed proper training for nurses. But how and where? And who would staff it and pay the bills? The problems seemed beyond solution. Then Janet Lacey, one of the founders of Christian Aid, responded to an invitation to come out and stayed for a week visiting many of our health centres and hospitals. She gave us wise advice:

> Get together with all the other churches involved in health work, then send a letter from all of you to the Christian Medical Commission (CMC) in Geneva and ask them for someone to come to see the challenges and suggest a plan.

We did exactly that. As far as I know, Catholics, Anglicans and Presbyterians had never had a joint meeting in the seventy and more years they had been working in Malawi, let alone the Seventh Day Adventists. Within a month or so they had all agreed to an invitation being sent to the CMC and in August 1965 Dr James McGilvray came. He visited every one of the twenty church hospitals and, in two weeks, secured their agreement to work together in the body now called CHAM – Christian Health Association Of Malawi. He spent his last night with us, having come from a hospital with a strong evangelical tradition. "I was asked by a missionary sister, 'Does this mean we might have a Roman Catholic nun working in this hospital?' I was so exhausted I just said, 'Don't worry, my dear, she wouldn't stay long!'" We were told later that CHAM was the first such body in the developing world.

The first Secretary of CHAM was Hugo Niemer, a tall gentle doctor from the Netherlands with a long grey beard. Under his guidance, CHAM forged much closer links with the Ministry of Health, which, ten years later, agreed to pay the salaries of all qualified Malawian staff. Its first conspicuous achievement was setting up ten nurse training schools, one at St Luke's, Malosa, in the Southern Region and one at St Anne's, Nkhotakota, in the Central Region. Unfortunately, Dr Niemer's work came to a sudden end a few years later when at midnight his car hit the weekly train at the Balaka level-crossing. Both Hugo and his daughter, who was driving, died instantly. In the 1980s, the Nursing Council decreed that midwives must also learn general nursing and St Anne's Training School came to an end. Everyone applauds the raising of standards but these have done little to end the high rate of maternal death in Malawi. In 2006, 807 mothers died in childbirth. In Britain, the figure was 11 per 100,000 live births. The training at St Anne's may have fallen short academically, but it did include two months at an outlying Health Centre with no electricity. Their experience was learned the hard way, in keeping with the hard life most Malawian women face.

In a country where only four percent of the population had access to electricity, the experience of delivering a baby by the light of a paraffin lamp was useful. This was far from ideal but it ensured that student midwives experienced the reality of childbirth in a village house which is the way most Malawians of today have come into the world.

Update (2021): The Christian Health Association of Malawi (CHAM) is the largest non-governmental healthcare provider and the largest trainer of healthcare practitioners in Malawi. CHAM provides thirty percent of Malawi's healthcare services and trains up to eighty percent of Malawi's healthcare providers.

Susan Cole-King and her family came to Malawi in 1964. Her husband, Paul, was the first curator of the newly established museum in Blantyre and wrote a number of excellent booklets about the history and pre-history of Malawi. Their four children overlapped with our two in ages.

Dr Susan Cole-King

Susan had had a vivid spiritual experience while still at school, which led her to train as a nurse. After completing her training, she met Dr Banda, then practising as a doctor in London, following which she decided she would train as a doctor and work in Malawi. Before arriving in Malawi, she had been stimulated by the ideas of Professor David Morley, known as the Under-5 movement. He said that the lives of millions of children could be saved and vastly improved by monitoring those under five years of age, teaching mothers about nutrition and childcare and immunizing children against killer diseases that killed and crippled children all over the developing world.

When Unicef began to publish their annual State of the World's Children reports, Malawi was seven places from bottom in a league table of all countries in the world. In Malawi, 320 out of every 1,000 children died without reaching the age of five. All the countries ranked lower than Malawi were at war, recovering from war or in the Sahel, the semi-desert region south of the Sahara. This laid the foundations for the continuing improvement in childhood mortality that we still see today.

Quietly, Susan, now employed by the Ministry of Health, put David Morley's theories into practice in a rural clinic near Chiradzulu, in the Southern Region. Within three years, the government was convinced of their soundness and the Under-5 campaign was launched with a series of seminars for health workers at the newly founded Chilema Ecumenical Lay Training Centre. A year or two later, Susan was given the job of launching the Under-5 clinic movement on a national scale. The fruits of her pioneering work, along with that of hundreds of Malawians, are that, in 2005, the death rate of children under five had fallen from 320 to 189 per 1,000.

In 1971, I was given a report on child health in the Domasi area, a small part of the Lake Chirwa plain which I could see every day from my study. The writers had interviewed 171 women about their children. Between them, they had lost 160 babies under one year old; a further 52 before they were five; and another 68 at a later age. The women recognised the symptoms of kwashiorkor – protein starvation, a common cause of child death. When asked what were the causes:

> 143 said "breaking a sexual taboo"
> 8 said "witchcraft"
> 25 said "don't know"
> 3 said "the wrong kind of food".

They all know only too well the symptoms of malaria, but only nineteen percent thought it was carried by mosquitoes. Thirty-six percent of these women had been to school as had sixty percent of their husbands.

This was not in a backwater. Zomba, until then the centre of government, was only ten miles away. Domasi, the leading government Teacher Training College, was adjacent to the area surveyed; Zomba Government Hospital and our own St Luke's were within easy reach.

The report made me think furiously. We were proud of our schools, which had some 50,000 children attending daily. Were they learning any of the simple lessons for their own children to survive? A few days later, I was to give the address at the national interfaith service for the Independence Day anniversary in Kwacha Hall, Blantyre, as I had done several times previously. The address, attended by all the Cabinet, would be broadcast throughout

Malawi. It was an opportunity to say something more than the bland platitudes customary on such occasions. I forget exactly what I said, but it included the gist of the report above, which I felt to be a challenge to all of us – churches, schools, hospitals and government. The result was unexpected. A motor-cyclist arrived the next morning summoning me to report to the Malawi Congress Party immediately. There I found most of the Party Executive awaiting me. I was not asked to defend or explain what I had said, just to understand that anything bordering on criticism was totally unacceptable, even if true.

The impetus of the Under-5 programme was unstoppable and the nurses and medical assistants at health centres and hospitals adopted it with enthusiasm. Whenever I visited one, I was told of new mobile clinics served by staff on bicycles. I would find nurses at out-patient clinics using the opportunity to teach Under-5 mums the basics of nutrition and protection against malaria. The task continues to be enormous.

Susan left Malawi after nine years to work at Sussex University. After a brief period with the World Health Organisation in Geneva, she became the Chief Medical Adviser to Unicef. During this time, she developed a wide understanding of HIV/AIDS.

Responding to a call long felt, Susan was ordained priest in New York in 1987. Taking part in the service were the Assistant Bishop of New York, together with Bishop Hugh Montefiore – who was a successor to Susan's father Leonard Wilson as Bishop of Birmingham, and myself, providing a link with her beloved Malawi.

Susan Cole-King's ordination in New York in 1987
From left: Donald Arden, Susan Cole-King, Dennis Walter, Hugh Montefiore

On 6 August 1998, the anniversary of the atom bomb falling on Nagasaki, the Archbishop of Japan asked Susan to preach to the bishops attending the Lambeth Conference. This was partly an acknowledgement of her gifts as a preacher but also honouring her father, Bishop Leonard Wilson, who, as Bishop of Singapore, had been a prisoner of war in the notorious Changi jail where he had confirmed one of his Japanese jailers. Susan's sermon on peace and reconciliation was said by many to be the highlight of the Conference.

Listening to Susan was James Tengatenga, Bishop of Southern Malawi. When Susan later asked him if there was anything she could do to help clergy and people in the diocese with the challenges they were facing over HIV/AIDS, he was clear that there was. For two years running, Susan spent several months in Malawi learning about the devastation of the pandemic and leading workshops for clergy and lay people. In these, she emphasised the important role for Christians in removing the stigma attached to AIDS and in supporting both those infected and the people looking after them. People who shared in these workshops said how much they helped build their understanding of Christian caring. Susan's premature and sudden death in 2001 was a great loss to people in Malawi as well as to her family and many others.

Leprosy

I encountered leprosy the week after my arrival in Pretoria in 1945. All "lepers" in South Africa were incarcerated in Westfort Leprosarium, on the edge of Pretoria. There were around a thousand people, mostly "Native" with a handful of "Coloureds" and "Europeans". Their only common meeting place was the chapel, where Pip Woodfield and I took turns at a weekly Eucharist. The accepted medical opinion was that leprosy was caught by contagion; you must never "touch a leper". I felt brave when I occasionally shook hands. There was little else you could do when you spoke only one of South Africa's ten languages and Katie was not with you.

Katie Volmink was a "Coloured" granny, almost blind, grossly disfigured who had only one leg. For the people of Westfort, she was the personification of Christ. When anyone, of whatever race, felt death approaching, they would just say, "Please send for Katie." Within a few minutes, she was alongside them, holding their hands and would stay with them till they had died, even if it was forty-eight hours later.

At our weekly Eucharist, Pip and I spoke in English and Katie would translate into Afrikaans, a second interpreter into Tswana and a third into Zulu or Xhosa (which are remotely similar). The leprosy bacillus had "burned itself out" in Katie, and after I left Pretoria she was discharged from Westport and spent her last years with her family. We kept in touch until her death.

UMCA had been concerned about the high incidence of leprosy in Malawi from the very beginning. Dr William Wigan, who served the people of Malawi for thirty-six years from 1911 to 1947, pioneered leprosy wards at Likoma, Likwenu, Malindi and Mponda's. The German government admired his dedication so much that even after the outbreak of the 1914 war, he continued to supply medical care to the leprosy patients on Lundu Island, off Sphinxhaven, as Liuli was then called, while the Germans provided the food. "An impressive example of enemy co-operation" as Michael King describes it.

Because of UMCA's initiatives and good work caring for people with leprosy on Likoma Island, Nkhotakota, in Tanzania and at Malindi, the government in 1926 gave UMCA three hundred acres of land at Likwenu for a leprosarium. This adjoined the site where Malosa Secondary School, the Diocesan Headquarters, Chilema Ecumenical Lay Training Centre and St Luke's Hospital, would later develop. In 1931, there were around one hundred patients, including "burnt out cases" who had settled on the edge of the mission land. The situation was similar in the 1960s, when Bill and Muriel Walters and Smythies Umande were in charge, supported by Lepra, the Leprosy Relief Association. Biti Kulanje was a leper village north of Malindi, where people who had recovered from leprosy were sent to live and cared for.

A sea-change came in 1966 with the arrival in Blantyre of David Molesworth of Lepra, with the incredible mission of wiping out leprosy in Malawi.

Dr David Molesworth

It was thought that 20,000 people had Hanson's disease, as leprosy was now renamed to help it shed its biblical image. David told me that leprosaria were the problem and not the answer. People would never accept treatment if it meant immediate removal from their home and family, perhaps for life. If we went mobile, leprosy could be eradicated. David set up a programme in a hundred square miles around Blantyre and within a few weeks had more patients under treatment than all the leprosaria in the country.

Likwenu was the next area. Bill and Muriel Walters, together with Smythies Merikebu, adopted the new policy enthusiastically. It was made known throughout the Kasupe (Machinga) area that a medical worker would, without fail, be at a certain store, school or tree at a certain hour on a certain day every fortnight. His job was to supply two weeks' worth of pills and hope.

Within two or three months, Likwenu and its satellite centres were looking after many hundreds of people with leprosy. Muriel died of cancer in January 1973 and was buried at the Leprosarium. Other churches and agencies, having seen the impressive results obtained at Likwenu and Blantyre, adopted the same strategy until the whole country was covered.

In 1976, Peter Garland, the former Principal of St Michael's Teacher Training College, Malindi, was ordained as a voluntary priest, joined Lepra and was based at Likwenu. He was also given responsibility for coordinating transport for all Lepra programmes. This was largely push-bikes and motor-bikes to keep down costs while making it as certain as possible that one of the leprosy teams would be under that tree on time. A little later, David Molesworth moved to another country and Peter, who had moved to Blantyre, became an Archdeacon and head of Lepra in Malawi.

Peter Garland (1997) with his Order of the Lion, which was the highest order awarded by the Malawi Government

I was visiting Blantyre in 1995 when it was officially announced that leprosy was no longer a threat in Malawi. This was a huge achievement for all the field-workers and staff of Lepra and for Peter's leadership. The odd case might occasionally appear – the borders with Mozambique were porous and the incubation period is long, but the campaign ended. The President of Malawi bestowed Malawi's highest award, the Lion of Malawi, on Peter in gratitude for his huge contribution to the eradication of leprosy in Malawi.

By the time we left in 1981, the Anglican church in Malawi was responsible for four hospitals and fourteen health centres. The four hospitals were St Luke's Malosa, St Anne's Nkhotakhota, St Peter's Likoma Island, St Martin's Malindi.

Malawi Against Polio

Malawi Against Polio (MAP) was conceived in the hills behind Mangochi in July 1977. Ibrahimu, aged fifteen, had crawled half-a-mile on hands and knees to be confirmed. He was completely normal except that he had never been able to walk because one leg stopped short at the ankle. Each week he had crawled half a mile to attend his confirmation class.

A simple operation and a cheap peg-foot were all he had ever needed for fourteen years to enable him to walk. But such things were not available in the remote Muslim village where he lived.

I was angry with his father and asked him why he had not tried to get medical help. "Ever since he was born, each time I come home from the Copperbelt in Zambia I carry him fifteen miles to Mangochi Hospital. Each time they say, 'Go home and wait till you are called.' But they have never called me." On the previous day at each of two confirmation services a girl had been carried up for the laying-on-of-hands. Both were paralysed as the result of polio, their legs useless bent sticks.

Boy with Polio – Chilipa 1963

Jan Borgstein and understanding the challenge

A few days later, still angry, I met Jan Borgstein, the Dutch senior surgeon in Malawi, at a reception on State House lawn. "Why are you doctors doing nothing about polio?" By the time we had finished talking we had agreed that Jan would look after the surgical side and that I would organise a small survey to make a case for action. How big was the problem? No one had any idea, though motorists knew that quite often they would have to slow down to allow a girl or boy to shuffle across the road on their hands and bottoms.

We decided on a sample survey of those within reach of the seventy-mile road from Malosa to Malindi on the eastern lake shore, with a detour to include Balaka. Letters were written to the few schools we knew of within reach of the road, asking for children with these problems to be brought on Saturday, 26 November 1977, to the roadside or to one of the schools, churches or health centres on the route that we intended to follow. We hoped that we might see perhaps a hundred youngsters.

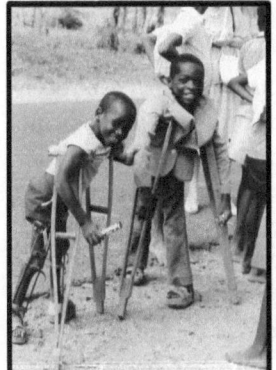

Boys with Polio

We began at St Luke's Hospital where there were 50. At Liwonde there were 60 and we decided to divide into two groups, one doing a detour to Balaka, the other carrying straight on. Some came crawling, some were carried, some on the backs of bicycles, some hopping on poles. None of us had ever seen so much needless suffering on any one day. Needless, because all the polio could have been prevented by three doses of vaccine and all the clubfeet could have been straightened while the children were still babies.

It took three Saturdays to complete our mini-survey. Five hundred youngsters with such problems had come to the roadside or to one of the health centres on our route, not counting another 60 who were blind or arthritic. Jan Borgstein's plan had been to give up his Saturdays to operate on those affected at St Luke's or at another hospital on the route. This would hardly make a dent in the problems the survey had revealed. There was no orthopaedic surgeon and only one physiotherapist in a country four times the size of Wales.

I wrote at the time in the Diocesan Newsletter:

> The good news is that nearly all the hundreds who came hopping on one leg, crawling or carried can even now be put back on their feet. Whose fault was it that this was allowed to happen? Nobody's.
>
> Whose fault if this goes on? Ours. If you are a leader in the church, please tell your people – "Polio can be prevented, club-feet can be

straightened, crippled children can learn to walk again. If you earn more than the average wage or live overseas please help us to buy the vaccine and the leg-irons. If you happen to be a physiotherapist or an orthopaedic surgeon we can think of lots you can do so that all of Malawi's children can go "walking and leaping and praising God" like the man Peter and John healed in the temple. You can read that story in Acts chapter 3.

An SOS was sent off to Save the Children and other agencies. Jan told us of an orthopaedic surgeon in Sydney called *Ron Huckstep* who had been interned in China as a child and had his first informal lessons in medicine while in prison. More recently he had headed a campaign against polio in Uganda. Having been trained as an engineer before becoming a doctor he approached problems as an engineer. Currently the only way of getting a pair of calipers was to visit the Queen Elizabeth central hospital in Blantyre. He would measure the child, who would then return home and report back a month later for a fitting. The Huckstep approach was to see that every rural clinic in Malawi had a stock of wooden calipers of different sizes.

Huckstep had visited Malawi some years earlier, but there was then no political will and nothing happened. This time he was more subtle. President Banda had recently made a large donation to the Royal College of Surgeons in Scotland, where he had trained as a doctor; in return they had made him an Honorary Fellow. Huckstep arranged to collect his medal in Scotland and bring it with him to Malawi. This gave him instant access to the Head of State instead of the usual month's delay. He was rewarded with the promise of an hour's broadcasting time each week on Radio Malawi, and the support of the chairman of the Malawi Congress Party in every village in Malawi who now had more power than the chiefs.

In his ten days with us Ron Huckstep visited the north to see the problem in remote village areas and held a non-stop seminar in Blantyre from Friday morning to Sunday night. This produced an action plan and more importantly, backing from every section of the community. It was resolved to form MAP – Malawi Against Polio. Miss Cecilia Kadzamira, President Banda's official hostess, was elected into the chair, Dr Jan Borgstein as medical adviser and myself as secretary. Now we had at least a framework but still no funds. I was asked to send an appeal to every charity I could think of.

Rotary donates money to kick off MAP
One of the reports was sent to my brother Felix in Queensland. When he

had arrived thirty-five years earlier as head of the Brisbane Children's Hospital, he was the only paediatrician in Queensland and the Northern Territory. He had been involved in public controversy about the treatment of polio and had visited us in Malawi more than once. What none of us in Malawi knew was that Clem Renouf, the new head of Rotary's world-wide programme for Health, Hunger & Humanity was a personal friend of Felix. He also had a problem: six million dollars in a bank in New York and no idea of how to spend them. Felix showed my letter to Clem with dramatic results. Funds quickly became available and a succession of orthopaedic surgeons came to Malawi and passed on their skills to clinical officers and nurses. World Orthopaedic Concern, founded by Arthur Eyre-Brook, an orthopaedic surgeon from Bristol, who visited Malawi, enabled his retired colleagues to teach their skills where they were desperately needed.

Michael and Elspeth King's *The Story of Medicine and Disease in Malawi* records that in the first two years after MAP was formed 21,167 patients with polio, clubfoot and other kinds of trauma were seen. Five hundred and seventy-two operations had been carried out, many by visiting volunteer surgeons, and 18,000 appliances issued, all made in four MAP workshops.

Jan Borgstein, who had inspired the whole campaign and whose dedication was total, saw none of the results of his vision. As I was flying back from Colorado in June 1979, Jan died of a heart attack climbing the 10,000-foot Mulanje Mountain. A message from his wife Ankie Borgstein was waiting for me asking if I would conduct his funeral, but please without any religious reference as he was an atheist on principle. I forget exactly what I said but in my mind was the reply Jesus made to his disciples when they told him they had stopped a healer from working because he was not "one of us": "He that is not against us is for us", Jesus told them. Six of Jan and Ankie Borgstein's seven sons have become doctors, including Eric who is now Professor of Surgery at the Queen Elizabeth Hospital where Ankie still works part time as paediatrician.

The campaign spread to other developing countries and was broadened to cover other contagious diseases. In 1985 Rotary reported that since 1979 their Health, Hunger & Humanity programme had assisted seventy new long-term projects in forty-three developing countries at a total cost of 21.4 million dollars. Forty-nine million doses of polio vaccine had been administered.

Michael King followed Jan Borgstein as senior surgeon. The book *The Story of Medicine and Disease in Malawi* published by him and his wife Elspeth includes a photograph of sixteen children on crutches going to school from the Rumphi clinic, started by Gwen Gibbs in 1978. Gwen was a do-it-yourself missionary physiotherapist who began the work of MAP at Lilongwe and then moved on to Rumphi in the Northern Region. Supported financially only by her mother in North London, she built and ran a hostel for thirty disabled school children before moving on to work with leprosy patients in Tanzania, where she later died.

One of my first pleasures when we moved to Uxbridge in 1981 was to meet with a local doctor, Paul Binks and his wife Margaret, who had worked with MAP in Malawi for a number of years. They were both Rotarians and, although Margaret had developed terminal cancer, had decided to return to Malawi in joint service to children with polio.

In 1996 Chris Lavy, now professor of orthopaedics at Oxford, decided with his wife Vicky, who was a GP, to work in Malawi for four years. He wrote:

> Many people ask why we went. We could give a spiritual answer about going where God guides – and that would be true – but the simplest answer would be that we were needed. The 12 million people in the Greater London area had 200 consultant orthopaedic surgeons. Malawi, with the same population, had none. We planned to stay for four years but after six we were building Malawi's first orthopaedic hospital in Blantyre and I had to stay to see this through. Before we knew it we had been in Malawi for ten years and had three children. That hospital is now the Beit CURE international teaching hospital with 66 beds specialising in treating the orthopaedic needs of children and adults.
>
> Was it worth it? I saw and operated on thousands of patients, ranging from wild animal trauma to untreated club-foot so severe that the patients' soles were facing the sky as they walked. I saw children with legs so bowed that their buttocks touched their ankles, and spines so twisted that their chest and pelvis faced different directions. They seemed happy as they went cheerfully away after the operation with the bent part generally straighter than before. Only the long term will tell whether the benefit was lasting.

Thanks to massive efforts by official institutions and Rotary International, polio in 2013 is found in only five countries – Kenya, Nigeria, Afghanistan, Pakistan, Somalia. More than two billion children have been immunized since 1988, with the co-operation of twenty million volunteers and international funding of the order of three trillion dollars.

Marriage and its problems

"Marriage discipline" in the African church had made me uneasy for twenty years. Now I was responsible for it. Girls seemed to graduate automatically from the confirmation class to the penitents' class as they became pregnant. In Pretoria I asked my elders and betters about the boys: they replied enigmatically, "Well, you can't tell." The rules seemed daft, but I had no power to change them. Now I could no longer dodge the challenge.

Soon after my arrival in Malawi, I was conducting a confirmation in a strongly Muslim area near Lake Malombe, in a congregation led by *Yohana*, a returned soldier. His wife Anna had been a Muslim but was baptized before she and Yohana married in church. They had three children before Yohana joined the army in the 1940s and was sent to Ethiopia. Family pressure brought to bear on Anna, who gave up her Christianity and was married again to a man of her old faith whom her family had chosen for her. She was now the second wife of a Muslim.

Yohana came back to his village after the war and made every effort to persuade Anna to rejoin him but without success. After two years of bachelordom, he married Mary, a Christian girl, by village custom. They had several children, two of whom I confirmed. The church elders and priest said that Yohana and his present wife were the mainstay of the congregation, now about a hundred strong. They had been together for fifteen years and their home was an example to Christians and Muslims alike. Both were "under discipline" – they could not receive communion.

After hearing their story, I lifted the ban. Then the priest asked, "Can they now be married in church?" I had to say "No." Church law saw him as still being married to Anna, now a Muslim; to marry Mary in church would be bigamy. I saw a string of unanswerable questions coming up, "Don't they need the grace of marriage? Doesn't the Bishop want them to be faithful to each other till death?"

On the way home I reflected on the women of Esizibeni, the smallest, newest and most vibrant of our congregations in Swaziland. Every one of its ten members were women who were married to men of Swazi traditional religion. All of them would have been excommunicated for life under existing Church law.

I wrote in the next *Ecclesia*:

Our marriage must express the spirit of the Good Shepherd who came to seek and save the lost. I came to Malawi from Swaziland where Christianity was often planted by Christian wives of polygamous husbands. It was a profound shock to learn that in Malawi none of them could have been baptized, not from any fault of their own but because they had the misfortune to belong to a society where polygamy was the rule. Changes are coming. One of them is that baptism will no longer be refused to a woman who is married to a polygamist.

I do not believe that the Christ who refused to condemn the woman caught in adultery would refuse the means of grace to a woman today who, caught in the meshes of an inhuman economic system, does the best that her conscience and her priest can tell her to do.

The "inhuman economic system" was of course migrant labour. At the time I wrote, 300,000 of Malawi's 600,000 men of working age at any one time were outside Malawi, on Witwatersrand gold-mines, on mines and farms in Southern Rhodesia (Zimbabwe) or on the Copperbelt of Northern Rhodesia (Zambia). In Mangochi District, where Yohana and Mary lived, women out-numbered men by two-to-one.

The Province considered all these problems and in 1969 one of many important decisions was to make it possible for a "non-christian man with more than one wife to be received into the church with his believing wives and children and in due course to be confirmed and to receive communion provided the local community gives its willing consent." This had been forbidden by the Lambeth Conference of 1888 and had caused much heart-burning, especially where we were working in Moslem communities such as the southern lake shore and the question had come to the fore in the researches by Adrian Hastings.

A new canon came into force, which provided for a small panel of three, usually the parish priest and two local lay-people to listen to the couple and make their recommendations to the bishop. I wondered how this would be received. Instead of the shock I expected, everyone seemed delighted. John Liomba, a teacher who had been ordained as a voluntary priest, had been going through his parish records at Malindi and wrote:

> Ellen Chuma's case I found the most fantastic. Ellen, now in her later fifties, was married to a faithful Moslem named Ngulinga some forty years ago. Hence she was excommunicated in the middle of 1931, in the days of Bishop Gerald Douglas. She has remained so until now. I

could not believe this. I felt water collecting in the corners of my eyes. Forty-two years! But whose fault was it? Could poor Ellen have made a better choice?

The answer was "No."

Ernest Chimpango was a victim of the harsh discipline of UMCA days, like so many Malawians he went to Southern Rhodesia to find work. He came back to the Ntchisi area after two years away, only to find his wife had found a new husband. He spent a year trying to persuade her to return, but it was too late.

Reluctantly he remarried and was promptly barred from communion. I went out to his village and found the whole congregation indignant. Women and men all agreed that a man could not live alone in a village. Ernest was their father-in-God in a huge parish with many congregations where a visit from the priest was a rarity. At a long meeting with the local clergy, they all agreed that he should continue as a lay leader in the congregation.

Ernest later moved to Blantyre, 150 miles from Ntchisi, and set himself three tasks: to build up the Chewa-speaking congregation at St Paul's; to found a new congregation at Chilomoni – some miles from St Paul's; to build a semi-circle of churches from Chileka airport to Magomero, where the first missionaries who had come with Bishop Mackenzie in 1861 lie buried. Ernest was working for Air Malawi when I ordained him as a voluntary deacon in 1977, together with Douglas Cook one of the leaders of the Thyolo congregation. Ernest's wife was now leader of the Chilomoni branch of the Mothers' Union in the congregation he had begun. On 18 February 1979, Ernest and Douglas were both ordained priests.

Chapamanga congregation on the Mozambican border in the south-west corner of Malawi, began in 1979. A member of the congregation approached Fr Antonio, a Catholic priest, saying that there were refugees from Mozambique who wanted to be baptized. He said he had too much work on hand and sent the request on to me, addressed to Likoma Island! The letter eventually reached me and I passed it on to two splendid laymen at Nchalo Sugar Estates, Gileburg Chiweko and George Mtsinje. One worked in their head office, one in the sugar plantations. For several months they struggled each Saturday by bicycle the fifty miles of sandy road to Chapamanga to instruct the new catechumens, and to lead Sunday worship. Then fifty miles back again. I was happy to be able to ordain them both soon afterwards as voluntary deacons and later as priests.

A year later Ernest Chimpango was called from Blantyre to baptise this group. In an interview with the editor of *Mpingo* (as *Ecclesia* had now been renamed) he said:

> It is fifty miles from Nchalo and it is a long way on a push-bike. I found that everything had already been organised by the two deacons. On the first day I failed to baptize all the 100 people, I only baptised seventy-two because I got tired standing up to the waist in water in the River Mwanza. It was good that the area was hot; if it had been Blantyre it would have been different (Blantyre is 800m higher).

Since then we have been visiting this place and we have more than forty-five Christians who were confirmed by Bishop Ainani on 25th May.

We left Malawi soon afterwards and I was not able to visit Chapamanga myself as I had a long visit to Botswana and Matabeleland to fit in. Ernest Chimpango kept up his work for many more years. I happened to be in Malawi when he died in 1997 and was proud to be asked to preach at his funeral in Blantyre, for which Justin Malewezi, Vice-President of Malawi, came down from his home in Ntchisi. I had been right to break the rules and restore Ernest.

Building Department

The Building Department was created by *Arthur Rawlings* a UMCA layman who arrived in 1937 with the job of Diocesan Builder responsible for maintaining buildings and creating new ones.
When I arrived Arthur was living at Nkhotakota concentrating on teaching young men how to build.
Writing in *Ecclesia* in 1962 he spoke of the need for social centres where Christians of all denominations could meet together. Putting words into action he went with twelve of his builders to Lilongwe to build a community hall next to St Peter's church.
Next on his list was to build the new diocesan headquarters at Malosa with its office and houses. This included improving the water scheme from the river which also supplied the secondary school and leprosarium. With the increasing demand for new buildings in different parts of the diocese Arthur recruited local contractors whom he oversaw to maintain his high standards.
I wrote in *Ecclesia* in November 1964:

> Arthur Rawlings is returning to England. The news was not unexpected, three years ago he had planned to work in England but stayed on with his usual unselfishness to build the new diocesan centre and to organise a building team that would carry on after he had gone. Many young men remember his patient teaching with gratitude, and many fellow-workers remember with affection one who was never too busy to listen to their troubles. Thank you Arthur for your twenty-seven creative and dedicated years of service in Malawi.

Walter and Norma *Fagan*, together with their three children arrived from Texas in June 1965. Walter to look after the Building Department and Norma to help me with correspondence. Walter was given the title "Master of Works", with responsibility not only for buildings but also for maintaining water and electricity supplies to Malosa Secondary School, Leprosarium, Chilema Ecumenical Lay Training Centre, Diocesan Headquarters and St Luke's Hospital.

The backbone of the Building Department were the builders who had been trained by Arthur Rawlings, the chief of whom was Dunstan Mzokomera. Alongside them were electricians, plumbers and mechanics trained at Malindi by Francis Bell, the gifted UMCA engineer who served there for thirty-eight years.

Working closely with Dunstan Mzokomera, who usually accompanied him, Walter travelled throughout the diocese checking on the three or more contractors building health centres.

Having been a colonel in the army, Walter was a good organiser but more importantly was quick to develop genuine friendships with people, especially the staff of the Building Department. He was always good at asking questions and listening to advice. After three years' hard work and making a huge contribution the Fagans returned to Texas.

Jane succeeded Walter as "Master of Works" assisted and guided by her deputy Dunstan Mzokomera. She had been drawing plans for the Building Department since 1965.

All non-government architects, concerned by the killings in the Congo following its independence in 1963, had left the country before Malawi became independent in 1964. Jane was guided by the people who would be using the buildings and had lessons from a friendly government architect seventeen miles away in Zomba. Some of the fruits were operating theatre, wards and staff houses for the new St Luke's Hospital, the "Aertex" buildings for St Thomas' Hostel for secondary school students in Mangochi – so named because of the open-brickwork providing ventilation and light.

Later buildings have included the new larger outpatients block at St Luke's and Kaphiridzinja, the diocesan cottage on the lake shore. The latter was largely funded by Christian Aid and friends of the diocese and planned to provide somewhere for diocesan staff to rest and recuperate. One of the first and regular users was Justus Kishindo, our tireless Education, and later Diocesan, Secretary and his family.

Oxfam, German and Dutch agencies kept Jane busy with her drawings and buildings for hospitals and health centres. Dr Maurice King, the author of the medical bible for the tropical world, had been visiting Malawi and recommended to the Ministry of Health that they build outpatient departments to Jane's St Luke's design at all government hospitals. He published her plan in the next edition of his book.

Dunstan Mzokomera as deputy Master of Works played a key role in coordinating the work of the four or more different contractors, ensuring their work met high standards. None of the buildings could have been completed without him.

Dunstan succeeded Jane after we left. One of the first jobs he was given was to build a new Church of the Ascension at Malosa, replacing the one earlier destroyed by fire, for which he received universal praise.

Jane at the drawing board

Ardens leave Malawi 1981

An abiding memory will be the day of the farewell party at our house in Malosa in February 1981 just before we left Malawi, we were all startled to see a large government lorry coming up the drive. A beaming Josiah emerged saying he had asked a friend to bring him as he couldn't possibly miss the party! It is my abiding hope that someone will write an adequate life story of this great man while memories are still fresh.

Editor: Bishop Dunstan Ainani delivered a speech at Bishop Arden's Farewell Party on 25th January 1981 at Chilema:

> Bishop D. Arden came to Malawi from Swaziland in 1961. He was consecrated Bishop of Diocese of Nyasaland on 30th November 1961 in the Church of the Ascension, Likwenu. At that time the Anglican Diocese included the whole country. This involved too much travelling on pastoral work by one bishop.
>
> In 1971 it was found necessary to divide the diocese into two, hence the formation of Diocese of Lake Malawi with its headquarters in Nkhotakota and Diocese of Southern Malawi with its headquarters at Malosa. Bishop Josiah Mtekateka was elected the first Malawian Bishop of Lake Malawi.
>
> Bishop Arden was then elected the Archbishop of the Province of Central Africa in 1971, following the tragic death of Archbishop Oliver Green-Wilkinson, which includes Zambia, Botswana and Malawi. This meant more work as it included the oversight of eight dioceses in the four countries, this at a very critical period when there was severe fighting in Rhodesia (now Zimbabwe).
>
> Bishop Arden's term of office has not been an easy one. He was consecrated Bishop only a few years before we gained our independence in 1964, during which time many Europeans who were not dedicated left the country. But Bishop Arden stayed and performed a wonderful service in Malawi which has earned him the honour of CBE by Her Majesty the Queen.
>
> During his term of office as Diocesan Bishop of Southern Malawi he has encouraged ecumenism among the Churches in Malawi which has resulted in the formation of institutions like:

Chilema Ecumenical Lay Training Centre
Christian Service Committee
Christian Council of Malawi
Christian Literature Association in Malawi
Private Hospital Association in Malawi
Theological Education by Extension in Malawi
Zomba Theological College jointly with the CCAP

Not only has he helped to improve relationships among Christians but he has gone further to coordinate with Government in some major development projects among which Malawi Against Polio is the most remarkable. This project is one of his last projects which has involved him in a number of meetings with high-ranking government officials.

Within Diocesan Institutions he has provided guidance to various Boards of Governors as an active chairman such as:

Malosa Secondary School
St Michael's Girls' Secondary School at Malindi
Medical Board of Dioceses of Southern Malawi
Anglican Council in Malawi
Urban Development project, just to mention a few.

We would be failing in our duty if we didn't give an account of what Mrs J. Arden has done alongside Bishop Arden to make his success. She took on a very difficult line which many men cannot manage – that of Master of Works. During her term of office the following have been built:

St Lukes's Hospital and Nurses Training School
Lulanga Health Centre at Makanjira
Mkope and Matope Health Centres
Chilipa and Gawanani Health Centres
Mposa and Nkasala Health Centres
Mkope Blind School
Monkey Bay FP School
Malindi Rural Centre

Has improved Malindi and Mponda's hospitals and many other Diocesan institutional buildings.

In the meantime the Building Department has been offered a contract to build Zomba Theological College.

She has been Chairman of the Mothers' Union both on Diocesan and Provincial levels. And she has always offered both material and moral support during moments of sorrow, especially at funerals. She has wept together with our women in our traditional way. That is something she will always be remembered for.

If I had to say everything which Bishop and Mrs Arden have done during their stay in Malawi it would take the whole day till midnight. We wish them all the best of everything in whatever God has prepared for them.

Having said all that, the Anglican Church wants to state categorically that all this progress has only been made possible because of the wise and dynamic leadership of our beloved Life President Ngwazi Dr H. Kamuzu Banda, who gives full support to the developments in the church. Apart from allowing freedom of worship he has personal interest in the activities of the church. May the Lord give him long life to lead this nation in peace and prosperity.

By the time I left Malawi in January 1981, Peter Nyanja was Bishop of Diocese of Lake Malawi and Dunstan Ainani had succeeded me as Bishop of Southern Malawi.

Bishops Peter Nyanja, Donald Arden, Dunstan Ainani, Josiah Mtekateka (1980)

Postscript

There are now four dioceses in Malawi.

Diocese of Lake Malawi (1971) – Diocese of Northern Malawi (1996) – Diocese of Southern Malawi (2002) – Diocese of Upper Shire (2002).

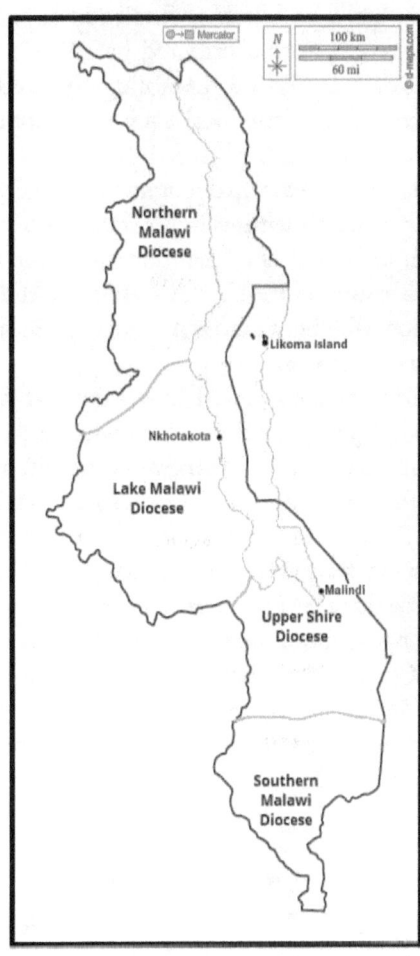

St Margaret's Uxbridge

For the first eight months of 1981 we were on "terminal leave" – ominous term! – spent in USPG houses in London available to missionaries. I started job-hunting, not easy when the Church of England was still on the old boys' network. Town jobs were mostly distributed by bishops to priests whom they knew from their days at Oxford, Cambridge or Durham. Rural posts depended on the patrons, often the local squire. A clapped-out Australian from Africa fitted into neither slot.

Tom Butler, a worker priest who had taught electronics at the University of Zambia and who had stayed with us in Malawi, was now Archdeacon of the Willesden Area in the Diocese of London and came to our rescue. At Uxbridge there was a town-centre church only a quarter of a mile from another. He didn't know whether to close it or give it one last chance. Would I give it a go and find out what to do?

In September I went to be interviewed. It was my first time in north-west London. They had said, "Just get off the train when it stops," but omitted to mention that the line branched at Harrow-on-the-Hill and I was halfway to Amersham when the penny dropped. I arrived at Uxbridge an hour late and there were Don Price and Fred Teather, the two churchwardens of St Margaret's, waiting to meet me and quite unperturbed. They were to be my right and left hands for the next five years and remained friends for life.

St Margaret's, I later found out, had been in existence at least from 1200 when Radulfus was Chaplain of Uxbridge but the present building dated from the late 1300s. It had a magnificent south transept – actually bigger than the nave – added around 1450, which was said to have the second finest timbered roof in Middlesex. It was in the heart of the town right opposite the underground station.

In the 1960s the congregation had been down to seventeen, but my predecessor had brought it back to life in the 1970s and Don and Fred left me in no doubt that things were happening. After a long talk they gave me a key and left me to explore for myself. It was a cold and drizzly winter's day and when I unlocked the old oak door the church smelled of decaying hassocks. I thought of Ezekiel in the valley of dry bones and his question: "Can these bones live again?" The story ended with the bones coming to life.

I said "Yes" and the door opened on a new chapter of our lives. Thanks to its position in the centre of the town, members of the congregation every Saturday morning welcomed passersby for refreshments, within a year, due to many volunteers, this welcome extended from Monday to Saturday.

A large hall owned by the parish was ten minutes away where a youth group, Brownies, Guides and community groups met. I floated the idea of selling the hall and using the proceeds to reorder the church, as was happening in a number of churches in London. Response from the PCC and congregation was enthusiastic. Young and old joined visits to five recently reordered churches, an architect was appointed and numerous meetings considered proposals.

While all this was going on members of the congregation met together in "clumps" providing pastoral care to people living in groups of roads. Youth groups increased their activities, including camping weekends in Wales. Young people arranged informal evening services, also enjoyed by the over seventies. Energetic bell ringers rang the eight bells twice a week.

Thanks to Tom Butler remembering Jane's work with the Building Department in Malawi, she was invited to fill an unexpected vacancy for a Buildings Officer at the London Diocesan Board for Schools with its one hundred and fifty-two schools. For the first three years she coordinated work maintaining schools and building several new ones. For the remainder of her fourteen years with the Board, she wrote handbooks summarising legislation and procedures for headteachers and governors, many of which were used nationally.

Clergy stop being paid when they are seventy. A few months before I was pensioned off, the PCC and Diocese agreed work could start on creating a two-floored flexible building for worship, coffee and much else. Together with others I had had the interesting part of helping this happen. The hard job of working with the contractor and architect to bring the plans to life was left to my successor. We had enjoyed every minute of our five years at St Margaret's and now had to find somewhere to live.

Fred Teather and Don Price at Uxbridge

St Alban's North Harrow

We had had nowhere to live after leaving Uxbridge. Once again Tom Butler came to our rescue. He wrote to all parishes in the Willesden Area asking if any had a spare house for a spare bishop. The Vicar and PCC of St Alban's North Harrow said, "We'll have him."

In April 1986 I began twenty-five happy years as an honorary curate at St Alban's and an assistant bishop in the Diocese of London. Raymond Jones, a spiritual and pastoral priest and his wife Jo, gave us a warm welcome. Very sadly Raymond died from Leukemia a few months after we arrived. Churchwardens Wally Packer and David Browning ensured I learned my new job.

Later in the year a fire destroyed the large hall next to the church. The insurance made possible the building of a new hall closer to the church, with a covered passage between the two.

Simon Farrer, the fulltime curate, looked after the parish until Peter Hemingway, vicar of a nearby parish, was appointed to succeed Raymond. He and his wife Babs helped to develop the parish. As a voluntary curate I did what I could to support Peter by helping with services, pastoral care and the work of the PCC.

Roger Davies and Paul Baguley were Lay Readers whose sermons and care for people always impressed me. Paul was later ordained and continued to serve St Alban's as a voluntary priest.

Thanks to twenty or so volunteer coordinators, Clusters came into being, each coordinator keeping in touch with people in a group of roads in the parish and alerting clergy to any particular pastoral need.

Bring and share lunches organised by a team of Cluster coordinators, led by Betty Cooper and Sheila Brownlee, assisted by Jane, became a regular feature of parish life. It was good to welcome people from other faiths and outside the parish to enjoy each other's company as well as the food.

I was always cheered by our quarterly meetings. Neville Johnson was an assiduous minute's secretary, and Valerie Rolph wonderful at keeping in touch with coordinators. Helping with Clusters was one of the joys of my time at St Alban's.

PCC meetings were not always such fun, but I was grateful to be able to keep in touch by attending them when I was not elsewhere. As a member of the pastoral team I particularly appreciated celebrating Communion in people's homes.

I always enjoyed and was encouraged by the weekly ecumenical meetings of ministers and clergy from the five different churches in the parish. We met in each other's houses, prayed together and supported each other.

Members of the congregation were patient about my continual description of our life in Malawi and in 2006 a group decided to go to see for themselves. Gerry and Marilyn Divine, who led the group, Eileen Eggington, Jai Mahadeo, Philip and Paula Crouch, Malcolm and Pam Grant spent two strenuous weeks meeting people and getting to know the country.

A year later Eileen Eggington, Joan Foster and our son Bazil led a group of twenty young people aged seventeen to twenty-five on a two week visit to Malawi. Several people from Malawi have since visited St Alban's and the congregation continues to support work there.

Eileen's enthusiasm for developing a partnership with people in Malawi knew no bounds, in 2008 she became a trustee of the Malawi Association for Christian Support (MACS) where Jane and I were also trustees, and in 2009 became its project officer which she continues to be.

Ordination of women

The ordination of women was something I had encouraged while in Malawi, I joined Movement for the Ordination of Women (MOW) immediately after returning to England. In 1987 Jane and I flew to New York where Bishop Hugh Montefiore, Bishop of Birmingham and I took part in the ordination of Susan Cole-King, who had become a friend during her twenty years as a doctor in Malawi. She was keen to have bishops from the Church of England take part in the service. There is more about Susan in the chapter on Health.

In 1994 I had the joy of ordaining ninety-two women as priests in St Paul's Cathedral on two consecutive days together with a different bishop each day.

In the following years I continued to ordain women as priests in several of London's five Episcopal Areas where the bishop was refusing to do so.

It was good to be able to welcome Joan Foster as Vicar of St Alban's in 1996 where she shared her many skills with the people in the parish and beyond. Joan's creative mind brought to life a delightful all-weather garden between church and hall, providing a popular extension to the hall. She also did much to enliven the vicarage garden where she and Jonathan welcomed Cluster and parish parties.

David Tuck, whom I met in Zambia during the five years he served there, was vicar of St John's church in the next-door parish of Pinner. I was delighted when he became an honorary curate at St Alban's in 2004. David was enthusiastic about interfaith relations and arranged for members of St Alban's to visit places of worship of the many different faiths living in Harrow. I was fascinated by those visits.

Leaving St Alban's

We said a very sad goodbye to the generous-hearted and kind people of St Alban's in January 2011. Our twenty-five years with them could not have been happier. It was the longest time I had ever spent in one place.

As an honorary curate it was possible for me to do a variety of things outside the parish, taking confirmations and ordinations throughout the Diocese but also being involved with other things, including becoming Visitor to the Magdalen Fellowship for clergy who had been divorced and Warden of the Friends of USPG.

Editor: A working-party from the congregation, chaired by Philip Crouch, arranged for a plaque commemorating Donald's service to be installed in the church in 2017.

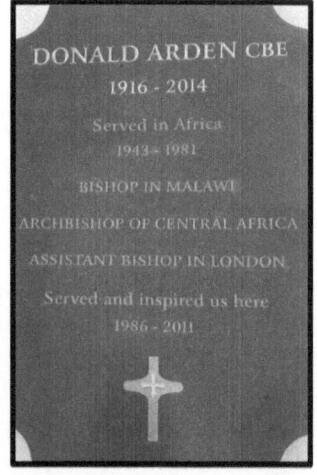

Donald Arden CBE 1916-2014
Served in Africa 1943-1981
Bishop in Malawi
Archbishop of Central Africa
Assistant Bishop in London
Served and inspired us here 1986-2011

St Alban's interludes

The following are excerpts from the diary I kept for the two weeks I visited Mozambique in June 1989.

After co-leading a team visiting Malawi, I took a plane packed with Muslims from Zambia and Malawi who were travelling to take part in a festival in Maputo, the capital of Mozambique. Dinis Sengulane had been elected Bishop in 1976 on the day after his thirtieth birthday. He was the charismatic Bishop of Lebombo in Southern Mozambique and had built many links with friends in Britain and America. The Diocese of Niassa in Northern Mozambique, where I spent most of my time, had few links with any other part of the world.

The Sengulane home, with its four young children, was a first floor flat in a big block in the Avenida Julius Nyere. People wandered in and out of the flat non-stop – a young man from Bloemfontein – a sad looking mother hoping Dinis had found an evening meal for her and her child.

There were street boys outside. Religious Sisters ran a soup kitchen for them, followed by Bible study and an hour of school work, aimed at preparing them to go back to school. They had hopes of starting a carpentry training course.

Dinis is exploring the possibilities of contacting the one credible leader of the MNR (Mozambique National Resistance) in the country and leader of Frelimo (Freedom and Liberation for Mozambique) fighting to rid the country of Portuguese rule. He feels strongly that the present policies are getting nowhere – they both remain strong and could go on for ever. There must be talk of peace. But with whom?

Dinis had a meeting with President Chissano this morning who said, "Only the Church can find a way to peace for us." The British Ambassador is also encouraging and willing to help when opportunity offers. It is an awful responsibility. The Christian Council of Mozambique is carrying on an extraordinary amount of work from its tiny headquarters building.

Monday 12 June

I flew 400 miles north to the Diocese of Niassa with Bertha Manhique, Bishop Paulino Manhique's daughter who was very shy about the English she had learned at school. The tourist book in the plane was bilingual; I read the Portuguese and was corrected by Bertha. She read the English and I corrected her. We got off at Nampula and were met by Bishop Paulino.

Bishop Paulino Manhique has many challenges in his Diocese. He has ten clergy now at Metangula falling over each other's feet. He could transfer a few to Tete and Nampula – but what to do with the rest? Northern Brazil has offered priests with special skills but Government will not grant a post to expatriates, so he has turned down the offer.

I went on to Nampula, halfway to the Indian Ocean. It is ringed by mini moon mountains. There was another party to meet us, led by Grace Zingani, full of excitement. She didn't know that I had a wife but was very anxious that I should give her love to Jane. In UMCA days missionaries were not allowed to marry and I think she is probably still laughing at the idea of Jane and I being married.

Four Sisters of Mother Teresa's Order came to greet us as we finished our Eucharist in Father Silulu's backyard. They came from India, Bangladesh, Uganda and Tanzania. To the three usual vows which Sisters make, these have added a fourth – to share what you have with the poorest of the poor.

Saturday 17 June

In Pemba I had an interview with the Portuguese Governor of the Province, very forthcoming but had no English. He was very appreciative of aid agencies, especially Oxfam. Transport was his great problem. "Don't go off the new tarred main road, there you will be safe from landmines."

Fifteen kilometres from Pemba we made a sudden diversion, they said it was too "gula, gula" nearby, to do some shopping. I thought they meant a few hundred yards – then I was told it was three-and-a-half km – then another ten minutes and we ended up 33 km from the main road. I was not too worried about safety as there were many people about – continuous villages, a bulldozer remaking the road and two check-points. Our destination turned out to be a tiny basket-making set-up, with six people working on the khonde (verandah) and the purpose was to buy me a new hat.

We left at 2.10 p.m., the programme said we had a meeting with the congregation at 2.30, a good hour away. At about 3.00 p.m. and 12 km from the main road, two men came running towards us – "Bandidos in the village!" We waited to see developments – then a third woman came reporting shooting. We headed back to alert the militia. They agree we should have an armed escort to test the road before we travelled on it. They said two other vehicles had passed safely but soldiers on the road reported that two people had been killed in an attack. We went on to another militia HQ at Mecufi, a deserted Portuguese small holiday resort. The very clued-up commandant offered us the alternatives of going now with eight militia or staying the night. As it was dark by now we decided to stay. We sat about in collapsed chairs at the militia HQ until 8.00 p.m. We were then taken to another house with a bed and loo and given an excellent meal of pasta.

Sunday 18 June

Off at 6.30 a.m. with eight militia armed with rifles and bazookas. When we reached the village of the night before – Murébue – we heard reports of two people having been killed and that the children had run away into the bush. Everything in turmoil. I asked to go and see what had happened. Beside a hut was the body of a young man of perhaps nineteen, shot through the chest. Three huts had been burned down, there was a burned-out lorry on the left and a burned-out army ambulance on the right half full of maize. The bandidos had attacked, shot wildly, threw one hand-grenade which did not explode, burned down huts and lorries and after looting, took fourteen captives. The whole village was in a state of shock.

On the other side of the road was another body covered with palm leaves on an overturned bed. They said he came from Pemba, was about 25 and was working on a firewood lorry. He had been shot through the neck and groin and abdomen. The bandidos had disappeared into the bush and the militia did not seem very interested in pursuing them. We took two on board our pick-up and 1 km down the road we passed a man being carried on a stretcher to a clinic 3 km ahead. Half of his jaw had been shot away and the rest was hanging down four inches. We loaded him on the pick-up, dropped the soldiers at the army post and took the patient to the small general hospital.

Then to the congregation who had been expecting us for mass in the Assemblies of God church at 7.00 a.m. ... It was now 8.30, too late for the service so we had a brief meeting in a nearby hotel. I talked in Chichewa and João translated. There were gifts from the Mothers' Union – a carved Madonna, a walking-stick and from Phineas a basket and hat, which had caused all the problems and wrecked the planned service. Everyone was apologetic and reproached Phineas in a variety of languages. To the airport and off about noon back to Maputo and on to London.

It was good to be able to share my experiences with the Willesden World Group when I got back.

In 1998 a Covenant was signed by the Bishop of Lebombo, Dinis Sengulane, Bishop of London, Richard Chartres and Bishop of Niassa, Paulino Manhique.

ALMA (Angola London Mozambique Association)
In 2008 the original Covenant was extended to include Angola. The partnership continues to go from strength to strength.

Retreats

With a little trepidation we signed up in 1990 for our first eight-day silent retreat spent on Bardsey Island, a teardrop in the sea off the tip of the LLeyn peninsular in North Wales. No books, no radio, only a bible and no turning back as the boat only crossed over on Saturdays, weather permitting. No talking, except for half an hour each day with one of the leaders to discuss the bible passage we had been with.

One wonderful night we "found God in all things" while we accompanied a RSPB worker ringing Shearwaters flying in at midnight to their hundreds of burrows on the hillside.

From then on we usually managed an eight-day silent retreat each year in different parts of the country.

Concern Universal

Was a fast growing fully ecumenical aid agency. I joined Concern Universal as a trustee after meeting one of its staff in Malawi during a return visit there. The agricultural work they were doing alongside people in the central region, and a similar project on the Mozambican lake shore, impressed me. They were also doing much to support a variety of water projects. In Sierra Leone staff were running a project for refugees.

I was a trustee for over ten years attending quarterly meetings in Hereford and was fascinated and encouraged by the contribution they were making in some of the poorest countries in the world.

Mines Advisory Group (MAG)

In 1994 as a member of the Mines Advisory Group (MAG) Board, I attended a meeting in the House of Commons on landmines – the anti-personnel variety. Ray McGrath an ex-SAS sergeant who trains mine lifters all over the world, laid out ten of the commonest types of these evil weapons; not designed to damage vehicles or buildings, but deliberately aimed at maiming and killing people. Made from plastic, different shapes and colours, some like powder-puffs. They mostly kill children as they look after goats, collect firewood and maim adults as they struggle to till the land.

One of my most moving days came in 1997 when I was listening to Chris Moon and Princess Diana speaking on landmines. Chris had a leg blown off lifting mines in Mozambique and this year ran one hundred and forty-three miles across Saharan sand-dunes to raise money for the cause. "You don't wibble when you get blown up" has gone into the memory bank.

MACS (Malawi Association for Christian Support)

I was invited to serve as Patron, which I did for many years attending meetings of trustees. The charity has been working alongside people in rural areas since 1993 with local people contributing self-help in local community, health, water, solar and education, http://www.malawimacs.org..

Norway

Three times in the 1990s we spent two weeks in Balestrand on the shores of Norway's largest fjord. The European Chaplaincy arranged for me to be chaplain to the English-speaking congregation in a beautiful hand-crafted wooden traditional style stave church. Every Sunday was like a mini-Taizé with over a dozen different nationalities filling the church.

But there was plenty of time to walk, climb, slip and slide over the snow on the peaks, gaze down over breathtaking views of mountains and fjord, clamber over a glacier using ice-axe rope and nail boots, marvel at the blue of the glacier and puzzle over why the water flowing from it was jade green.

At the end of two weeks we would explore more remote places. In the spectacular Jotunheimen national park, one of the hostels we reached after a day's walk, received its supplies of tinned food once a year by helicopter. We enjoyed watching the reindeer and learning how to crush tins.

Over an evening meal in another hostel, four skilled Norwegian climbers wanted to know where we had done our training for the Besseggen walk we had completed that day. They were adamant I should be profiled in the press for having done it as an untrained eighty-one-year-old. We didn't tell them about my spectacular bruising from hip to knee! The most hilarious time was Jane doing the last ten metres on her backside and I doing ditto twenty seconds later.

November 30th 2011 was the Golden Jubilee of Donald's consecration as bishop. The Bishop of London, Richard Chartres invited Donald to celebrate the Eucharist in St Paul's Cathedral, preached and served as deacon. Donald's robe was made in Malawi.

Romsey and Postscript

Romsey

Romsey is a friendly market town between Winchester and Salisbury and on the edge of the New Forest. In 2011 we moved into a small terraced cottage five minutes from its thousand years old glorious abbey and centre of the town. Chris and Nadine live twenty minutes away and Bazil and Zoe an hour and a half.

I enjoy being back in Hampshire and showing the family the house in Boscombe, where I was born. There is lots to explore, life in the abbey is vibrant and a number of interesting groups in the town to join.

Postscript

Editors: Donald never got to finish his memoir.

On 30th November, the fiftieth anniversary of his consecration as a bishop, Donald presided at a Communion service in St Paul's Cathedral. Richard Chartres, Bishop of London was keen Donald mark this milestone and preached at the service.

Within three years, Donald died peacefully at home on 18 July 2014. The Bishop of the Diocese of Upper Shire in Malawi spoke during a Thanksgiving Service in the Abbey in September.

Some of the people who knew Donald said of him:

> He was really our loved Father; a wonderfully loving and caring priest; a man of God; a wonderful irritant for the Kingdom; the most remarkable and inspiring person I have ever met; his quiet wisdom and impish wit; I always came away feeling better about the world and myself; his twinkling eyes and infectious smile; his wonderful voice and singing sea-shanties.

Malawi

In 2015, at the request of the Bishop of the Diocese of Upper Shire, some of Donald's ashes were interred in a small stone pillar where he had lived. Bazil and Christopher attended the dedication ceremony.

Bishop of Upper Shire, Jane, High Commissioner for Malawi, Macdonald Banda, Bishop Trevor Mwamba

Donald's Memorial in Malosa, Malawi

Bazil and Chris went out for the memorial service in 2015

Appendices

Staff List - March 1962	222
Four Outstanding Clergy	224
Canon Oswald Chisa	224
Canon Barnaba Chipanda	225
Fr Jerome Bai	227
Fr Lloyd Chikoko	227
The building of Likoma Cathedral	231
Petro Kilekwa – Slave Boy to Priest	239
The SS *Chauncy Maples* and my Uncle Ernest	241
Archdeacon Christopher Lacey 1905-1968	244

Staff list March 1962

Mothers' Union Margaret Woodley
Diocesan Office, Mponda's William Towers, Edwin Kaposah
Printing Office, Likoma Swithun Noakes and
Staff Engineering Dept, Malindi Francis Bell and staff
Nkhkotakota Works/training Arthur Rawlings
Malosa Works Norman Holland
Ordinands

NYASALAND STAFF LIST MARCH 1962

Bishop Donald Arden
Vicar General Christopher Lacey

Nkhotakota Archdeaconry
Archdeacon: Guy Carleton
Parish Priest-in-charge Assistant Priest
Nkhotakota Oswald Chisa, Yohana Kapeta
Kayoyo Bernard Mbiza
Charundu Bartolomayo Msonthi, Francis Nkongojo Madanjala, Cyprian Liwewe
Chia John Mwassi
Mlala Krispo Machili, Jerome Bai (at Bua)

Shire Highlands Archdeaconry
Archdeacon: Christopher Lacey
Likwenu – Malosa John Rashidi, Frank Mkata
Christ the King, Soche Mattiya Mseka
St Paul's Blantyre Edward Hardman, John Parslow
Holy Innocents, Limbe & St Matthew's Chichiri
St Andrew's, Mulanje; All Saints, Thyolo; St George's, Zomba
Matope Paul Lundu, Barnaba Chipanda

Shire Archdeaconry
Archdeacon: Habil Chipembere
Malindi Habil Chipembere, Joseph Chikokota
Mponda's Ron Tovey, Martin Malasa
Samama Augustine Chande
Nkope Hill Michael Zingani, Dunstan Chizito

Likoma Archdeaconry
Archdeacon and Dean: Gerald Hadow
Jameson Mwenda, Nathan Mtaya
George Ambali
Ordinands at St John's Seminary, Lusaka Nathaniel Aipa, Benson Msonthi
Lloyd Chikoko, Edward Nanganga, George Mchakama, Peter Sauli (Deacon)
George Msakwiza

Medical Department
Likoma Hospital (St Peter's) R.H. Mumford, Gladys Snell
Malindi Hospital (St Martin's) David Stevenson, John Chandiamba
Nkhotakota Hosp (St Anne's) Beatrice Anderson
Mponda's Hospital Joan Knowles, Christine Moss, Smythies Merikebu
Nkope Hill Health Centre Geoffrey Chioko
Likwenu Hospital Richard Kapala
Likwenu Leprosarium Bill and Muriel Walter

College and Schools
St Michael's Teacher Training College Wilfred Stringer
Malosa Secondary School Hilda Evans
Nkhotakota Hill primary schools Steere Kaphambe
Southern Province primary schools Justus Kishindo
Likoma primary schools Alban Chilalika
Various

Four Outstanding Clergy

Canon Oswald Chisa

Oswald Chisa was a courageous and much loved priest whom I wish I had known better. He had been imprisoned by the colonial government in 1959 and had been released before my arrival in November 1961. At the beginning of 1961 he was made Priest-in-Charge of All Saints, Nkhotakota, working with Fr Yohana Kapeta and Fr Guy Carleton.

Oswald had two careers. In 1927 he joined the medical course under Dr Wigan on Likoma Island and after qualifying in 1934 worked as a medical assistant (the core of the medical services of Malawi, as Dr Michael King describes them) at Kayoyo, Likoma and Messumba in Mozambique. After his ordination as a priest in 1949, he served in Tanganyika and Mozambique before coming to Nkhotakota in 1958. He retired in 1964 because of ill health and was made an honorary canon by Bishop Josiah Mtekateka in 1972, three years before his death in 1975. Liz Payne, who was working as a midwife and tutor at St Anne's hospital was one of the many who packed the large church for the all night vigil preceding his funeral and wrote in *Ecclesia*:

> During the all-night vigil the church (now the cathedral of Lake Malawi Diocese) was packed. Prayer was offered spontaneously and I myself was moved to pray. At the graveside behind the church so many people prayed, sang and wept – Christians, Muslims, those of African Traditional Religion and children – all friends of Oswald Chisa. This was a great tribute from the Nkhotakota community on 20 May 1975. One felt that the peace of the Lord was with all who had gathered.

Canon Barnaba Chipanda

Serving in a country the length of Scotland and England put together, there were twenty-one Anglican clergy belonging to the country and seven expatriates when I arrived in 1961. Of the twenty-one, twelve were in their sixties and building their retirement homes. Barnaba was one of the nine on whom the future depended. He and his wife Fedge, to whom he was devoted, both came from Malindi.

Barnaba was born in 1917, trained as a teacher at St Michael's College and taught for sixteen years until he joined St Andrew's Theological College on Likoma Island. He was ordained in 1960 and apprenticed to Paul Lundu at Matope, when I arrived. Soon afterwards he was put in charge of the Chilipa parish area, which later became a separate parish. Two weeks later he was sent on a two-month course for radio and script writers at Mukono in Uganda. I privately wondered how anyone so shy and retiring could become a radio star. How wrong I was! A letter came describing his first flight:

> I made myself look downwards and saw something like a snake. My companion told me it was the River Shire! I was almost taking off the belt from my waist and kneeling to pray. Then I remembered what St Paul wrote, "Be ye therefore firm!" so I sat firmly and happily.

In only two months, the course turned this shy young priest into one chosen by Malawi radio for a regular slot every Sunday at 6.30. Radio Gospel Addis Ababa broadcast him to the whole of Africa every evening for three months.

Barnaba had a mind of his own. Although I had spoken of the need to revise our rules on discipline, I had no clear ideas about polygamy. It was Barnaba who first raised the issue. In a letter to *Ecclesia* he set out the problem of a Christian with two wives, one Christian and one of African Traditional religion. This man repaired the broken door of Chilipa church and the Christians had even bought a special chair for him, inscribed GIFT. Barnaba ends:

> Thanks to this man, our church building is in good condition. Yet the children of his second wife cannot attend catechumens' classes and he may not receive the sacraments. I pass this question to your readers: "What should we do?"

The only reply printed in *Ecclesia* is just signed, "Another Shepherd." It says in brief:

- synod said last year that his wife and children could be baptised;

- polygamy is a sin, but not worse than neglect of a family;
- a man who cares for a second wife and children is better than the man who has sexual relations with anybody, not bothering about the results;
- he cannot now just abandon his second wife and her children, even though he was wrong to have taken her.

I hope that some readers will try to answer the hard question: "What would Christ do?"

Barnaba was one of the first of the Malawi clergy to show enthusiasm for growing involvement with Blantyre Presbyterian synod. He writes about a joint conference of ministers and clergy:

> This was the first time that shepherds of both churches were able to meet and discuss their problems and to worship together. We talked as friends and discussed our differences and problems. The climax was the last day when both groups knelt in front of God to adore him.

In October 1970, Barnaba was appointed Archdeacon of Shire and priest-in-charge of Mponda's. In the following year he was invited to join a radio workshop sponsored by the Catholic Church in East Africa. In the first week seventy radio programmes were recorded, and in the second week articles were written for publication in Malawian newspapers and magazines. Other participants included Fr Dunstan Ainani, who later became Bishop of South Malawi, and Fr George Ndomondo, the former MP for Fort Johnston West, who was ordained after his release from detention following the Henry Chipembere rebellion. Barnaba later became Vicar-General, and worked at Nkope, Balaka and Monkey Bay until his retirement in 1987.

Fr George Ndomondo, his former MP, writes:

> He was fond of taking snuff but remained a smart priest. Snuff made him a lot of Moslem friends, who loved and respected him. While he was in retirement at Mponda's he continued to witness, not only in church but also when taking funerals. He knew what the cross had done for him and therefore what it will do for everyone else. He always had a message when he stood to preach, not a single person could go to sleep. In his long sermons each point was explained with emphasis, sometimes by hitting any object near, sometimes by hitting his chest. He was a man of prayer. Though he was short, his powerful voice made him a powerful preacher. Mponda's experienced a good

catch from the net. Fr Chipanda used to fish people along the shore of our waters of Galilee, the Shire River.

Canon Chipanda's sudden death on 2 October 2002 was a great shock. A vast crowd showed the respect and affection with which this godly man was held by Christians and Moslems alike. Christians miss his lovely chanting. May he and his Fedge rest in peace!

Fr Jerome Bai

At Liwaladzi, twenty miles north of Nkhotakota, the priest, Jerome Bai had formerly been a medical assistant and his wife a nurse and they were performing prodigious service to the community by treating some 10,000 patients a year, using their own home as a clinic.

The people in response were anxious to build a new home for them, but the Diocese had no funds to provide more than a new roof. Nothing daunted, the congregation went ahead and built a home considerably larger than the standard plan at less than half the standard cost. The rest came from parish funds and free labour. Clearly there was energy in the local church waiting to be recognised.

Fr Lloyd Chikoko

Self-propagation was another mark of a truly indigenous church. Here a fine example was being set by Lloyd Chikoko. Lloyd came from Chongole, south of the Chia Lagoon in central Malawi. Most of his working life had been spent in industry in Rhodesia and South Africa, where he was ordained in the African Orthodox Church. Since returning to Nyasaland two years earlier, he found himself a widower and became a voluntary helper to Father John Mwassi.

The team interviewing new students for St John's Seminary in Lusaka gave him a good report, which I happily accepted. At the end of his first term there was a shock. A letter came from the Principal, John Weller, "We all love Lloyd, but think you should consider his report before sending him back for another term." Attached was his exam report showing twelve percent for New Testament, seven percent for Old Testament ... I said a few prayers, consulted others and sent back a telegram, "Lloyd returning."

He went back and was ordained priest on 21 December 1965 with others who became excellent pastors – George Mchakama, Peter Sauli and John Masano. Taking part in the ordination was Canon Petro Kilekwa, then ninety-six, the slave-boy who became a priest and the first Malawian to be posted to an area away from the lake shore.

Lloyd was unequalled as an evangelist. Long walks did not deter him. The Anglican students at Don Bosco Teacher Training College were so impressed that he had walked seventy miles to celebrate the Eucharist for them, they wrote to *Ecclesia* saying that not only they but the two Catholic priests on their staff wanted to pay tribute to him:

> All this has been achieved because of regular evangelism undertaken by Fr Chikoko and his voluntary helpers. If all Church Elders and other faithful Christians also regarded themselves as ambassadors of Christ, we would certainly bring to him many who do not know him. Your prayers, and regular visits by our bishops – that is what we need.

A layman, Mr J.W. Chiteje, from Lloyd's parish at Dwambazi wrote:

> The small and scattered flock of Anglicans from Chizumulu Island and Mozambique was looked after by priests from Nkhotakota, but until Fr Chikoko there were few church buildings and converts. This year alone Dwambazi has shown big developments. Two new churches have been built, one at Ngala and another at Liuzi. Liuzi has built a catechist's house and a small rest-house for the present. Eighty-nine adults were baptized on St Bartholomew's day. There were also one hundred and six people who received the cross (as Hearers, beginning their baptism preparation) and a large number of children have been baptized.

In January 1970 Bishop Josiah Mtekateka wrote:

> I went to confirm the first fruits of Fr Lloyd Chikoko's work in the mountains near the Vipya Plateau. To reach the place we had to pass through Iwawa Forest. We left the car at the nearest camp – before we arrived we saw much game. From there we walked for four hours, but on our way back the next morning we walked only two hours.
>
> Fr Chikoko told me that when he first started going through those mountains he met the Group Headman called Chikumi, who said, "You cannot baptise any person in my area, first of all baptise me." Fr Chikoko answered, "We do not baptise any person until he/she has received all instructions, we need to know that he understands. I shall baptise you later on after you have been taught everything we

wish you to know and understand." Then Fr Chikoko was allowed to go around some of his villages. When he came to Muwawa Village, he first met a young maiden, Wainesi by name, and after talking to her she said, "Let me go and find others for you, not only myself alone." So she went and brought six with her, three men and three women and they joined the class.

This, my first time there, I confirmed 45 candidates including the Group Headman himself. Here there is a very hard work for the catechist as well as Fr Chikoko, going through those mountains and he goes to each of the villages, but he cannot go home the same day when he visits his villages every week. He is doing this because it is very hard for him to return on the third day because of the long way, hills and mountains and for the benefit of the congregations. The catechist's name is Mr Samuel Chimulu and he has six places to look after.

Fr Chikoko has thirty-four villages to go round and he has six catechists, many of them scattered in the hills and mountains. In October Fr Chikoko was ill for a month and received many injections. The Roman Catholic Father from Nkhata Bay, who knows him well, said, "Fr Chikoko must be ill because he walks so much. I am afraid that if he will be taken from here, our work will die."

I wish you to remember Fr Chikoko in your prayers, together with his catechists and the people in this remote area.

In 1972 Lloyd was transferred to Chiruwa parish, between Salima and Chia. The same story was repeated. Mr Amoni wrote an article for *Ecclesia* headed "Chiruwa Parish is Outward Looking;"

Between Chiruwa and Salima is a small island called Mbeje. Many people go there to catch and buy fish for sale. No priest has made an effort to visit these people. Since the arrival of Fr Lloyd Chikoko in the parish, however, he has been visiting this island to celebrate Holy Communion.

He also visits people on the main land who are not Christians. While he is making these visits, Christians from Mtosa, the head station, and from other congregations, take it in turns to conduct services.

Other priests should think of doing this. Bishop Josiah Mtekateka also spent several days with us. This was really encouraging.

I sometimes reflect on the fruits of Lloyd's ministry when I receive appeals from ordinands for sums of money equal to Lloyd's salary for six months to purchase massive tomes by Karl Barth to enable them to take a degree. Lloyd was made a canon by Bishop Josiah in 1974 and retired in 1979.

I last saw him at his home in the hills behind Chongole when visiting Malawi in 1992. He was totally blind, but was still celebrating the Eucharist from memory and planning the building of a new church in the little hilltop village where he lived. Lloyd died in 1997 the finest evangelist I have ever known."

The Building of Likoma Cathedral

The first section is summarised from: 1903-1955 volumes 1-3 of the *History of the Universities' Mission to Central Africa* (published from 1859 to 1957).

In 1899 Mr Frank George, an architect, came out and took over the building work of the Mission, all amateurs falling into line under him. Under his auspices the whole station had been rebuilt with stone. The native stone is granite – very hard to work; and the mortar is dothi – white ant earth.

The white ant or termite does the work that the European earthworm does, in turning over the earth and bringing it to the surface. They construct long earthen tunnels, under cover of which the ants advance and work, and their huge homes are of earth, bound with their saliva and hardened by the air.

This makes very good mortar, especially that of Likoma; a mixture of earth and sand, which the women dig out, moisten and tread under foot. This hardens when dry. But alas! It has one fault. Rain softens it, and unless there are deep eaves to carry off the rain, the walls often fall down. Bright hopes exist that roofs might even last fifteen years with care.

Early in 1903 Mr George brought his band of masons and carpenters, who had already built Kota Kota and Unangu churches, to Likoma to collect material. That band of workmen, trained and instructed by him and aided by Albert Crabb, was responsible for one of the most notable structures of our time. Such a building would be a credit to England, but on a comparatively desert island it can only be called wonderful.

Likoma provided nothing but granite, which had to be quarried. All other materials had to be sought on the mainland of Portuguese East Africa (Mozambique) and brought over in boats – the bricks made, the lime burned, the trees felled.

Owing to the great distance from the source of supply, the enormous cost of freight and the length of time to wait for things to be sent from England, the cathedral has been built without a number of things usually looked upon as necessary. Only cement, iron for the roof, and glass were sent from England. The building of it marks a stage in the growth of the Church in Central Africa and shows that it has taken root in the land.

All those employed on the building were Christians or catechumens. The work started each morning with a short service held specially for the work people, asking for a blessing on the day's labour. The builders were a fine body of men and women who took an extraordinary interest in their work. All the stone, brick and other material had been carried to its place on the heads of porters, a large number of whom were women.

It was to be a large cruciform building, covering an area of 17,600 square feet. When quite complete – that is when the chapter house, library and cloisters were finished – it would cover 37,000 square feet. It would measure from east to west three hundred and twenty feet, north to south wall of transept eighty-five feet.

A retreat for forty members of the mission was held before its dedication at Michaelmas 1905. As a child expressed it: "Many Europeans began to be in retreat. They were silent, they assembled together and prayed to God in their hearts. Two Europeans were set apart that day as deacons and we had very many prayers."

Then on St Michael's Day, to the strains of Laetatus sum (I was glad), a goodly congregation passed up the aisle of the new cathedral. Some of them were thinking what a venture of faith was that building of Jerusalem in Likoma's Isle; and how they had hardly dared to say, "Our feet shall stand in thy gates, O Jerusalem."

In September 1908, the bells were hung in the south-west tower and the clock was put together by Edwin Ayers and started. Unfortunately December brought very heavy storms of wind and rain and the upper parts of two buttresses of both towers were brought crashing to the ground. Happily no one was hurt but many hours were spent taking down the clock and chimes as a precaution against any further damage.

Then on 2 February 1909 another of the buttresses of the tower came down and it was definitely decided that the height of the towers must be reduced and the whole plan of the west front re-arranged.

In November 1911 there took place what should have been an occasion of unalloyed joy and thanksgiving for the whole diocese – the consecration of the Cathedral. But the event was saddened by the tragic death of the Rev. Arthur Jeffreys Douglas, principal of St Michael's College, at the hands of the Portuguese officer in charge of Kobwe where the College was situated. He was angry at being told that arms could not be carried on the *Charles Janson* and fired shots at the College. At that moment Arthur Douglas came out of the college chapel to investigate and the officer shot through the heart at five yards range. The motive was probably revenge as Arthur Douglas had remonstrated with him on behalf of girls whom the officer wanted. "Africans," wrote Bishop Fisher, "are quite clear that he died for them."

On 14 November 1911, the Cathedral Church of St Peter was consecrated by Thomas Fisher, Bishop of Nyasaland.

The first service of the gathering was a Solemn Eucharist of requiem for former workers.

A very large congregation filled the great nave. The sermon was preached in Chinyanja by Bishop Hine. The bishop had as chaplain Deacon Yohana Tawe, one of the earliest Christians on Likoma. Another deacon, Leonard Kangati, who had been prepared for baptism by Dr Hine in 1889, was also present. All the Yao clergy, headed by Padre Yohana Abdallah, were there, as well as Padre Augustine Ambali, who had been ordained priest with Padre Eustace Malisawa on St Thomas's Day, 21 December 1906.

The blessing of the new library took place on the same occasion, an excellent octagonal building, put up by Albert Crabb from plans by Frank George.

Heavy rains and storms still took their toll and in March 1912 the parapet of the south transept fell with part of the wall. This was rebuilt with a safe roof by Albert Crabb before the next rains, but a year later the parapet on the south side of the Lady Chapel fell, bringing with it all the outer stone wall below.

Half way through 1913, Frank George was back again at Likoma after eighteen months' work in the Diocese of Northern Rhodesia. He had always regarded the parapets at best as a very doubtful experiment and had built them rather under protest. The bishop now gave him a free hand to make the building safe.

The parapets were done away with; the roof was extended so as to cover the walls completely and protect them from the weather. The cathedral lost some of its exterior effect, but it was made safe and its interior beauty was unaffected.

In addition to this work, Frank George was also busy with the Chapter House, which had been included in his original design for the Cathedral and was now being built as part of the memorial to Father Douglas.

Archdeacon Frank George first went to Nyasaland in 1899 as a layman. He was a qualified architect and his first services were given in that capacity. His great monument is the Cathedral at Likoma, but he was architect and builder of many other churches, not only in the Diocese of Nyasaland but also in Northern Rhodesia and Zanzibar. In 1916, after training at Bishops'

College, Cheshunt, he was ordained deacon by Bishop Hine in England. In 1917 Bishop Fisher ordained him priest in the cathedral at Likoma which he had designed and built.

From that time he worked at Liuli in Tanganyika and in 1928, after the death of Archdeacon Johnson, he became also archdeacon of Niassa. "Under him," Canon Wilson wrote, "the work grew and grew until Christians were numbered by thousands."

In 1933 he had so serious a breakdown in health that his life was despaired of. The devoted nursing of Ethel Hall and the skills of Dr Wigan and of Dr Nye of Livingstonia saved his life but he could no longer work in Africa.

In 1950 Bishop Frank Thorne asked Mr Wolfenden, architect at the tung plantations at Mzuzu, for his advice about two cracks in the south transept. His report was mildly reassuring. Provided there were no serious earth-tremors, the Cathedral ought to stand for a good many years yet.

The building was put to the test in February 1952 when over eight inches of rain fell in one night and there was also an earth tremor which shook the south-west tower, yet without calling for major repairs. Many other buildings at the headquarters and many houses on the island were severely damaged by the tremor or the rains.

In 1955 the grass-covered iron roof was leaking so badly that much of it had to be replaced.

Gerald Hadow, dean of the Cathedral from 1950, may have felt that he had inherited a poisoned chalice but set himself to tackle it robustly. White ants had attacked some of the purlins to which the roof sheets were nailed, so he constructed a long bath filled with pentachlorophenol into which every piece of timber being used for the roof was soaked for 24 hours.

For further information:

https://missiology.org.uk/pdf/e-books/anderson-morshead/history-universities-mission.pdf

There is also the book, *History of Likoma Island 1800 to 2016* published in 2016.

A tower collapses – time for repairs 1962–63

On my first visit in 1962 there was a crash in the middle of the night and I woke to find that one corner of the smaller tower had collapsed. Fearing further falls, I asked for the tower to be roped off. This was not well received by the cathedral council who said the new bishop was despising their cathedral.

There was more trouble while I was away in March 1963. Christopher Lacey, the Vicar General, wrote: "Christopher Roderick, one of our VSOs, has gone to Likoma to help Fr Hadow. As a result of the incessant rain, earth tremors and wind, the smaller of the two towers has begun to fall in an alarming fashion. This necessitates extensive repair work which Fr Hadow cannot possibly do on his own."

Clearly the cathedral was in big trouble and we asked for help from Ian Reeler, architect of the splendid new Lusaka Cathedral in Zambia. His report was presented to DSC by Mr J.T. Thawe, lay representative from Likoma in March 1966 and reported in *Ecclesia* in April:

- Shorter tower: severe cracks make it dangerous. Demolish it.
- Heavy buttresses at the transepts: useless. Demolish.
- Library: severe crack in the octagonal wall needs attention.
- Drainage: the ditches could not deal with water from the high ground. A wall and cement paving is needed on the north side.
- Lady Chapel: rain coming in, termites active. Overhaul the roof.

The reaction of the DSC is not recorded. Skill and money were needed, and both were in short supply. Any new resources were already committed to growth on the mainland.

It was not until two years later that demolition of both towers began, in December 1968. *Ecclesia* records tersely:

> The demolition of the towers of Likoma Cathedral (both of which had begun to crumble) has begun and shows the towers to be in a very poor condition.

My own feelings at the time were expressed in the editorial of *Ecclesia* for July 1969 where I recalled that the first baptism in the gospels was in a river and the first Eucharist, followed by the first ordination, in the upstairs room of a private house. I quoted Mark Gibbs in *God's Frozen People*:

Buildings, clergy and theological colleges we take for granted. We cannot conceive of the Church existing without them. What did the early Church do when it did not have these things? It converted the Roman Empire.

I went on to tell of an enthusiastic young priest who suggested to his priest- in-charge a procession of witness on Good Friday with Christians of other churches to the places in the township where people gathered. His suggestion received the crushing reply: "Anglicans do not preach out of doors." I ended: We certainly need buildings where people can meet protected from rain and sun. But if this means retreating into the safety of a church building to avoid meeting non-christians in the places where they are, then a series of carefully organised fires may be what our diocese most needs!

My hesitations about cathedrals were not prompted by the experience of Likoma, still less about the zeal Likomans showed for spreading the gospel. In Salima, Blantyre and elsewhere our church was known as Chalichi cha Likoma, the Church of Likoma.

There were times however when the Likoma dialect caused problems. In 1961 it was used in all services. Because of UMCA links with Tanganyika, theological words such as "sacrament" and "Holy Spirit" were Swahili words with Arabic roots and unintelligible to non-Anglicans. This did not make evangelism easier and was reversed at our first elected synod in 1962. It was the generosity of the Presbyterian Synod of Livingstonia that made the huge task of re-roofing and rebuilding the cathedral possible. They had a large building programme and had asked the Presbyterian Church of Ireland for help. In response a young Irish builder had come from Belfast, Danny Mckee, but their work was not yet ready to start. Generously they offered his services free of charge for the next few months, which extended to fifteen months.

Ecclesia August 1971:

> On 24th July 1971, 50 tons of cement, steel and other building materials left Blantyre on their 300-mile journey to St Peter's Cathedral, Likoma Island. Mr Daniel McKee hopes to arrive on the Island at the beginning of August to begin the repair work to the towers and the main structure of the cathedral.
>
> We are very grateful to the Beit Trust (and later the Dulverton Trust) for having given K14,000 (roughly £14,000) for this work, and to the Presbyterian Church of Ireland for providing the salary for Mr McKee. The generous donation of K1,000 made by the President is to be put into the Cathedral Maintenance Fund to provide recurrent money over the years.

In May 1972 Bishop Josiah Mtekateka reported briefly in *Ecclesia*:

> The work of rebuilding the Cathedral is going on well. The shorter cathedral tower is already finished and the tall tower half-way done."

Two years later, in April 1974 he reported again in *Ecclesia*:

> Last month I went to Likoma Island to see the progress on the Cathedral repairs. I noticed that a few places were not completed. Some timbers in the roof at the nave have been eaten by termites and need to be replaced by iron rafters. This is the only part left.
>
> The cathedral was rededicated on 10 October 1976, fourteen years after I witnessed the collapse of part of the smaller tower. It was my first time to visit Likoma since Josiah Mtekateka's enthronement as Diocesan Bishop in 1971. I wanted the new diocese to know that it had its own bishop, born on the same island in the same year that the cathedral began.
>
> Sixteen members of Texas Diocese attended, led by their Suffragan Bishop, Roger Cilley. The team included Bill Sterling, who had spent a month with Bishop Josiah in the Central Region in 1965. He was now chairman of the overseas division of Texas diocese which had been a generous supporter of the rebuilding fund.

Ecclesia November 1976:

> Certainly Likomans appreciated their newly rebuilt cathedral. A church-warden reported in January 1980: "Christmas collections were over K141 (about £140) for the first time and the Cathedral now has no problems about paying our priest. We meet our quota and there are plenty of fish in the Lake."

Augustine Chande was dean of the cathedral from 1978 until his sudden death and told *Ecclesia* in January 1978:

> We had difficulties travelling to the mainland to buy wafers, so we bought the things for making them from the Catholic Sisters in Lilongwe and trained Mrs Kacholola and Mrs Chikwemba to make our own and are even supplying our brothers in Messumba. We barter wafers for firewood from Mozambique!

A brief account of the 1971–1976 rebuilding

Since writing the above I have come across a briefer account of the rebuilding, written at the time to a personal friend in California who died in 2008, Deaconess Esther Davis. My letter is dated 17 October 1976.

I have spent a fortnight in Lake Malawi diocese, assisting Bishop Josiah in dedicating the rebuilt cathedral.

It is an astonishing piece of work. The rebuilding was master-minded by a young Irish Presbyterian builder, Danny Mckee, who had come to Malawi to assist the Synod of Livingstonia. His personal expenses and costs for the 15 months he was on the island were paid by the Presbyterian Church of Ireland as a free gift.

With only $20,000 available for the work on Likoma Cathedral and for all the cement, steel girders, other building materials and their transport by rail and steamer to Likoma, Danny and the Likoma building team have done an unbelievable job.

They pulled down both towers to ground level after photographing all the intricate brickwork. I have no idea how many different patterns of bricks had been used. Then they put in new reinforced concrete foundations and rebuilt the two towers so carefully that only an expert could work out what is original 1903 work and what was rebuilt in 1975 and 1976.

They then stripped the entire roof off the cathedral and replaced all the chiswe-infested tie-beams and purlins with new steelwork. Other work was done on the transepts and the Lady Chapel but I know no details as I have not been on Likoma for five years.

Visiting Likoma 2005

Jane and I visited Likoma in 2005 to share in the centenary celebrations of the Cathedral.

For more on the history of the church and island at Likoma, see W.T. Manjano Chirwa, *History of Likoma Island 1800 to 2016* (2016 ISBN 978-99908-940-4-2)

Petro Kilekwa – Slave Boy to Priest

Present at my consecration was Canon Petro Kilekwa. Petro had been captured as a slave in Eastern Zambia as a young boy in the 1870s, marched nearly a thousand miles to Zanzibar, sold in the market there and taken in an Arab dhow to the Persian Gulf. A British naval ship came alongside the dhow, released Petro and his friends, after which Petro became the Admiral's Cabin Boy. Petro was eventually ordained and did wonderful work as a priest in Malawi. On a shelf in his thatched village house at Mtonda sat a Victorian travelling clock with the inscription To Petro, with grateful thanks from Admiral Benbow.

When Bazil was three months old, we took him to see Canon Petro Kilekwa, then aged 94 or 95. He was up a ladder re-thatching his house and came down to greet us. His story encapsulates something of the intertwined history of Islam, the Yao people among whom we lived and the focus of Anglican mission in Malawi. His story is taken from *Slave Boy to Priest* which he had written 30 years earlier.

Petro Kilekwa with Bazil – 1965

Petro must have been eleven or twelve when he was captured as a slave near Lake Bangweula in north-eastern Zambia. His mother tried to ransom him with three yards of calico but the "coastmen" demanded eight. A yoke was fitted to his neck and they marched him away, alert to attacks by Angoni raiders from Zululand and lions. After walking some hundred and fifty miles they arrived at Samama on the western shore of Lake Malawi, just north of Mponda's. There his Arab owner developed smallpox and called to Petro to lie close to him, saying, "If I die, we die together. If I live, we live together."

The next morning the Arab died, but Petro survived and was sold to Yao traders who dealt in slaves. A year later he was resold, marched 500 miles to the Indian Ocean coast at Yikindani, put on board an Arab dhow to sail to the Persian Gulf.

One morning there was panic. A small boat was coming towards them. The Arabs shouted, "Get below in the hold! These are bad men who eat black boys!" Petro and his friend leapt into the hold as the hatch-covers were put on and lay on the bottom of the boat, hardly daring to breathe. Eventually Petro and a friend were transferred to a man-of-war on anti-slavery patrol, HMS *Osprey* and were landed at Muscat in 1885. They sailed up the Euphrates to Basra and then to Bombay. Petro was then transferred to the flagship, HMS *Bacchante*. Petro became the punkah boy to Admiral Lord Charles Scott, pulling a rope that moved overhead curtains, making a light breeze. His companion, Mwambala, was only punkah boy to the captain, said Petro with a smile.

They sailed again to Bombay for Queen Victoria's jubilee in 1887, then to Colombo, Aden, Madagascar and finally to Zanzibar. As the Baccante was heading for England, Petro and his friend were put into St Andrew's College, Kiungani, built by the UMCA to help released slaves. He stayed there for six years, eventually training as a teacher. He returned to work in Nyasaland, arriving in 1899. As a teacher, he opened the first school at Ntchisi in 1907, and later came back there as deacon and priest. But most of his ministry was in Islamic areas at Nkhotakota and on the eastern and southern lake shore.

Petro was priest-in-charge of Nkope and Sani for eighteen years, 1930-1948, which included the whole forty mile stretch from Monkey Bay to Mponda's where many of the people were Muslim.

Canon Petro retired to Mtonda, near Monkey Bay, building a house on a plot of land given to him by the government in recognition of his fine work in Africa. He called the house Kiungani after the place in which he had spent so many years after being released by the slave-traders. Petro died in 1967.

Editor: In 2019 Bazil came across this story of Petro Kilekwa in the Slavery museum in Zanzibar.

Petro Kilekwa summary in Slavery Museum in Zanzibar

The SS *Chauncy Maples* and my Uncle Ernest

Lake Malawi is approximately the days of the year long and the weeks of the year wide and sits in the southern end of the great Rift Valley that stretches from the Red Sea to Zimbabwe. In the days before roads, travelling by boat around the lake was the obvious way for missionaries to do their work.

In 1890 my uncle, Ernest Crouch, joined the Universities' Mission to Central Africa (UMCA) as a ship's engineer. He first served on the *Charles Janson* a small steamer built fourteen years earlier. While working on the *Charles Janson*, Uncle Ernest, was asked to prepare specifications for a new larger steamer. As well as supplying the lake shore mission stations, *Chauncy Maples* was to be a floating teacher-training and theological college. She was to be named after Bishop Chauncy Maples who had drowned on his way to his consecration in the cathedral on Likoma Island in 1895.

Uncle Ernest was sent to Scotland to order a ship to his specifications. She was "mocked-up" on the Clyde, taken to pieces, each of her plates numbered and sent off to be galvanized. She was then packed into 3,500 crates, except for the huge boiler, which could not be taken to pieces. All these were sent by cargo steamer to Quelimane, the Indian Ocean port at the mouth of the Zambezi River. Then 400 miles up the Zambezi and Shire River into Nyasaland.

This southern end of Nyasaland, known as the Lower Shire, is 1,500 feet lower than Lake Nyasa and the Shire River cascades over a series of non-navigable rapids. The crates containing the C.M. were converted into 4,500 head-loads to be carried through the bush to lake level. The boiler was dragged by 450 Angoni men on a carriage made out of cart-wheels. This they pulled 100 miles, climbing 1,500 feet singing and making the road as they went. When they reached Matope "the place of mud", the Shire became navigable again. Eventually the whole lot arrived at Mponda's, just where the river runs out of the lake.

450 men transporting the boiler Lower to Upper Shire rivers (Photo courtesy of Lady of the Lake)

To his horror Uncle Ernest discovered that in the process of galvanizing, all the numbers on the plates had been wiped out! Only he knew the pattern.

At Mponda's mission on the banks of the Shire, they cleared and levelled a one acre site and laid out the pieces. The next few months were spent on a steamer-sized jig-saw puzzle – "That plate belongs over there, that one's part of the bridge ..." I don't know what the hippos who plodded out of the river each evening in search of food, thought of these strange inedible shapes.

The only mistake in Glasgow was not using galvanized rivets and that is the only reason why she failed her MOT 95 years later. The plates are still as good as when they were assembled in 1900 but the rivets that held them together have rusted. She was one of the world's longest serving steamers, working commercially on lake or sea.

The vision that the *Chauncy Maples* would be a floating teacher-training and theological college did not work out as the students became sea-sick. But from 1901 to 1957 she steamed around the lake paying monthly visits to missions and centres in Portuguese East Africa (Mozambique), Tanganyika (Tanzania) and Nyasaland (Malawi). For many years she provided the only link between these centres as there were no roads, carrying people, stores, medicines, produce, animals, chickens and anything else you think of.

Likoma Island was the headquarters of this large diocese extending into four countries – Tanganyika (Tanzania), Portuguese East Africa (Mozambique), Northern Rhodesia (Zambia) and Nyasaland. After leaving UMCA in 1901, Uncle Ernest became chief engineer of Bristol docks and built the present dock gates.

Ernest Crouch at Mponda's with boiler ready to be put into position

The boiler on the *Chauncey Maples* was fired by wood and in 1957 it became clear it was no longer practical to do this, so she was pensioned off. By that time she was probably one the world's oldest ships still in active service.

The fact that she remained in good health for so long and especially during the 1939-45 World War, was largely due to a remarkable UMCA missionary, Francis Bell, who, for forty years in his workshop on the lake shore at Malindi serviced the *Chauncey Maples*, making a spare part if it was not possible to buy it. Francis was also in demand from local people for his skill in despatching marauding lions.

In 1967 the British government refitted her as a present to the Malawi government so that she could assist the MV *Ilala* as a second passenger ship on the lake. His Excellency the Life President of Malawi, Dr H. Kamuzu Banda took part in the re-launching ceremony at Monkey Bay and I was asked to lead the prayers and to bless her in her new work. Uncle Ernest must have been smiling down on us all.

She continued to sail around the lake until 1990 when the rivets holding the plates, which had not been galvanised, began rusting and made her unseaworthy.

A book entitled *The Lady of the Lake* written by Vera Garland, a friend of ours who lived in Malawi, provides a fascinating account of the life of the *Chauncy Maples*. Vera was unaware that Ernest Crouch was my uncle.

Archdeacon Christopher Lacey 1905-1968

I suspect the only reason Christopher had not been elected bishop was that he was chairing the three-person commission to whom the Elective Assembly had delegated the election when it had failed to secure a two-thirds majority.

There were no half measures about Christopher. He had intended to be an agriculturalist and was half way through his course when he decided to train for the priesthood instead. When he arrived in Nyasaland in 1937, he was posted to Likoma Island, in charge of the most isolated cathedral in the world.

A former parishioner on Likoma wrote:

> It was on Likoma that Fr Lacey got his nickname "Achirwa". The clan name Chirwa was the commonest on the island. It was because of his friendship with many people on the island, together with his cheerful and friendly manner that people came to look on him as one of themselves and to call him Achirwa – the "A" being a friendly form of address.

The words that best describe Christopher are gaiety, simplicity, spontaneity. Life for him seemed to be full of surprises: he never quite understood why people should want to love him and give him things, like the new typewriter that came just at the end of his life. He was the epitome of UMCA at its best, firmly rooted in a magnificent tradition and in the gospel virtues of simplicity and singleness of mind and love.

You would never imagine there had been any price to pay. When we were living together at Mponda's he could be found sitting at the side of the road waiting for one of the passing cars to give him a lift to a congregation fifty miles away. He gave the impression that he preferred to travel that way because it was more fun and you met new people. Christopher would say, "Did archdeacons in other places really have cars to do their visitations?"

Many of the good things that had begun to happen started from his visions. He played a large part in the founding of the Presbyterian/Anglican Lay Training Centre at Chilema and the discussions on unity with the Christian Council and Roman Catholic Church.

When he was transferred to be parish priest of Limbe and Archdeacon, it was – among other responsibilities – to be warden of a hostel for young men who had come to work in the city from places such as Likoma and Mponda's that he knew so well. He was always concerned that people should see Christ the Redeemer as well as Christ the Judge.

It is symbolic that this last brief illness began at a service in the Presbyterian church in Blantyre and was aggravated when, against medical advice, he drove 62 miles to Malosa for discussions in preparation for a meeting of the Catholic-Anglican joint committee.

A wholly characteristic story I heard only after his death: how after his operation, with drainage tubes and drips going in all directions, he had turned to a visitor and said: "We must have a new verse in the Benedicite: all ye Pipes and Tubes, bless ye the Lord, praise him and magnify him for ever." He was buried in the graveyard at Limbe.

In a letter to me in 1962 Christopher wrote: "It would be silly and wrong to stay on till one is old and decrepit." God saw to it that he never became either. It was wholly right that his Requiem Mass was that of Easter Day. For him, life was perpetually springtime and in his presence, we were constantly reborn.

Index of Names & Organisations

People
Abdullah/Abdallah, Yohana............99,233
Ainani, Dunstan........106,161,172,200,204, 206,226
Aipa, Nathaniel............................100,223
Alderson, Cecil........................44,108,139
Allen, Roland...............79,84,100,173
Ambali, George........................222,233
Amoni, Mr.....................................229
Anderson, Beatrice.........................223
Andrews, C.F....................................24
Antonio, Father..............................199
Armitage, Robert...........................126
Ayres, Edwin..................................232
Baguley, Paul..................................210
Bai, Jerome..............................222,227
Baker, Colin...................................128
Banda, Aleke..................................132
Banda, Hastings Kamuzu..........43,44,48,59, 69,71,81,101,102,125-128,130-132,134,145, 185,194,206,245
Banda, Macdonald..........................220
Banda, Malango..............................171
Bandaranaike, Solomon....................38
Barker, Anthony & Mags.............43,76
Barnes, Father........................15,16,18
Bayne, Stephen........61,66,70,72,78,133
Baxter, Richard.................118,158,160
Bell, Francis......48,88,130,202,222,245
Bickersteth, Julian.............................14
Biggers, Jack.....................................74
Binks, Paul & Margaret...................196
Bishop of London............................59
Bishop of St Alban's.........................24
Blackwood, Michael..........................65
Blignaut, Dr....................................158
Bolt, John.......................................128
Borgstein, Jan & Ankie.............192-195
Boucher, Claude......................118,119
Brand, Stuart & Sue..........................70
Braund, George................................70
Brown, Lawrence............................115
Brown, Leonard..............................135
Brown, Leslie..................................178
Browning, David............................210
Brownlee, Sheila.............................210
Burrough, Paul...................141,145,149
Burtwell, Peter......................32,62,63

Buthelezi, Gatsha..............................43
Butler, Tom & Barbara..........3,5,19,208-210
Cairns, James..................................145
Carama, Clement..............................85
Carlisle, George...............73,83,108,133,154
Carleton, Guy..............81,105,121,222,224
Carver, Maurice...........................77,85
Chadwick, Paul.................................80
Chakaipa...151
Chambombe, Yonathan..................107
Chande, Augustine....................222,237
Chandiamba, John..........................223
Chartres, Richard..................5,216,219
Chikanga..56
Chikoko, Lloyd & Georgina............106,147, 148,171,172,223,227-230
Chikokota, Joseph.....................123,222
Chikoma, Robert............................107
Chikumi, Headman...................228,229
Chikwemba, Mrs............................237
Chilalika, Alban........................102,223
Chilinkwambe, Alice..................171,172
Chindongo, Mr & Mrs...................154
Chimpango, Ernest..........................199
Chimulu, Samuel............................229
Chioko, Geoffrey............................223
Chiona...142
Chipanda, Barnaba.............167,222,225-227
Chipanda, Fedge......................225,227
Chipembere, Catherine.........128-130,132
Chipembere, Habil..........48,61,63,82,87,88, 100-102,104,123,128-131,163,165,181,222
Chipembere, Henry....48,82,88,101,102,104, 123,125-129,132,226
Chirwa, Orton........43,44,82,102,125,126,132
Chirwa, Vera..................................132
Chisa, Oswald...............105,106,121,222,224
Chiteje, J.W.....................................228
Chitila, Frank...................................64
Chiume, Kanyama.....................125,128
Chiweko, Gileburg..........................199
Chizito, Dunstan............................222
Choo, Dunstan........66,101,102,104,105,169
Chuma, Ellen............................198,199
Chunga, Victor..........................117,118
Cérésole, Pierre................................20
Cilley, Roger...................................237
Clayton,..141

Clutton-Brock, Guy 139
Coggan, Donald 111
Cole-King, Susan & Paul 90,134,185-188, 211
Cook, Douglas 199
Cooper, Betty 210
Covin, Tom 99,162
Crabb, Albert 231,233
Cripps, Arthur Shearly............................... 138
Crofton, Mel & Brigid....... 49,50,62,63,69,92, 97,129
Crofton, Nigel & Nicola 88
Crouch, Ernest 43,50,241,243ff
Crouch, Philip & Paula....................... 211,212
Cumberland, Leslie 19
Davies, Roger... 210
Davis, Esther.. 238
Divine, Gerry & Marilyn........................... 211
Dobson, Jack.............. 32,33,35-37,61,63,100
Douglas, Arthur Jeffreys 232,233
Douglas, Gerald 198
Duke of Edinburgh.................................... 101
Eccles, David 64
Eggington, Eileen 211
Elizabeth, Queen Mother 110,115
Evans, Hilda... 223
Eyre-Brook, Arthur 195
Fady.. 160
Fagan, Walter & Norma..................... 201,202
Faith, Margaret 155
Farrer, Simon 210
Fenton, Bill... 21,22
Fenwick, Jeffrey... 139
ffrench-Beytagh, Gonville........................ 139
Fisher, Geoffrey 134
Fisher, Thomas 233,234
Forbes, Mikka 18
Foster, Joan & Jonathan............................ 211
Fox, Ann 70
Francis, Marjorie 167
Garland, Peter..................................... 190,191
Garland, Vera... 245
George, Frank..................................... 231,233
Gibbs, Gwen... 196
Gibbs, Humphrey 140
Gilmore, Norman & Barbara..................... 68
Grant, Malcolm & Pam............................ 211
Green-Wilkinson, Oliver.... 3,76,102,108,137, 138,141-143,204
Hadow, Gerald 105,222,234,235
Hall, Ethel.. 234
Hammond, David 104
Hardman, Edward..................................... 222
Harker, Hugh 19
Harrison, Geoff.. 32
Hastings, Adrian 116,198

Hatendi, Peter.. 150
Hemingway, Peter & Babs 210
Hepburn, Hamish..................................... 158
Herrick, Dick 19
Hewitt, George.. 145
Hicks, Cannon 117,167
Hine, John 72,99,111,132,233,234
Holland, Norman...................................... 222
Hoods, Willie 30
Hotblack, Gerry & Joan...............89,173,174
House, Anderson 71
How, John 155
Howard, Robert... 180
Huckstep, Ron 194
Huddleston, Trevor................................ 43,79
Hunter, Rodney 144
Ingram, Cecil & Maude Winnginton 59
Ions, Jean 33
Jalasi, Sheldon 105-107
Jali, Wilmot & Rosamund 31-33,39
Janson, Charles 53
Jones, Glyn....................................52,81,126-128
Jones, Helene 169
Jones, Raymond & Jo.............................. 210
Johnson, Neville.. 210
Johnson, William Percival. 53,58,62,103,122, 158,234
Johnston, Art & Nan................. 73,90-92,183
Kadzamira, Cecilia............................. 125,194
Kacholola, Mrs 237
Kalilombe, Patrick...................................... 89
Kalino, Dennis 124
Kamaliza, Michael.................................... 107
Kampango aka R.Phiri............................. 146
Kamungu, Leonard 103,122,145
Kangati, Leonard 233
Kapala, Richard... 223
Kapeta, Oswsald Chisa Yohana........ 222,224
Kaphambe, Steere..................................... 223
Kaposah, Edwin 222
Kariuki, Obadiah................................. 44,178
Kaunda, Kenneth..........112,141,143,145,171
Khama, Ruth & Seretse............................ 152
Kilekwa, Petro 45,54,106,123,228,240ff
King, Maurice 202
King, Michael & Elspeth 195,224
Kingsnorth, John... 56
Kishindo, Justus..48,65,160,162-165,202,223
Knowles, Joan & Jonathan.................. 48,223
Kulanje, Biti 189
Küng, Hans 76,159
Kunkwenzu, George................................. 184
Lacey, Christopher 51,62,63,80,81,88,176, 222,235,246ff
Lacey, Janet... 77,184
Lamont, Donald 141

Lawes, Robert 55,158
Lawrence, John 77
Lavy, Chris & Vicky 196
Leake, John & Alison 70,118,160,164
Lees, Laurence 104
Liomba, John 123,129
Livingstone, David 53,69,106,122
Liwewe, Cyprian 106,222
Luchs, Louis 71
Lunda, James 106
Lundu, Paul 222,225
Machili, Krispo 222
Mackenzie, Charles 45,53,122,199
Macleod, George 24
Macmillan, Harold 52,179
Madota, Catechist 124
Magombo, Rev 161,166
Mahadeo, Jai 211
Makandanje, Stephen 34,79,166,173
Makhulu, Khotso 152
Malasa, Martin 166,222
Malewezi, Justin 200
Malidadi, Robert 47
Malisawa, Eustace 233
Mallory, Shannon 152
Manhique, Bertha & Paulino 214,216
Maples, Chauncy 156
Maputwa, Maxwell 117,162,167-169
Marama, Clement 65,77,132
Mataka, Filemon 142
Masano, John 228
Mauwa, Wesley 114
Mazingaliwa, Alston 146
Mbandzeni 31
Mbiza, Bernard 222
Mchakama, George 100,223,228
McGilvray, James 184
McGrath, Ray 217
McKee, Danny 236,238
Mercer, Robert 151
Merikebu, George 118
Merikebu, Smythies 190,223
Minter, Kathleen 180
Mizeki, Bernard 122
Mkata, Frank 222
Mkomawanthu, Frank 111,174
Moffatt, John 139
Molale, Michael & Joyce 152,153
Molesworth, Anthony 32,35,37
Molesworth, David 189,190
Moon, Chris 217
Montefiore, Hugh 187,211
Morley, David 185,186
Moss, Christine 49,223
Mott, Tony 55
Mseka, Soche Mattiya 222
Msakwiza, George 223
Msekawanthu, Mathias 111
Msonthi, Bartolomayo 222
Msonthi, Benson 223
Msonthi, John 82
Mtaya, Nathan 222
Mtekateka, Josiah 102,106-111,113-
116,123,142,144,148,154-161,175,204,206,
224,228,230,236-238
Mtiesa, Swinny 180-183
Mtsinje, George 199
Mugabe, Robert 3
Mumford, R.H. 223
Muzorewa 150
Mwamba, Trevor 220
Mwassi, John 222,227
Mwenda, Jameson ... 55,148,161,221,161,222
Mzokomera, Dunstan 81,202,203
Nanganga, Edward 100,223
Ndomondo, George 126,144,226
Nemeleyani, Edward 180
Newbigin, Leslie 77
Ngoma, Elizabeth & Peter 170-172
Niemer, Hugo 184
Nkomo, Joshua & Grace 61,139,149
Nkongojo, Francis 222
Nkrumah, Nkwame 69
Noakes, Swithun 222
Nxumalo, Simon 41
Nyanja, Peter 168,206
Nye, Dr 234
Nyerere, Julias 125
Nyirenda, Joyce 105,169,170,171
Olang, Festo 153
Onaika, David 168
Packer, Wally 210
Paget, Edward 138,139
Palmer, Marion 156
Parslow, John 134,222
Paton, David 78
Pattison, Ken 158
Payne, Liz 224
Peterkins, Dorothy 132
Pike, Jim 74
Piper, Herb 15
Poole-Hughes, John 54,107
Potter, Jean 132
Price, Don 208
Princess Diana 217
Ramsey, Michael 47,48,137,175
Rashidi, John 222
Rawlings, Arthur 81,201,202,222
Ray, Bob (Rufus) 18
Renouf, Clem 195
Reeler, Ian 235
Richardson, Milton 73,133,154

Riddle, Gerald 88
Riddle, Jane 49,63,88
Ridley, H.N. 9
Roderick, Christopher 235
Rolph, Valerie 210
Ross, Ronald 179
Rubadiri, Alec 55,100
Rubadiri, Grace 132
Runcie, Robert 166
Ryan, Michael 183
Salmon, Anthony 32
Sangaya, Jonathan 67,99,131,142,158
Sauli, Peter 223,228
Savage, Tom 31,41,44,53,173
Schiffmayer, Jeff 71,104
Schultz, Roger 176
Scott, Charles 241
Scott, Michael 134
Sengulane, Dinis 213,216
Sibiti, Erica 177
Silulu, Father 214
Sim, Arthur Frazer 99,122,156,157
Sinker, George 111
Siyachitema, Jonathan 151
Skelton, Kenneth 139,141,145
Smith, Ian 3,112,137,140,141,149,152
Smith, Victor 131
Snell, Gladys 223
Sobhuza II 31-33,37
Southcott, Ernest & Margaret 19,69
Sterling, Bill 237
Stevenson, David 45,223
Stringer, Wilfred 223
Taylor, John 78,177
Tatlock, Dick 19
Tawe, Yohana 233
Teather, Fred 208,209
Temple, William 24
Tengatenga, James 188
Thawe, J.T. 235
Thorne, Frank 47,51,59,63,69,84,101,108,
113,137,179,234
Thupa, Bob 163
Tidey, George 19,20
Todd, Garfield 149
Tovey, Ron 48,51,222
Tredgold, Robert 139
Trefusis, Francis 145
Tuck, David 211
Umande, Smythies 189
van Asdonck 159
van Culin, Sam 71,72
Viner, Leonard 144
Volmink, Katie 188,189
Walker, Braz 154
Walter, Dennis 187

Walters, Bill & Muriel 189,190,223
Welensky, Roy 52,137
Weller, John 144,227
Westrop, Arthur 53
White, Doreen 114
White, John 138
Whitehead 139
Wigan, William 189,224,234
Williams, Noel 149
Wilson, Canon 234
Wilson, Harold 179
Wilson, Leonard & Mary 134,135,187,188
Wolfenden, Mr 234
Wood, Mark 140,145
Woodfield, Pip 25,29,188
Woodley, Margaret 169,183,222
Workman, John 136
Wrankmore, Bernard 42,62,63
Yeppe, Douglas 114,124
Young, Dick 65,66,70,71
Zingani, Joy 164
Zingani, Grace 214
Zingani, Maxwell 65,135,161,162,164-167
Zingani, Michael 222

Organisations
African Ecclesiastical Review 116
African Methodist Episcopal Church 151
Angola London Mozambique Association 216
Beit Trust 236
Cowley Fathers 71
Christian Aid 77,184,202
Christian Medical Commission (CMC)... 184
Christian Missionary Society 78,177
Churches of Christ .. 57,88,101,131,149,160,161
Church of Scotland 55
Concern Universal 217
Council of Anglican Provinces of Africa (CAPA) 153
Aga Khan Ismaeli Sect 27
Dutch Reformed Church 25,145,158,161,166
Guides 51,131,132
International Voluntary Service for Peace (IVSP) 20
Leoprosy Relief Association (Lepra) 189,190
Malawi (Nyasaland)
    Anglican Council of Malawi 113,114
    Boatie Paul 54,56,83,102,137
    Charles Janson 243
    Chauncy Maples 43,45,48,50,53,56,60,61,243

Christian Health Association of Malawi (CHAM) 99,184,185
Church of Central Africa Presbyterian (CCAP) 67,82,99,117,118,131,142,143, 158,165,172
Diocesan Standing Committee ... 61,64,90, 100,105,106,112,114,134,165
Ecclesia .... 51-52,72,74,77,85,117,118, 121-124,135,156,164-166 *Mpingo* 168, 171,174,197,200,201,225,228,229, 235-237
Ilala 55,83,96,110,245
Lion of Malawi award 191
Malawi Against Polio (MAP) 4,192ff, 205
Malawi Congress Party (MCP) 82,83 130,194
Mothers' Union 101,119,148,150, 152,166,169-172,199,205
Radio Malawi 194
Methodists 158
Mines Advisory Group (MAG) 217
Mother Teresa's Order 214
Movement for the Ordination of Women (MOW) 211
Order of Epiphany 180
Oxfam 202,214
Pineapple Growers Association 3,34-36
Quakers 20,162
Radio Gospel Addis Ababa 225
Rotary 195,196
Rubber 9,10
Save the Children 194
School Feeding Scheme (SA) 27
Scouts 14,27,28-30,35,41,50,53,131,132
Second World War 3,21,143,173
Society for the Propagation of the Gospel (SPG) 20,24,37
SS *Bendigo* 12,18
Student Christian Movement 24,76
Unicef 185,187
United Kingdom (UK)
 Anglican People Association 19,69
 Bardsey Island 216
 College of the Resurrection at Mirfield. 15,18,70,112,140
 Diocesan Board for Schools 5
 Diocese of London 3,4
 Holy Trinity Church, Potten End 23,24
 Iona community 24,99,118,158,160,162
 Lambeth Conference 86,95,111,114, 115,144,147,154,175,188,198
 St Alban's, North Harrow 3,5,210ff
 Malawi Association for Christian Support (MACS) 211,217
 St Catherine's Hatcham 21
 St Edward's School, Oxford 11
 St Margaret's, Uxbridge 4,208ff
 St Mary's, Kennington 21
 St Paul's Cathedral 5,69,211,219
 Southwark 3,5,19,21,69
 Willsden World Group 216
United Reformed Church 131,160
United States of America
 Episcopal Church of USA 65,71-73, 133,134
 Overseas Mission Society 71,73
Universities Mission to Central Africa (UMCA) ... 43,49-51,53,56,59,61,65,66,69,70, 84,103,120,121,130,155,158,161,162,163, 180,181,183,189,199,201,202,214,241,243, 245,246
USPG 3,69,156,174,183,208,212
White Fathers 112,118
World Council of Churches 56,67,68,78
World Health Organisation 187

www.ingramcontent.com/pod-product-compliance
Lightning Source LLC
Chambersburg PA
CBHW032126160426
43197CB00008B/534